A-Z BROMLEY

CONT

Key to Map Pages	2-3		35
Map Pages	4-34		...ards

REFERE

Motorway	M25
A Road	A21
B Road	B230
Dual Carriageway	
One-way Street Traffic flow on A roads is indicated by a heavy line on the drivers' left. Large Scale Page Only	
Junction Name	KESTON MARK
Restricted Access	
Pedestrianized Road	
Track & Footpath	
Residential Walkway	
Railway	Station, Level Crossing, Tunnel
Croydon Tramlink The boarding of Tramlink trams at stops may be limited to a single direction, indicated by the arrow.	Tunnel, Stop
Built-up Area	BOND RD.
Local Authority Boundary	
Posttown & London Postal District Boundary	
Postcode Boundary (within posttown)	
Map Continuation	18 / Large Scale Town Centre 35

Airport	
Car Park (Selected)	P
Church or Chapel	†
Fire Station	■
Hospital	H
House Numbers (A & B Roads only)	2 33
Information Centre	i
National Grid Reference	5 40
Park & Ride	Bromley P+
Police Station	▲
Post Office	★
Toilet with facilities for the Disabled Disabled facilities only	
Educational Establishment	
Hospital or Hospice	
Industrial Building	
Leisure or Recreational Facility	
Place of Interest	
Public Building	
Shopping Centre or Market	
Other Selected Buildings	

SCALE

Map Pages 4-34
1:19000 3.33 inches to 1 mile
0 ¼ ½ Mile
0 250 500 750 Metres
5.26cm to 1km 8.47cm to 1 mile

Map Page 35
1:9500 6.67 inches to 1 mile
0 ⅛ ¼ Mile
0 100 200 300 Metres
10.53 cm to 1km 16.94 cm to 1 mile

Fairfield Road, Borough Green, Sevenoaks, Kent TN15 8PP
Telephone: 01732 781000 (General Enquiries & Trade Sales)
01732 783422 (Retail Sales)

www.a-zmaps.co.uk

EDITION 4 2006

KEY TO MAP PAGES

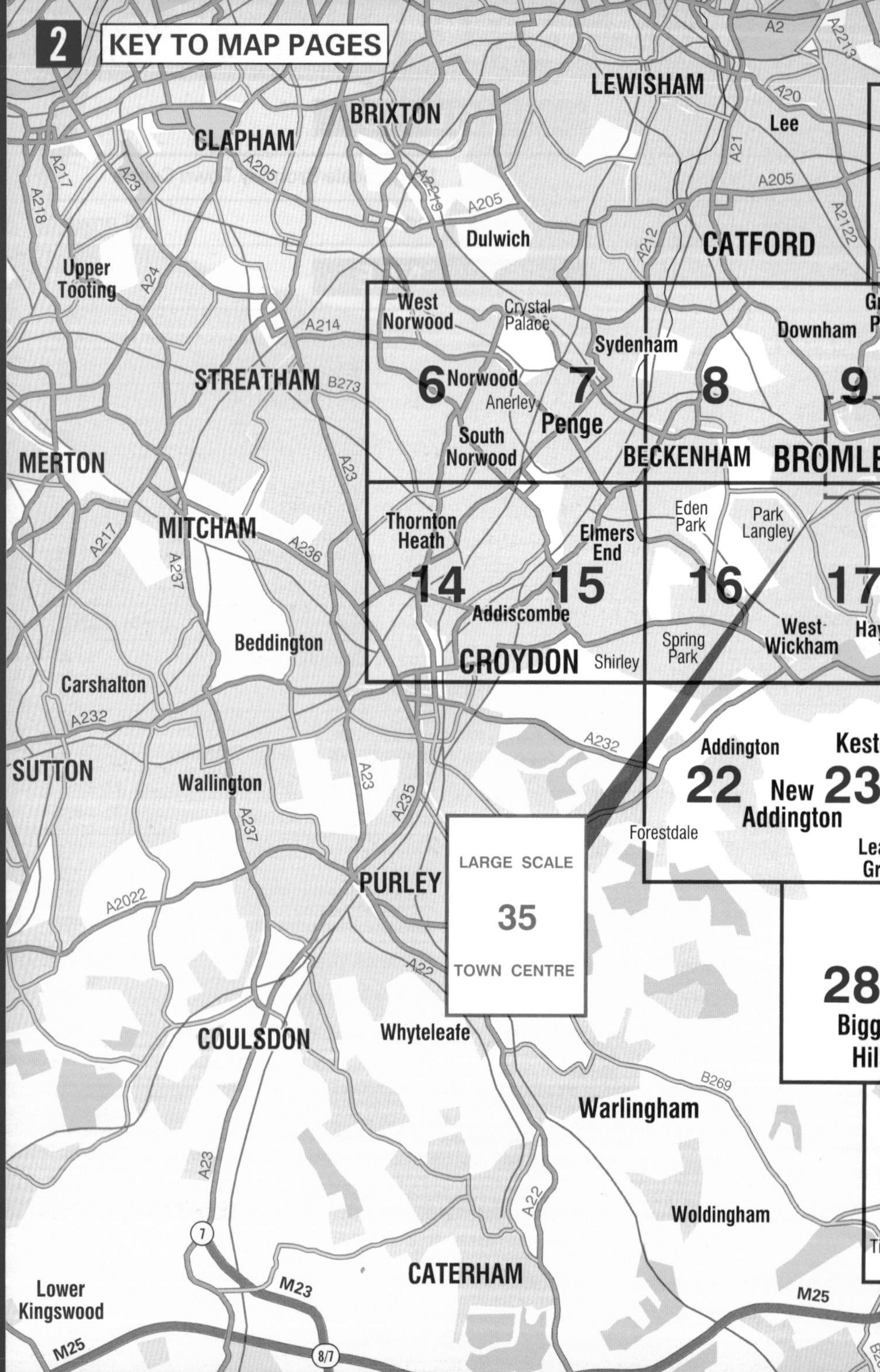

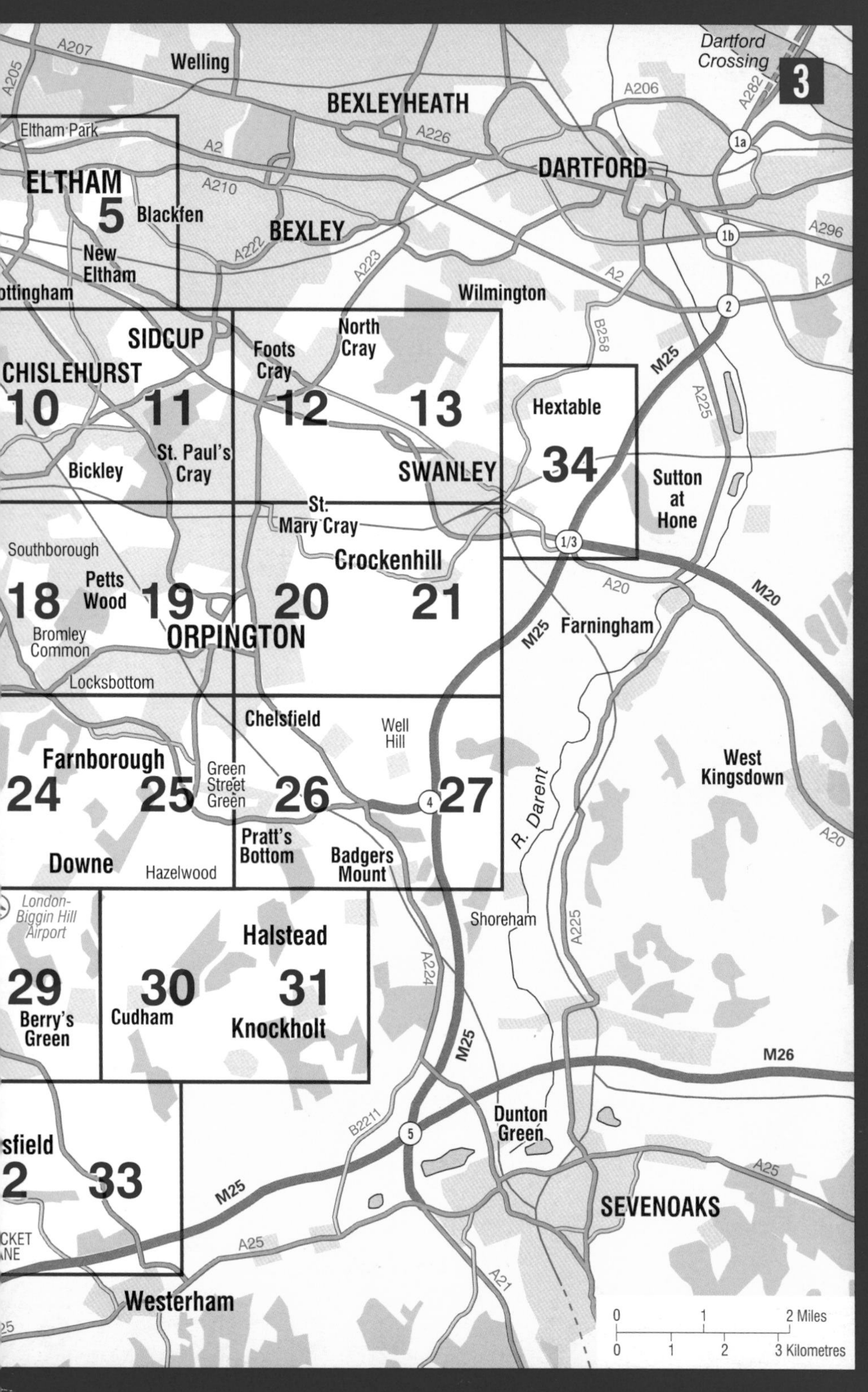
Dartford
Crossing
Welling
BEXLEYHEATH
DARTFORD
ELTHAM
5
Eltham Park
Blackfen
BEXLEY
New
Eltham
Wilmington
SIDCUP
CHISLEHURST
10
11
Foots
Cray
North
Cray
12
13
Hextable
34
Bickley
St. Paul's
Cray
SWANLEY
Sutton
at
Hone
St.
Mary Cray
Crockenhill
Southborough
18
Petts
Wood
19
20
21
Bromley
Common
ORPINGTON
Farningham
Locksbottom
Chelsfield
Well
Hill
Farnborough
24
25
Green
Street
Green
26
27
West
Kingsdown
R. Darent
Downe
Hazelwood
Pratt's
Bottom
Badgers
Mount
London-
Biggin Hill
Airport
Halstead
Shoreham
29
30
31
Berry's
Green
Cudham
Knockholt
Dunton
Green
33
SEVENOAKS
Westerham
A207
A205
A206
A282
A2
A226
A210
A222
A223
A296
B258
M25
A225
A20
M20
A224
M26
B2211
A25
A21
1a
1b
2
1/3
4
5
0
1
2 Miles
0
1
2
3 Kilometres

4
A
B
C
D
E
1
2
3
4
5
6
7
Kidbrooke
KIDBROOKE ESTATE
TILBROOK RD.
WINCHCOMB GARDENS
ROCHESTER WAY
ROCHESTER
WELL HALL ROAD
A205
WELL HALL ROUNDABOUT
KIDBROOKE PARK ROAD
A2213
TUDWAY
SE3
Nature Res.
Support Cen.
David Lloyd Leis.
Golf Driving Range
Sports Ground
Quaggy River
PINTO WAY
LYME FARM RD.
Meadowside Leis. Cen.
MEADOWSIDE
AVENUE
A2
Sports Ground
Tennis Courts
Tudor Barn
Bowling Green
Eltham
SUTCLIFFE PARK
Harrow Meadow
Sutcliffe Park Athletics Track
Football Ground
Roan School Playing Fields
A20
ELTHAM ROAD
A210
WESTHORNE AVENUE
ELTHAM HILL
YORKSHIRE GREY
Eltham Green Sch.
Playing Field
Moatbridge Sch.
ELTHAM
Eltham Coll.
Queenscroft Park
Eltham Hill Sch.
Swim. Pool
COURT ROAD
A208
Horn Park
Colfes Sch.
Playing Field
CROWN COURT
ABERGELDIE
SIDCUP ROAD
ELTHAM PALACE RD
Sports Ground
Bowling Grn.
Spts. Grd.
GROVE ROUND
Eltham Palace
Institute of Army Education
SE9
KING JOHN'S WALK
Community Centre
SE12
Horn Park Prim. Sch.
Horn Park
GREENWICH
LEWISHAM
BROMLEY
WESTHORNE AVENUE
SIBTHORPE
Comm. Cen.
WINN ROAD
MOTTINGHAM LA.
MOTTINGHAM ROAD
SHRUBSALL CL
AVENUE
Mottingham
Bird Sanctuary
The Tarn
Hadlow Coll. (Mottingham Centre)
Mottingham Hall
Mottingham Farm
Eltham College Jun. Sch.
Playing Fields
Eltham Coll.
Eric Liddell Spts. Cen.
MOTTINGHAM
MOTTINGHAM
COURT RD.
Sports Ground
Bannatyne Health Club
Sports Ground
Running Track
Sports Ground
Playing Field
Rec. Grd.
Sports Ground
Sports Ground
BARING ROAD
A2212
GROVE PARK
Depot
Comm. Cen.
CHINBROOK ROAD
Grove Park
Chinbrook Meadows
GROVE PARK
B226
DUNKERY ROAD
9
41
10
42
Marvels Wood
FRAMLINGHAM
Sec. Sch.
72
73
74
75

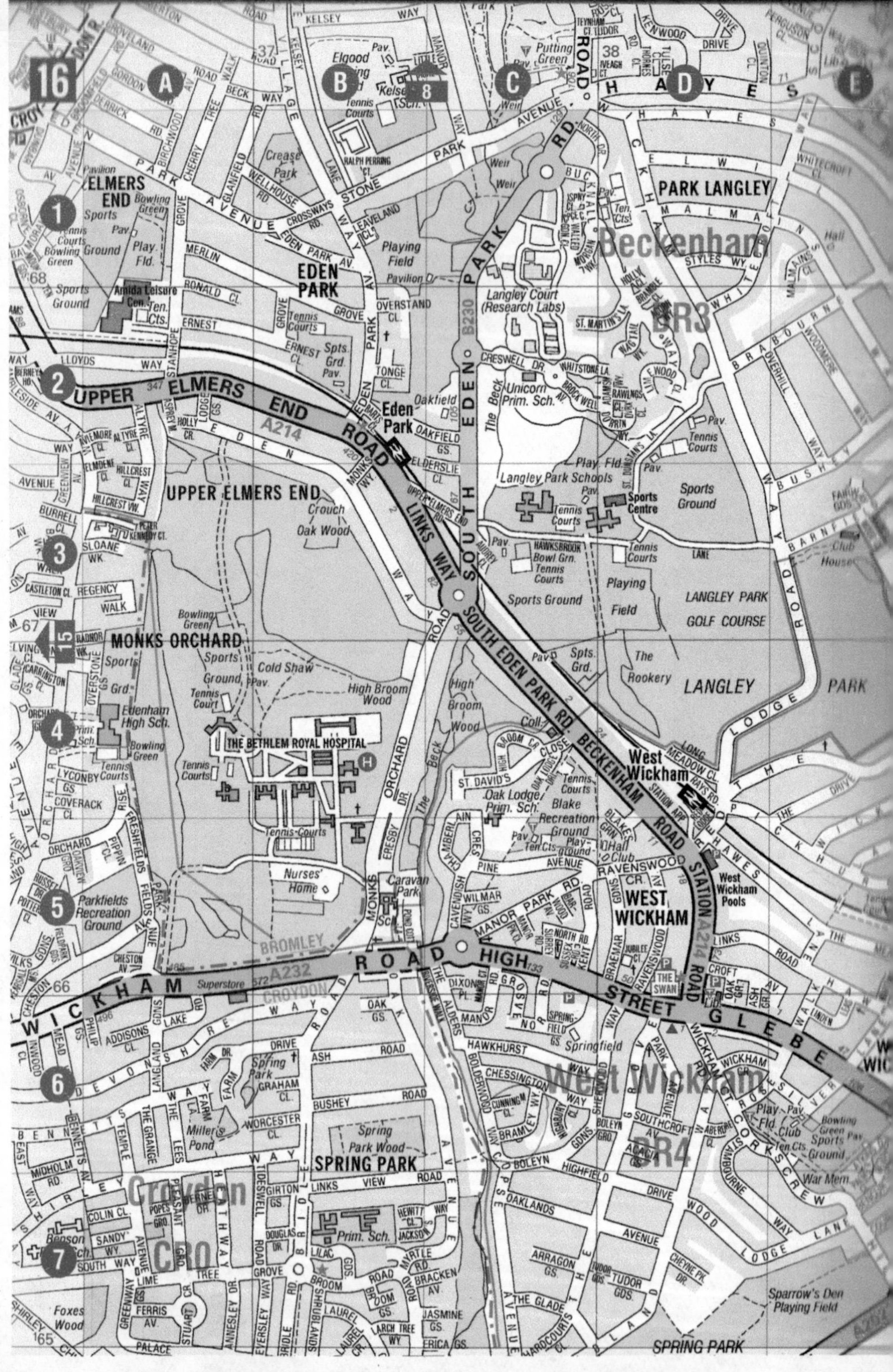

16
A
B
C
D
E
1
2
3
4
5
6
7
8
15
ELMERS END
EDEN PARK
PARK LANGLEY
Beckenham
BR3
UPPER ELMERS END
MONKS ORCHARD
WEST WICKHAM
West Wickham
BR4
SPRING PARK
Croydon
CR0
UPPER ELMERS END ROAD
A214
LINKS WAY
SOUTH EDEN PARK RD.
SOUTH EDEN PARK ROAD
B230
BECKENHAM ROAD
STATION ROAD
WICKHAM ROAD
CROYDON ROAD
A232
HIGH STREET
GLEBE WAY
HAYES WAY
PARK AVENUE
STONE PARK AVENUE
WICKHAM WAY
LANGLEY PARK
LANGLEY PARK GOLF COURSE
LODGE LANE
THE BETHLEM ROYAL HOSPITAL
Langley Court (Research Labs)
Langley Park Schools
Eden Park
West Wickham
West Wickham Pools
Edenham High Sch.
Parkfields Recreation Ground
Blake Recreation Ground
Oak Lodge Prim. Sch.
Unicorn Prim. Sch.
Crouch Oak Wood
Cold Shaw
High Broom Wood
Spring Park Wood
Miller's Pond
Sparrow's Den Playing Field
Foxes Wood
Springfield
Amida Leisure Cen.
Kelsey Sch.
Elgood Playing Fld
Crease Park
The Rookery
Superstore
THE SWAN
BROMLEY
CROYDON

5
44
545
F
G
H
J
K
1
2
3
4
5
6
7
10
11
ELTHAM PARK
SHEPHERDLEAS WOOD
Playing Field
ELTHAM PARK NORTH
ELTHAM PARK SOUTH
Falconwood Field
Falconwood
FALCONWOOD
WELLING WAY
FALCONWOOD Coll.
Welling DA16
ROCHESTER WAY
EAST ROCHESTER WAY
RELIEF ROAD
A2
Eltham Cemetery
Eltham Crematorium
ELTHAM WARREN GOLF COURSE
Club House
Nature Study Centre
Crown Woods School
Playing Field
BEXLEY ROAD
A210
BLACKFEN ROAD
University of Greenwich (Avery Hill Campus)
AVERY HILL
AVERY HILL PARK
AVERY HILL RD.
B2214
Alderwood Prim. Sch.
Parish Wood
Halls of Residence
Sidcup DA15
HALFWAY STREET
BLACKFEN
Sparrow's Farm Leisure Cen.
Sports Ground
Playing Fields
FOOTSCRAY ROAD
A211
Superstore
Comp. Sch.
Spts. Cen.
STREET
GREEN LANE
B263
New Eltham
Cricket Ground
St. Olave's Prep. School.
Dulverton Prim. Sch.
Old Farm Park
Wyncham Stream
NEW ELTHAM
FIVEWAYS
A20
SIDCUP ROAD
MAIN ROAD
SIDCUP BY-PASS
LONGLANDS
World Of Golf at Sidcup Pitch & Putt Course
Flamingo Park Sports Grd.
Chislehurst
Rec. Grd.
Netball Courts
Playing Field
Prim. Sch.

6
A
B
C
D
E
1
2
3
4
5
6
7
West Norwood
WEST NORWOOD
West Norwood Crematorium
Cemetery
Library
SE27
SE21
SE19
SW16
CR7
Sydenham Hill
Gipsy Hill
NORWOOD NEW TOWN
NORWOOD
UPPER NORWOOD
Thornton Heath
THORNTON HEATH
NORWOOD PARK
Kingswood Prim. Sch.
KINGSWOOD ESTATE
CROWN LA.
CROWN DALE
CENTRAL HILL
A214
A215
A212
A2199
B232
B273
B266
KNIGHTS HILL
NORWOOD HIGH ST.
ELDER ROAD
GIPSY HILL
SOUTH CROXTED RD.
DULWICH WD. PK.
COLLEGE RD.
CRYSTAL PALACE
ANERLEY
WESTOW HILL
CHURCH RD.
BEULAH HILL
GRANGE ROAD
SOUTH NORWOOD HILL
NORWOOD LANE
PARCHMORE ROAD
GREEN LANE
Rec. Grd.
Playing Fields
Biggin Wood
Downsview Prim. Sch.
St. Joseph's RC Jun. & Inf. Schs.
St. Joseph's College
Convent Wood
Rockmount Prim. Sch.
Senior Sch.
Recreation Ground
Tennis Courts
Temple
Westwood Language Coll. for Girls
David Livingstone Prim. Sch.
The Lawns
Harris City Technology Co
Beaulieu Heights
TV Station
Cypress Inf. Sch.
Cypress Jun. Sch.
Spurgeon's College
Grangewood Park
Coun. Offs.
Kensington Avenue Jun. & Inf. Schs.
Sports Ground
Comm. Cen.
RC Prim. Sch.
Rec. Ground
Nature Park
Training Cen.
Super store
Westow Park
Crystal Palace FC (Selhurst Park)
WHITEHORSE
14

7
F
G
H
J
K
1
2
3
4
5
6
7
8
15
UPPER SYDENHAM
Sydenham Wells Park
KIRKDALE
A212
SYDENHAM HILL
SYDENHAM ROAD
Sydenham
SE26
SYDENHAM
LWR. SYDENHAM
Mayow Park
DACRES ESTATE
Recreation
Bowling Grn.
Tennis Cts.
Home Park
Sports Ground
Lib. Hall
WESTWOOD
CRYSTAL PALACE PARK RD.
A234
Fisherman's Gate
Intermediate Lake
CRYSTAL PALACE PARK
The Maze
Sydenham Entrance
Crystal Palace National Sports Centre
Crystal Palace Athletics Stadium
Crystal Palace
Tennis Courts
Play. Fld.
Penge Entrance
Lower Lake
Anerley Entrance
St. Christopher's Hospice
The Haven
NEWLANDS PARK
A213
LEWISHAM
BROMLEY
Alexandra Rec. Grd.
Alexandra Jun. Sch.
Playing Field
Penge East
Penge West
HIGH ST.
PARISH LANE
LENNARD ROAD
KENT HOUSE ROAD
CATOR PARK
Spts. Grd.
Sports Grd.
New Beckenham
Kent House
Beckenham Road
Clock Ho.
PENGE
SE20
GREEN LA.
BECKENHAM RD.
ANERLEY
Anerley
A214
ANERLEY ROAD
Betts Park
Civic Halls
Anerley Sch.
Orchard Lodge (Remand Centre)
James Dixon Prim. Sch.
Nursing Home
Orchard School Sports Centre
TH & Lib.
CROYDON RD.
A213
PENGE RD.
Bromley Junction
ELMERS END
Avenue Road
Birkbeck
Beckenham Crematorium
Harrington Rd.
Blind Corner
SOUTH NORWOOD COUNTRY PARK
Elmers End
Beckenham
BR3
CROYDON RD.
A222
Playing Field
Depots
Rec. Grd.
Superstore
The Kentwood Cen.
Arts Cen.
The Spa

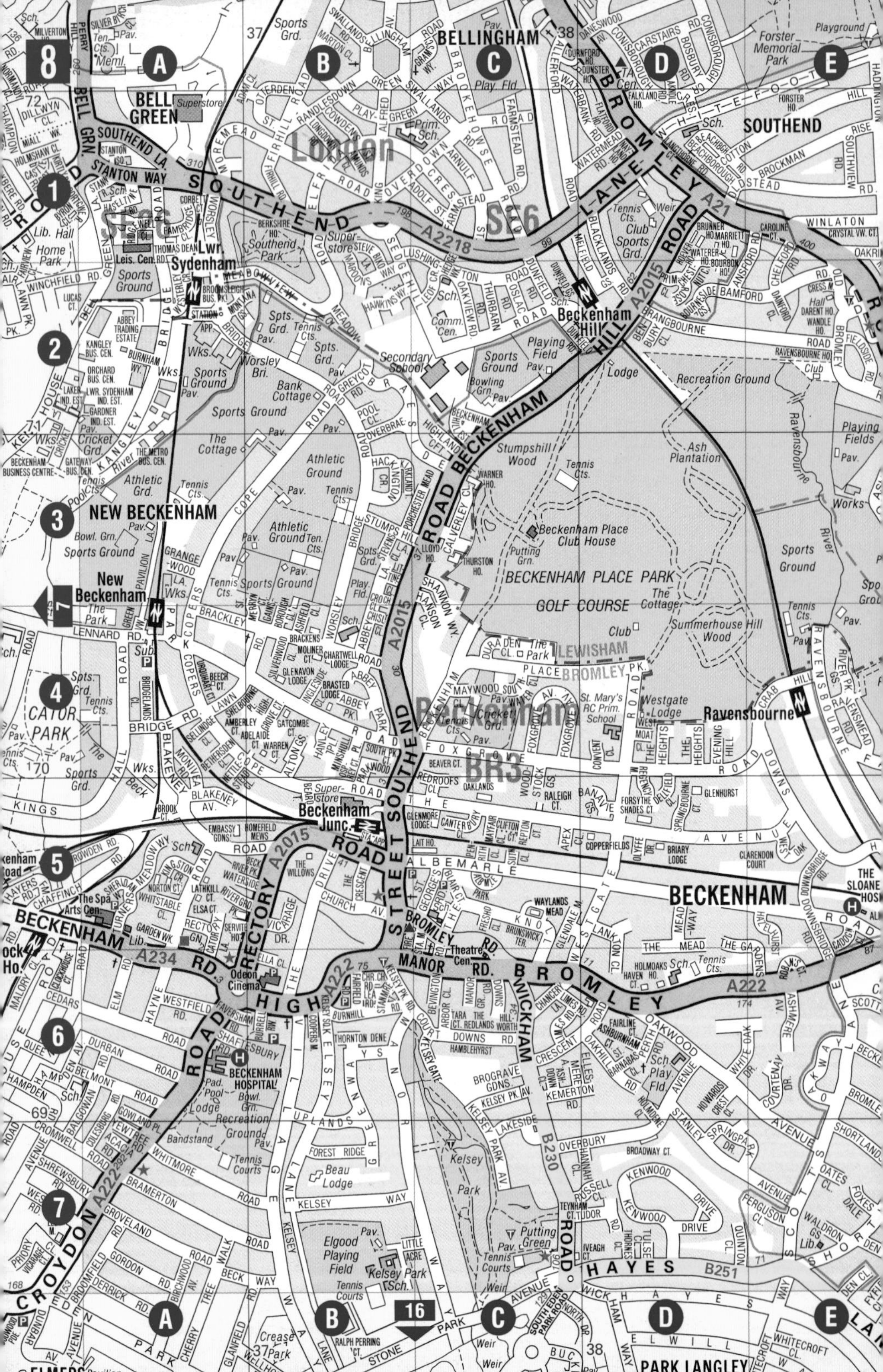
8
A
B
C
D
E
1
2
3
4
5
6
7
BELL GREEN
BELLINGHAM
SOUTHEND
London
SE6
SOUTHEND LA.
STANTON WAY
SOUTHEND
A2218
BROMLEY
LANE
BROMLEY ROAD
A21
Lwr. Sydenham
Beckenham Hill
BECKENHAM HILL ROAD
A2015
NEW BECKENHAM
New Beckenham
7
BECKENHAM PLACE PARK
GOLF COURSE
Beckenham Place Club House
Stumpshill Wood
Summerhouse Hill Wood
Ash Plantation
Recreation Ground
Ravensbourne
LEWISHAM
BROMLEY
Beckenham
BR3
CATOR PARK
SOUTHEND ROAD
Beckenham Junc.
RECTORY ROAD
A2015
BECKENHAM
BECKENHAM RD.
A234
HIGH
A222
MANOR RD.
BROMLEY
WICKHAM
A222
BECKENHAM HOSPITAL
Odeon Cinema
CROYDON ROAD
A222
Kelsey Park
Elgood Playing Field
HAYES
B251
B230
PARK LANGLEY
16
Crease Park
37
38

10
A
B
C
D
E
4
5
9
18
1
2
3
4
5
6
7
72
71
170
69
42
43
SE9
BR1
Bromley
ELMSTEAD
ELMSTEAD WOOD
Elmstead Woods
CHISLEHURST WEST
CHISLEHURS
Chislehurst
BICKLEY
Bickley
Sundridge Park
SUNDRIDGE PARK
GOLF COURSE
CAMDEN PARK
CHISLEHURST GOLF COURSE
Widmore Green
WIDMORE
Playing Field
Lower Marvels Wood
Marvels Wood
Grove Park Cemetery
LEWISHAM
BROMLEY
Castlecombe Prim. Sch.
Youth Cen.
Sports Ground
Ravensbourne College
Garden Wood
Training Centre
High Grove
Sundridge Park Mansion
Botany Bay
Rockpit Wood
Kyd Brook
Sira Institute
Red Hill Prim. Sch.
Whyte's Woodland
Bird Sanctuary
Camden Place (Club House)
The Cedars
Hangman's Cnr.
Cricket Grd.
Caves
Chalkpit Wood
Bullers Wood Sch.
St. Cecilia's
Scotts Park Prim. Sch.
Rifle Range
Birch Wood
Gosshill Wood
Pond Wood
Avalon
Bickley Junc.
Chislehurst Junction
Blackbrook Wood
Recreation Ground
Holmes Place
The Widmore Cen.
Hadlow
School
Rec. Grd
Works
Depot
WHITE HORSE HILL
RED HILL
HIGH
A208
A222
B264
B265
B263
MOTTINGHAM ROAD
WIDMORE RD.
BICKLEY RD.
BICKLEY PARK ROAD
CHISLEHURST RD.
PAGE HEATH LA.
HOMESDALE RD.
SUMMER HILL
OLD HILL
CAMDEN PARK ROAD
WILLOW GROVE
LOGS HILL
SUNDRIDGE AVE.
ELMSTEAD LANE
DUNKERY RD.
MARVELS LANE
FRAMLINGHAM CR.
CASTLECOMBE RD.
WALDEN RD.
HAWTHORNE ROAD
WOODLANDS RD.
AVENUE RD.

LONGLANDS
World Of Golf at Sidcup
Pitch & Putt Course
Kemnal Manor
Ashen Grove
Partridge Shaw
Esporta Health & Fitness
Beaver's Wood
Chislehurst Cemetery
Hoblands Wood
Foxbury
Playing Field
Old Elthamians Sports Club
Beaverwood Sch. for Girls
Athletic Ground
Sports Ground
Garden Centre
Chislehurst
Darul Uloom London Islamic Sch.
Farringtons & Stratford House
Icehouse Wood
PARK WOOD
SCADBURY PARK (Nature Reserve)
Square Clump
Bushy Clump
Bank's Shaw
Little Wood
Irish Plantation
Moat
Archway
Midfield Prim. Sch.
The Meadow School Playing Field
Youth Club
Hadresham
The Fantails
Holbrook Wood Lodge
Peasons
The Larches
St. Peter & St. Paul RC Prim. Sch.
Playing Field
The Gorse Children's Home
St. Paul's Cray Common
Hoblingwell Wood
Brackenwood
ST. PAUL'S CRAY
Recreation Ground
Leesons Prim. Sch.
Coll.
Marjorie McClure School
Playing Field
Hawkwood Estate
Tongs Farm
Walk Wood
Edlmann Memorial Wood
PETTS WOOD
Willett Memorial Wood
SIDCUP
Sports Ground
Resource Centre
Sidcup Green
Sidcup Place
Sidcup Place Park
St. Mary & St. Joseph's Catholic Sch.
Sixth Form Coll.
QUEEN MARY'S HOSPITAL
Wall Ho.
Frognal Ho.
Chestnut Ho.
Black Clump
FROGNAL CORNER
Spring Shaw
Orpington
MAIN ROAD
SIDCUP BY-PASS
A20
A211
A222
A208
PERRY STREET
BROMLEY LANE
ST. PAUL'S CRAY ROAD
ORPINGTON ROAD
CHISLEHURST RD.
SIDCUP HIGH ST.
DA14
DA15
BR7
BR5
F
G
H
J
K
1
2
3
4
5
6
7
5
11
12
19
545
46

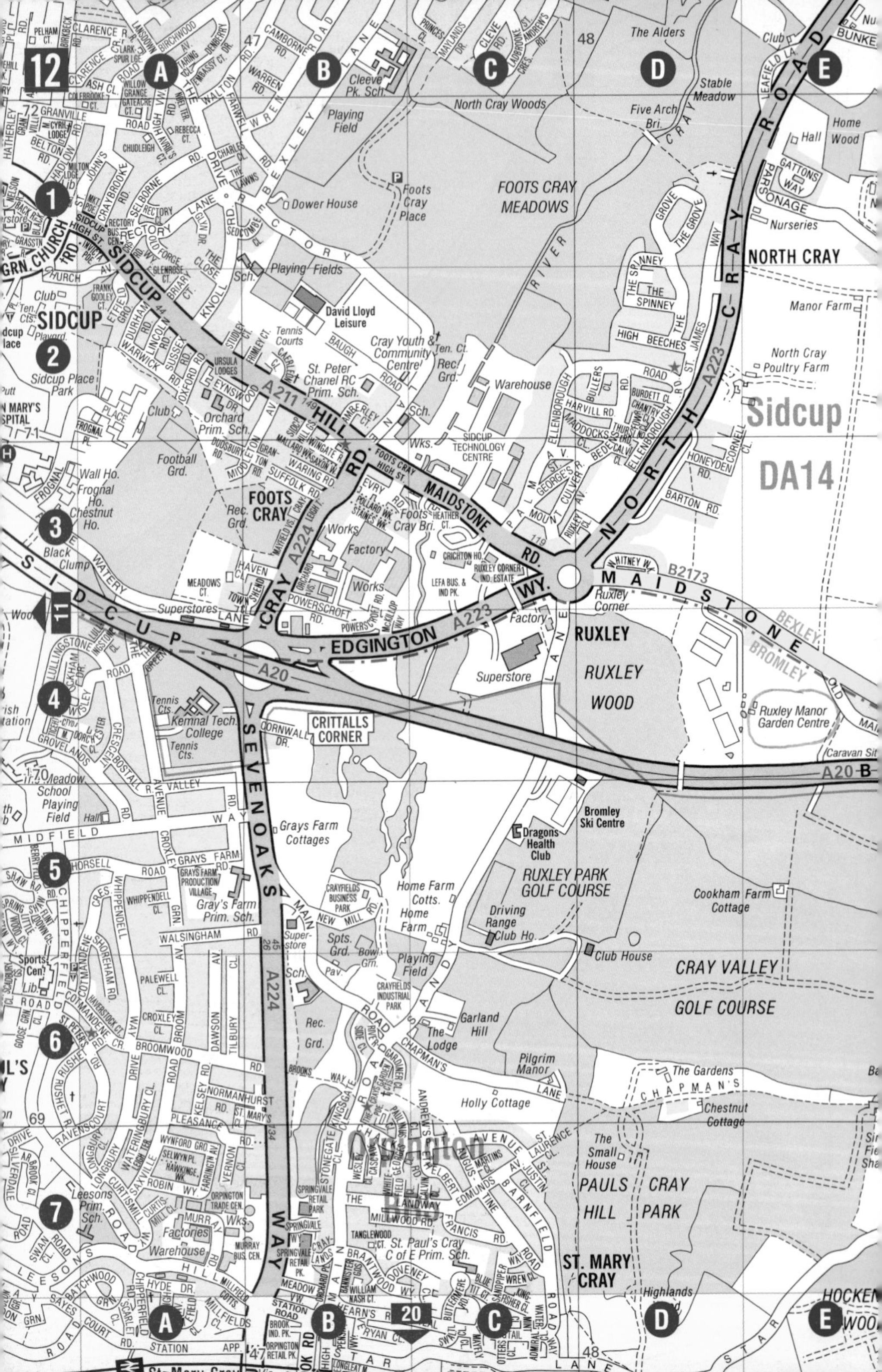

A
B
C
D
E
1
2
3
4
5
6
7
47
48
72
71
70
69
SIDCUP
SIDCUP HIGH ST.
Sidcup Place Park
FOOTS CRAY MEADOWS
North Cray Woods
The Alders
Stable Meadow
Five Arch Bri.
Home Wood
Hall
Nurseries
NORTH CRAY
Manor Farm
North Cray Poultry Farm
Sidcup
DA14
Cleeve Pk. Sch.
Playing Field
Foots Cray Place
Dower House
Playing Fields
David Lloyd Leisure
Tennis Courts
Cray Youth & Community Centre
St. Peter Chanel RC Prim. Sch.
Warehouse
SIDCUP TECHNOLOGY CENTRE
Orchard Prim. Sch.
Football Grd.
Wall Ho.
Frognal Ho.
Chestnut Ho.
Black Clump
FOOTS CRAY
Foots Cray Bri.
Works
Factory
CRICHTON HO.
RUXLEY CORNER IND. ESTATE
LEFA BUS. & IND PK.
MAIDSTONE RD.
NORTH CRAY ROAD
A223
A211
A224
A20
B2173
SIDCUP HILL
EDGINGTON WY.
SIDCUP BY-PASS
SEVENOAKS WAY
MAIDSTONE
Ruxley Corner
RUXLEY
RUXLEY WOOD
Superstore
Superstores
BEXLEY
BROMLEY
Ruxley Manor Garden Centre
Caravan Site
CRITTALLS CORNER
Kemnal Tech. College
Tennis Cts.
Meadow School Playing Field
Grays Farm Cottages
Bromley Ski Centre
Dragons Health Club
RUXLEY PARK GOLF COURSE
Driving Range
Club Ho.
Club House
Cookham Farm Cottage
CRAY VALLEY GOLF COURSE
Home Farm Cotts.
Home Farm
Playing Field
CRAYFIELDS BUSINESS PARK
CRAYFIELDS INDUSTRIAL PARK
Spts. Grd.
Rec. Grd.
Garland Hill
The Lodge
Pilgrim Manor
Holly Cottage
The Gardens
Chestnut Cottage
The Small House
PAULS CRAY HILL PARK
ST. MARY CRAY
Highlands
Gray's Farm Prim. Sch.
GRAYS FARM PRODUCTION VILLAGE
Sports Cen.
Lib.
Leesons Prim. Sch.
Factories
Warehouse
ORPINGTON TRADE CEN.
MURRAY BUS. CEN.
SPRINGVALE RETAIL PARK
St. Paul's Cray C of E Prim. Sch.
Orpington
STATION ROAD
BROOK IND. PK.
ORPINGTON RETAIL PK.
STATION APP.
20
11
CHAPMAN'S LANE
STAR LANE
MIDFIELD WAY
LEESONS HILL
CRAY
RIVER

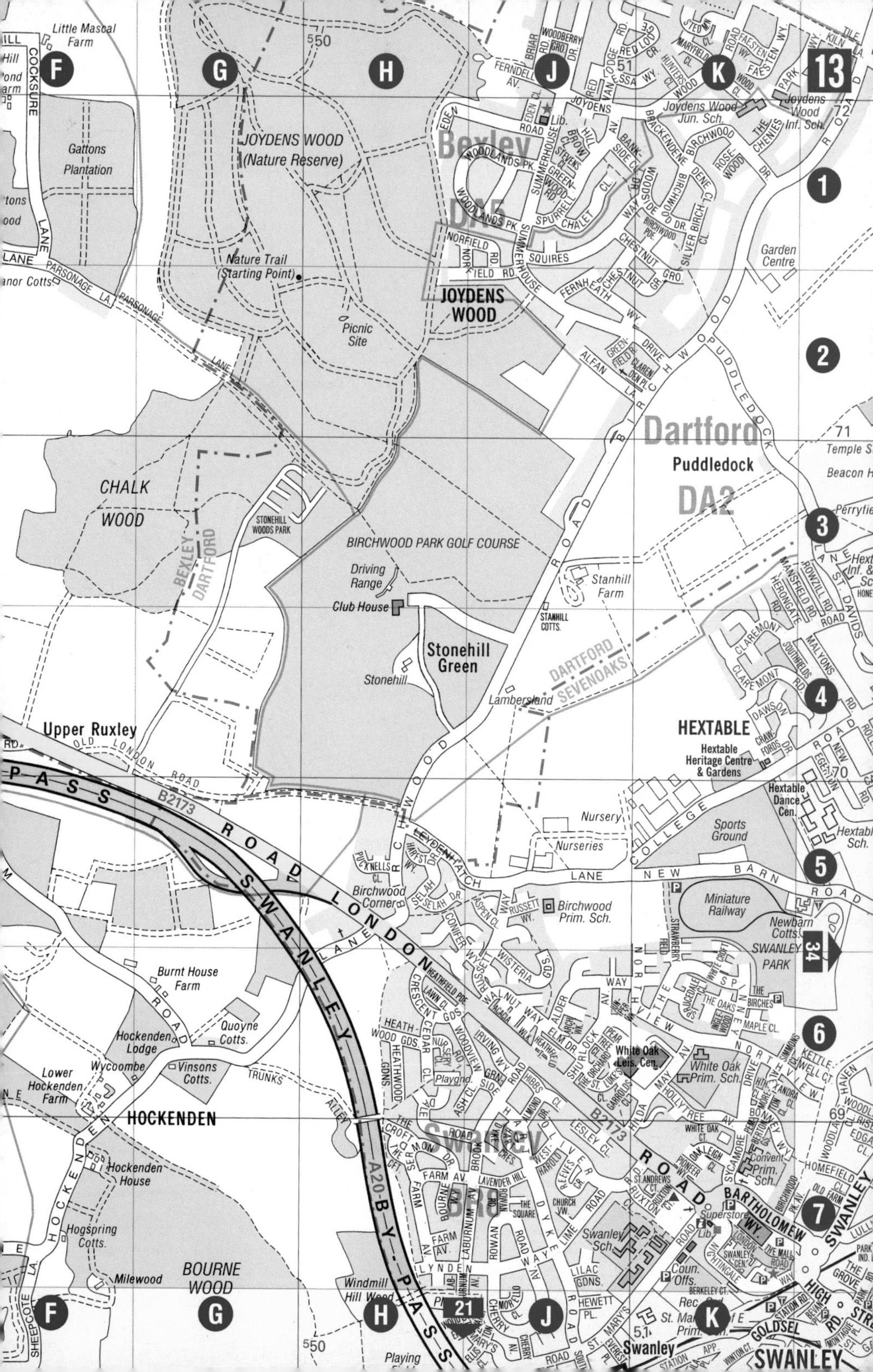

13
34
21
Joydens Wood
Bexley
DA5
Dartford
DA2
Puddledock
JOYDENS WOOD (Nature Reserve)
Nature Trail (Starting Point)
Picnic Site
JOYDENS WOOD
Gattons Plantation
Little Mascal Farm
CHALK WOOD
STONEHILL WOODS PARK
BIRCHWOOD PARK GOLF COURSE
Driving Range
Club House
Stonehill Green
Stonehill
Stanhill Farm
Lambersland
HEXTABLE
Hextable Heritage Centre & Gardens
Hextable Dance Cen.
Sports Ground
Miniature Railway
Newbarn Cotts.
SWANLEY PARK
Nursery
Nurseries
Birchwood Corner
Birchwood Prim. Sch.
Upper Ruxley
Burnt House Farm
Quoyne Cotts.
Hockenden Lodge
Vinsons Cotts.
Wycoombe
Lower Hockenden Farm
HOCKENDEN
Hockenden House
Hogspring Cotts.
Milewood
BOURNE WOOD
Windmill Hill Wood
White Oak Leis. Cen.
White Oak Prim. Sch.
Swanley Sch.
Convent Prim. Sch.
Superstore
Coun. Offs.
Swanley
SWANLEY
A20 BY-PASS
B2173
LONDON ROAD
Joydens Wood Jun. Sch.
Joydens Wood Inf. Sch.
Garden Centre
Temple St
Beacon H
Hextable Sch.
DARTFORD SEVENOAKS
BEXLEY DARTFORD

14
A
B
C
D
E
6
1
2
3
4
5
6
7
Thornton Heath
THORNTON HEATH
Thornton Heath
CR7
SE25
Crystal Palace FC (Selhurst Park)
Selhurst
SELHURST
MAYDAY UNIVERSITY HOSP.
Queen's Rd. Cemy.
BROAD GREEN
CROYDON
West Croydon
East Croydon
Wellesley Rd.
George St.
Church St.
WADDON
WANDLE PARK
Wandle Park
Reeves Cnr.
Lebanon Rd.
Sandilands
Fairfield Halls
Heavers Farm Prim. Sch.
St. Chad's RC Prim. Sch.
Heavers Farm Centre
Recreation Ground
Ecclesbourne Jun. & Inf. Schs.
Bensham Manor Sch.
Sports Ground
Coombe Cliff (Educ. Cen.)
Cambridge Tutors Coll.
Davidson Primary Sch.
Centrale Shop. Cen.
Whitgift Sq.
Croydon Coll.
Mag. Courts
BRIGSTOCK
LONDON ROAD
WHITEHORSE ROAD
WINDMILL RD.
ST. JAMES'S RD.
SELHURST RD.
LOWER ADDISCOMBE ROAD
WELLESLEY ROAD
ROMAN WAY
OLD TOWN
CROYDON FLYOVER
DUPPAS HILL RD.
COOMBE RD.
PARK LANE
PARK HILL ROAD
MORLAND ROAD
CHERRY ORCHARD ROAD
A212
A213
A222
A232
A235
A236
B266

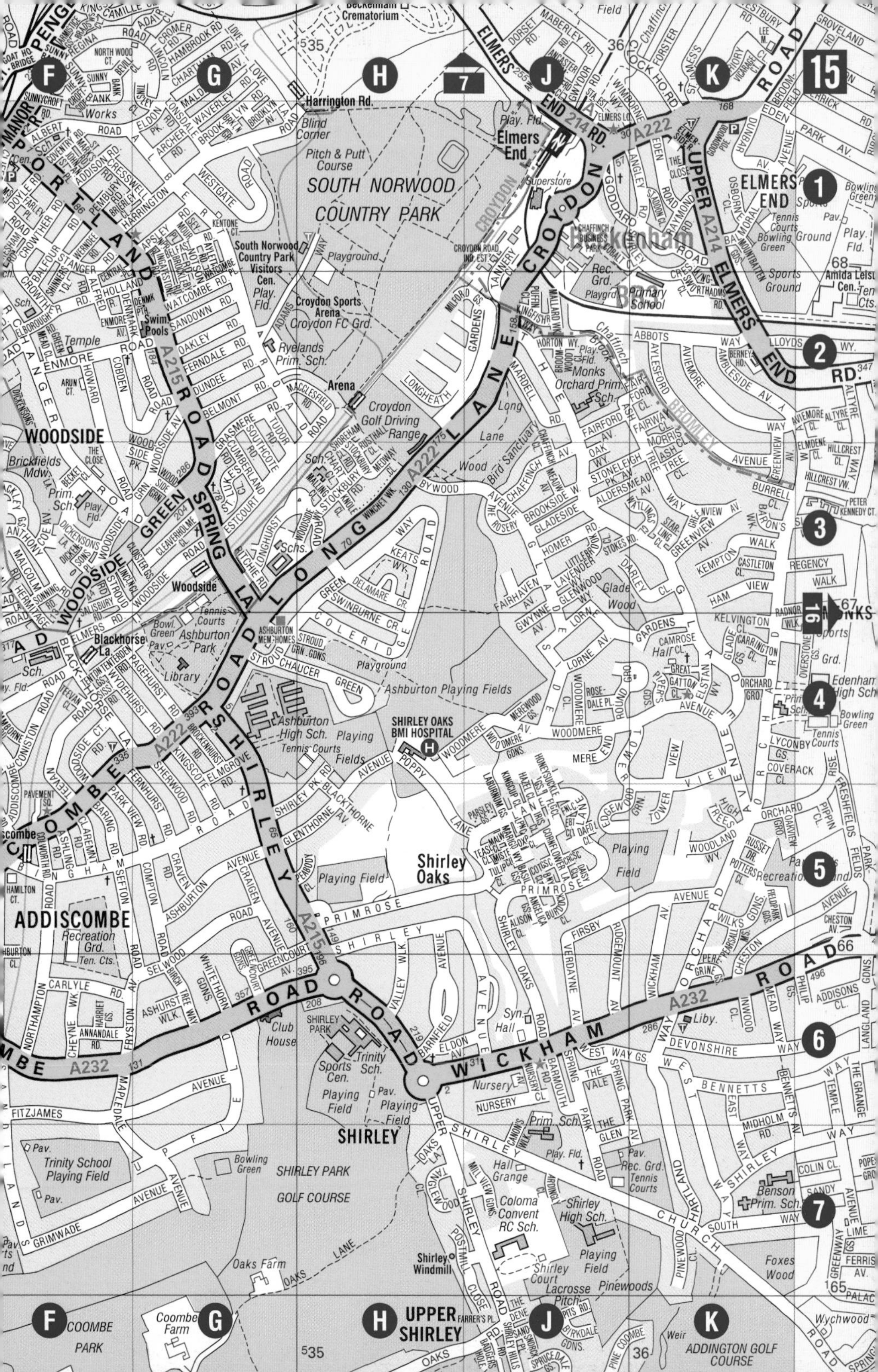

15
F
G
H
J
K
7
16
1
2
3
4
5
6
7
Beckenham Crematorium
Harrington Rd.
Blind Corner
Pitch & Putt Course
SOUTH NORWOOD COUNTRY PARK
South Norwood Country Park Visitors Cen.
Play. Fld.
Playground
Croydon Sports Arena
Croydon FC Grd.
Ryelands Prim. Sch.
Arena
Croydon Golf Driving Range
Elmers End
ELMERS END
ELMERS END RD.
CROYDON RD.
Superstore
Chaffinch Business Park
Beckenham
Rec. Grd.
Primary School
UPPER ELMERS END RD.
Tennis Courts
Bowling Ground
Bowling Green
Sports Ground
Amida Leisure Cen.
Monks Orchard Prim. Sch.
Long Lane Wood
Bird Sanctuary
LONG LANE
PORTLAND RD.
SPRING LANE
WOODSIDE GREEN
WOODSIDE
Brickfields Mdw.
Prim. Sch.
Play. Fld.
Temple
Swim. Pools
Woodside
Blackhorse La.
Sch.
Tennis Courts
Bowl. Green
Ashburton Park
Library
Ashburton Mem. Homes
Playground
Ashburton Playing Fields
Ashburton High Sch.
Playing Fields
SHIRLEY OAKS BMI HOSPITAL
Glade Wood
Edenham High Sch.
Playing Field
Shirley Oaks
Recreation Grd.
SHIRLEY ROAD
ADDISCOMBE
Recreation Grd.
Ten. Cts.
Addiscombe
ADDISCOMBE RD.
WICKHAM ROAD
Club House
Shirley Park
Trinity Sch.
Sports Cen.
Playing Field
SHIRLEY
Syn. Hall
Liby.
Nursery
Prim. Sch.
Play. Fld.
Rec. Grd.
Tennis Courts
Benson Prim. Sch.
Trinity School Playing Field
Pav.
Bowling Green
SHIRLEY PARK GOLF COURSE
Hall Grange
Coloma Convent RC Sch.
Shirley High Sch.
Playing Field
Shirley Windmill
Shirley Court
Lacrosse Pitch
Pinewoods
Foxes Wood
Oaks Farm
Coombe Farm
COOMBE PARK
UPPER SHIRLEY
Weir
ADDINGTON GOLF COURSE
Wychwood
A222
A214
A215
A232

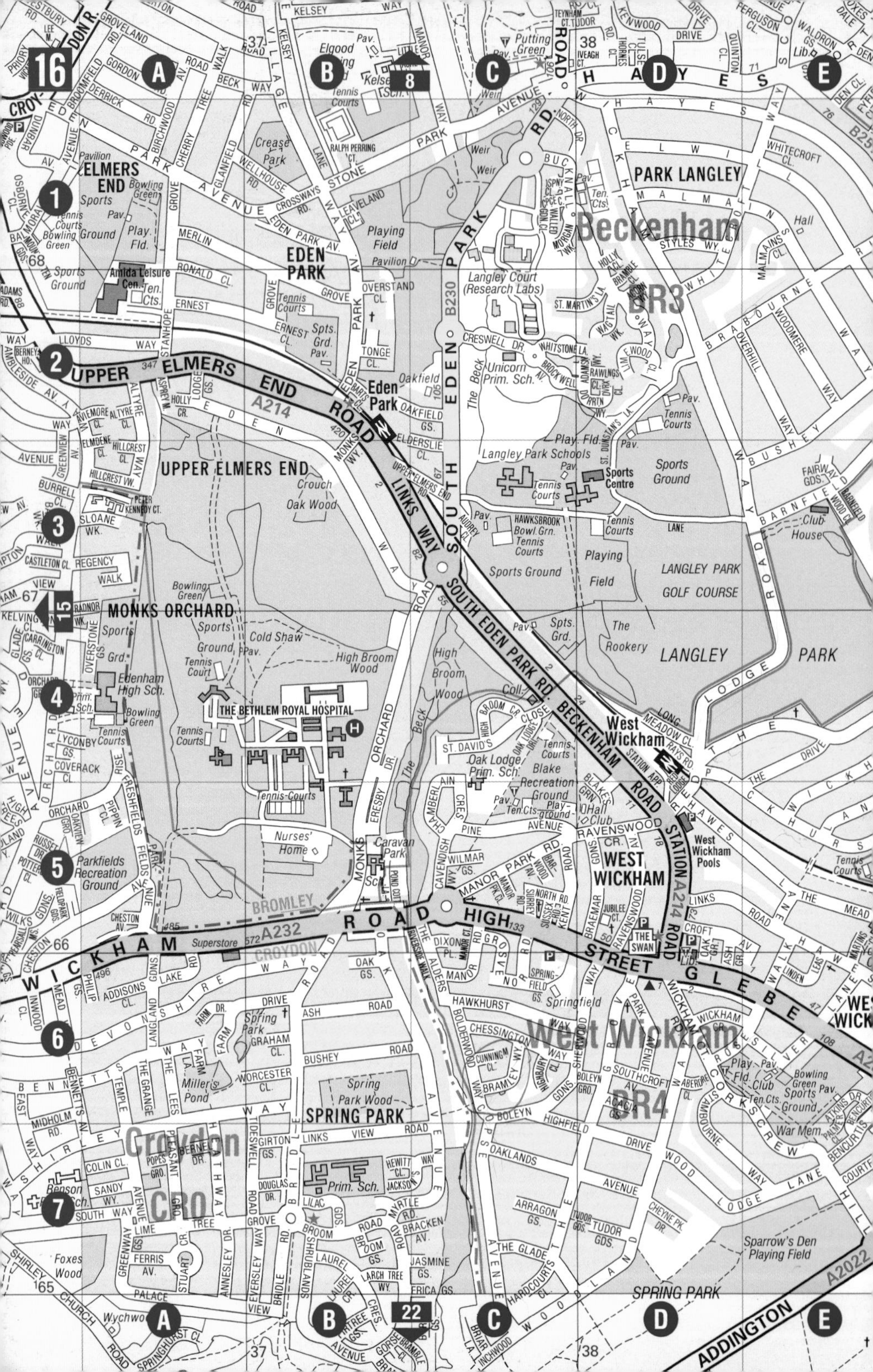

16
A
B
C
D
E
1
2
3
4
5
6
7
8
15
22
37
38
ELMERS END
Sports Ground
Play. Fld.
Amida Leisure Cen.
EDEN PARK
Crease Park
Elgood Playing Fld.
Kelsey Sch.
Tennis Courts
Playing Field
Pavilion
PARK LANGLEY
Beckenham
BR3
Langley Court (Research Labs)
Unicorn Prim. Sch.
Langley Park Schools
Sports Centre
Sports Ground
UPPER ELMERS END ROAD
A214
UPPER ELMERS END
Crouch Oak Wood
LINKS WAY
SOUTH EDEN PARK RD.
SOUTH EDEN PARK ROAD
B230
BECKENHAM ROAD
HAWKSBROOK Bowl. Grn.
LANGLEY PARK GOLF COURSE
The Rookery
LANGLEY PARK
West Wickham
MONKS ORCHARD
Cold Shaw
High Broom Wood
THE BETHLEM ROYAL HOSPITAL
Edenham High Sch.
Bowling Green
Parkfields Recreation Ground
Nurses' Home
Caravan Park
Oak Lodge Prim. Sch.
Blake Recreation Ground
WEST WICKHAM
West Wickham Pools
WICKHAM ROAD
A232
HIGH STREET
GLEBE WAY
BROMLEY
CROYDON
Superstore
THE SWAN
Springfield
West Wickham
BR4
Spring Park
Miller's Pond
Spring Park Wood
SPRING PARK
Croydon
CR0
Prim. Sch.
Benson Prim. Sch.
Foxes Wood
Sparrow's Den Playing Field
A2022
ADDINGTON
SPRING PARK
Bowling Green
Sports Ground
War Mem.
Play. Fld.
HAYES WAY
WICKHAM WAY
STATION ROAD
CORKSCREW HILL
LODGE LANE

17
Bromley South
SHORTLANDS
F
G
H
J
K
9
35
1
2
3
4
5
6
7
18
67
23
41
66
68
WESTMORELAND ROAD
HAYES ROAD
HAYES LANE
MASONS HILL
BROMLEY COMMON
HOMESDALE RD.
B228
B2212
B265
A21
B251
A232
CROYDON ROAD
CROYDON RD.
WEST WICKHAM
PICKHURST LANE
HAYES HILL
STATION APP.
RIDGEWAY
WARREN ROAD
BASTON ROAD
COMMONSIDE
FIVE ELMS ROAD
BARNET WOOD ROAD
GEORGE LANE
HAYES ST.
CHATHAM AVENUE
BOURNE WAY
CONEY HALL
CONEY HILL RD.
ADDINGTON RD.
MEAD WAY
Recreation Ground
Playing Field
Cricket Ground
Bromley FC Ground
Fishers Wood
Ravens Bourne
NORMAN PARK
Norman Park Athletics Track
Scrogginhall Wood
Rookery Lake
BROMLEY COMMON
Bromley Coll. of Further Educ.
Bromley
BR2
HAYES
Hayes Street Farm
Brook Wood
Mazzards Wood
Woodcock Grove
Bolds Wood
Hayes Prim. Sch.
Baston Pre - Jun. School
Hayes Sch.
THE PRIORY HOSPITAL, HAYES GROVE
Sports Ground
The Warren Bowl. Gn.
Hayes Court
HAYES COMMON
Five Elms
Gorsewood
Simpson's Cotts.
Colyers Wood
Barnet Wood
West Wickham Common
Cupola Wood
Pickhurst Jun. & Inf. Schs.
Pickhurst Green
The Ravensbourne Sch.
Hayesford
South Hill Wood Rec.Grnd
Hast Hill
Baston Manor
Padmall Wood
Lodge Coney Hall Rec. Grd.
Hayes
Bromley (Oct. to Jan.)

18
10
17
24
A
B
C
D
E
1
2
3
4
5
6
7
42
43
68
67
66
165
Bickley
BR1
BR2
Bromley
SOUTHBOROUGH
BROMLEY COMMON
LOCKSBOTTOM
KESTON MARK
Chislehurst Junction
JUBILEE COUNTRY PARK
Blackbrook Wood
Bromley High School
Thornet Wood
Recreation Ground
Holmes Place
Depot
Whitehall Pleasure Ground
Bowl. Grn.
Sports Ground
Bromley College of Further & Higher Education
Lord's Wood
Oakley House
Mazzards Wood
Woodcock Grove
Ravens Bourne
Barnet Wood
Playing Field
Ravens Wood Sch.
Simpson's Cotts
Padmall Wood
Southborough Prim. Sch.
Playing Field
Southborough Open Space (Rec. Grd.)
St. James' RC Prim. Sch.
Youth Cen.
Cemetery
Parkfield Recreation Ground
BROMLEY GOLF COURSE
Club House
Bishop Justus C of E Secondary School
Princes Plain Prim. Sch.
Prince's Plain
Scrubs Farm
Sparrow Wood
Sparrow Common
Crofton Heath
Clay Wood
Oakley Farm
Bus Depot
Nursery
Nobody's Wood
Pokeridden Wood
Knowlehill Wood
The Spinney
Knowlehill Farm
Hollydale Recreation Grounds
Depot Sports Grd.
Tennis Courts
Farnborough Recreation Ground
PRINCESS ROYAL UNIVERSITY HOSP.
Superstore
THE FANTAIL
A21
A233
A232
BROMLEY COMMON
HASTINGS ROAD
OAKLEY ROAD
FARNBOROUGH COMMON
CROYDON ROAD
CROFTON ROAD
SOUTHBOROUGH LANE
OLDFIELD ROAD
SOUTHLANDS ROAD
BLACKBROOK LANE
MAGPIE HALL LANE
TURPINGTON LANE
BARNET WOOD ROAD
GRAVEL ROAD
FARRINGDON AVENUE
CRESCENT AVENUE

19
F
G
H
J
K
11
25
20
1
2
3
4
5
6
7
Chislehurst
BR7
BR5
BR6
PETTS WOOD
Petts Wood
Edlmann Memorial Wood
Willett Memorial Wood
St. Mary Cray Junction
St. Mary Cray
ORPINGTON RD.
CHISLEHURST ROAD
A208
PERRY HALL RD.
POVEREST
Poverest Prim. Sch.
Orpington
ORPINGTON
Covet Wood
Recreation Ground
Bowling Green
Perry Hall Prim. Sch.
BROOM HILL
CROFTON
Crofton Jun. Sch.
Crofton Inf. Sch.
Petts Wood Recreation Ground
Lakeswood Hall
Gumping Common
A232
STATION ROAD
SPUR RD.
SEVENOAKS ROAD
A223
Civic Halls
Leisure Cen.
Priory Gardens
Newstead Wood
Newstead Wood Sch. for Girls
Playing Field
Darrick Wood
Tubbenden Jun. & Inf. Schs.
Ontario Centre
Hospice
Playing Field
Prim. Sch.

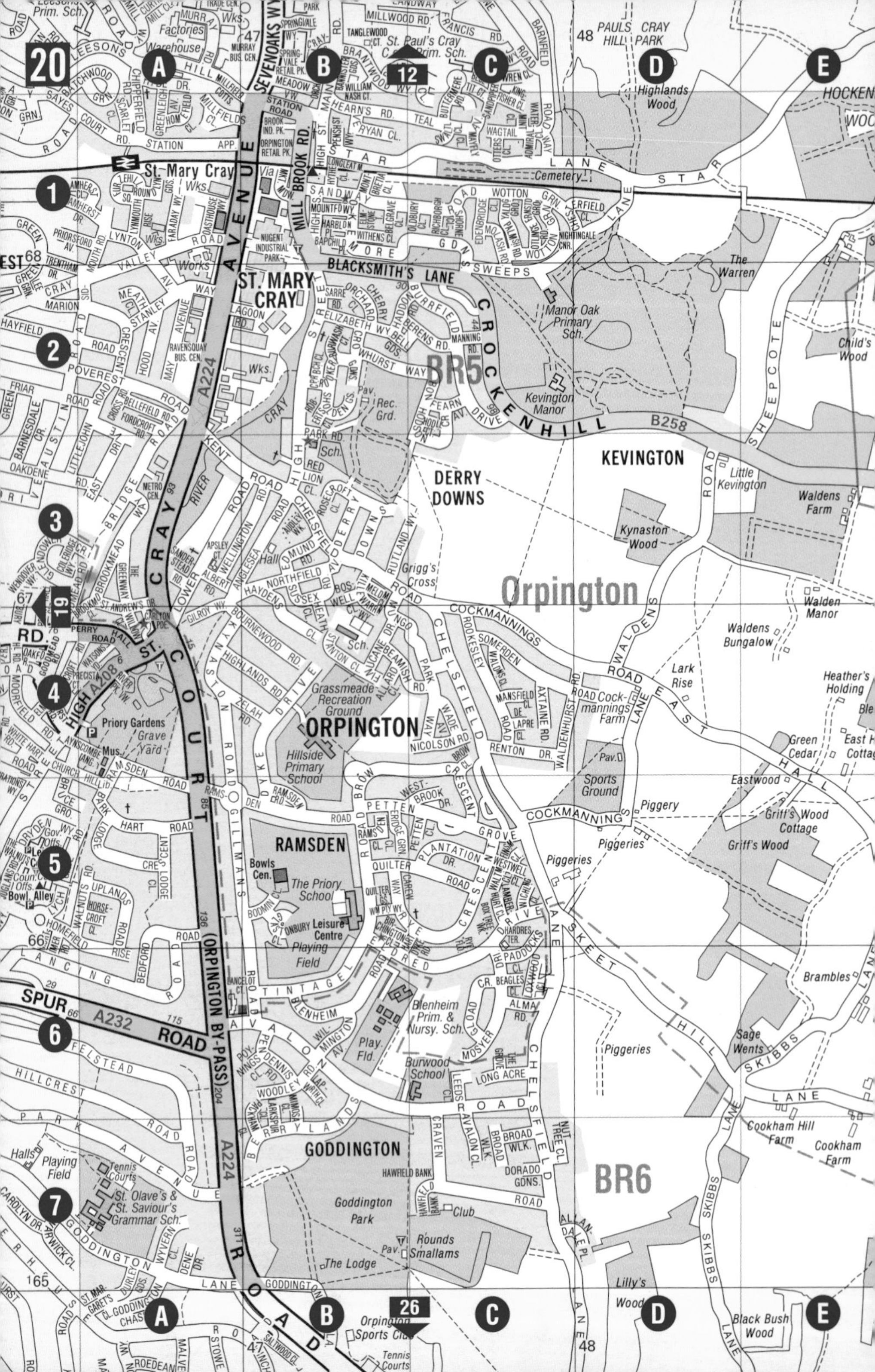

20
A
B
C
D
E
12
1
2
3
4
5
6
7
19
26
St. Mary Cray
ST. MARY CRAY
BR5
BR6
Orpington
ORPINGTON
KEVINGTON
DERRY DOWNS
RAMSDEN
GODDINGTON
Cemetery
Highlands Wood
PAULS CRAY HILL PARK
HOCKEN
Manor Oak Primary Sch.
Kevington Manor
The Warren
Child's Wood
Little Kevington
Waldens Farm
Kynaston Wood
Grigg's Cross
Walden Manor
Waldens Bungalow
Lark Rise
Heather's Holding
Cockmannings Farm
Sports Ground
Piggery
Piggeries
Green Cedar
Eastwood
Griff's Wood Cottage
Griff's Wood
Brambles
Sage Wents
Cookham Hill Farm
Cookham Farm
Lilly's Wood
Black Bush Wood
Grassmeade Recreation Ground
Hillside Primary School
Priory Gardens
Grave Yard
The Priory School
Bowls Cen.
Leisure Centre
Playing Field
Blenheim Prim. & Nursy. Sch.
Play. Fld.
Burwood School
Goddington Park
The Lodge
Rounds Smallams
Club
Orpington Sports Club
Tennis Courts
St. Olave's & St. Saviour's Grammar Sch.
Playing Field
Halls
CRAY AVENUE
A224
COURT
CRAY
(ORPINGTON BY-PASS)
ROAD
SPUR ROAD
A232
A208
CROCKENHILL
B258
STAR LANE
SHEEPCOTE
WALDENS ROAD
COCKMANNINGS ROAD
HALL ROAD EAST
SKEET HILL LANE
SKIBBS LANE
CHELSFIELD LANE
BLACKSMITH'S LANE
SWEEPS
MILL BROOK RD.
HIGH STREET
STATION APP.
COURT RD.
LEESONS HILL
SEVENOAKS WY.
WOTTON GRN.
MORE GDNS.
KENT ROAD
CHELSFIELD ROAD
COCKMANNINGS
LANCING ROAD
FELSTEAD
HILLCREST
PARK AVENUE
GODDINGTON LANE
BERRYLANDS
AVALON ROAD
TINTAGEL ROAD
HART ROAD
RAMSDEN ROAD
PETTEN GROVE
CRESCENT
PLANTATION DR.
NICOLSON RD.
RENTON DR.
HAWFIELD BANK
DORADO GDNS.
BROAD WLK.
LONG ACRE
ALMA RD.
MOSYER
48
47
68
67
66
165

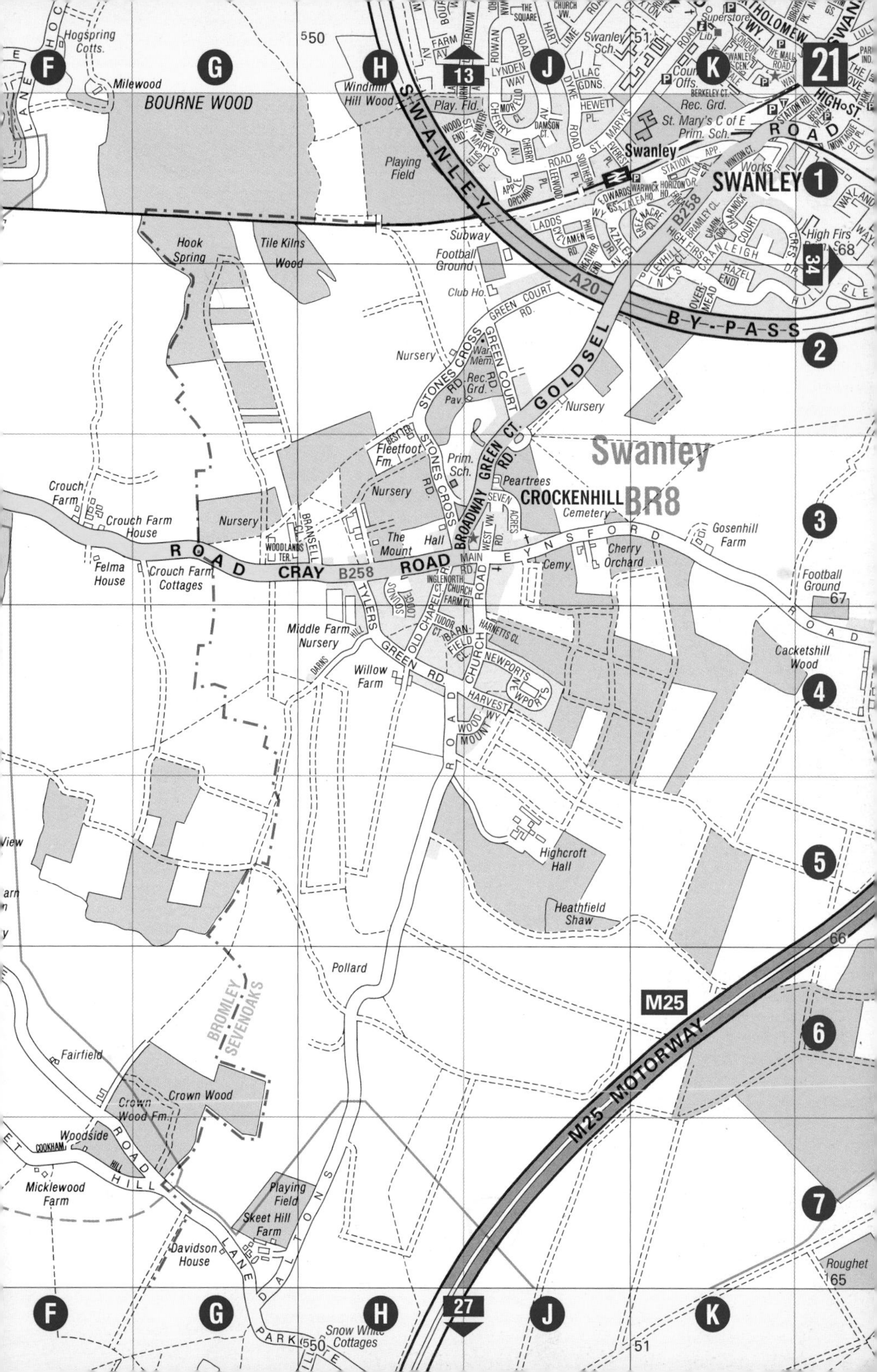
21
F
G
H
J
K
13
34
27
1
2
3
4
5
6
7
Hogspring Cotts.
Milewood
BOURNE WOOD
Windmill Hill Wood
Playing Field
SWANLEY BY-PASS
A20
Swanley
SWANLEY
St. Mary's C of E Prim. Sch.
Rec. Grd.
Superstore
Lib.
Court Offs.
Swanley Sch.
HIGH ST.
STATION RD.
High Firs
Hook Spring
Tile Kilns Wood
Subway
Football Ground
Club Ho.
GREEN COURT RD.
STONES CROSS RD.
War Mem.
Rec. Grd.
Pav.
Nursery
GOLDSEL RD.
GREEN CT. RD.
Swanley
BR8
CROCKENHILL
Peartrees
Cemetery
Prim. Sch.
Fleetfoot Fm.
Crouch Farm
Crouch Farm House
Felma House
Crouch Farm Cottages
ROAD CRAY B258 ROAD
EYNSFORD ROAD
Gosenhill Farm
Football Ground
Cherry Orchard
Cemy.
The Mount
Hall
BROADWAY
MAIN RD.
CHURCH ROAD
Middle Farm Nursery
Willow Farm
GREEN RD.
TYLERS
Cacketshill Wood
NEWPORTS
HARVEST
Highcroft Hall
Heathfield Shaw
Pollard
BROMLEY
SEVENOAKS
M25
M25 MOTORWAY
Fairfield
Crown Wood Fm.
Crown Wood
Woodside
COOKHAM HILL
Micklewood Farm
Playing Field
Skeet Hill Farm
Davidson House
DALTONS
Snow White Cottages
PARK
Roughet
550
51
66
67
68
165

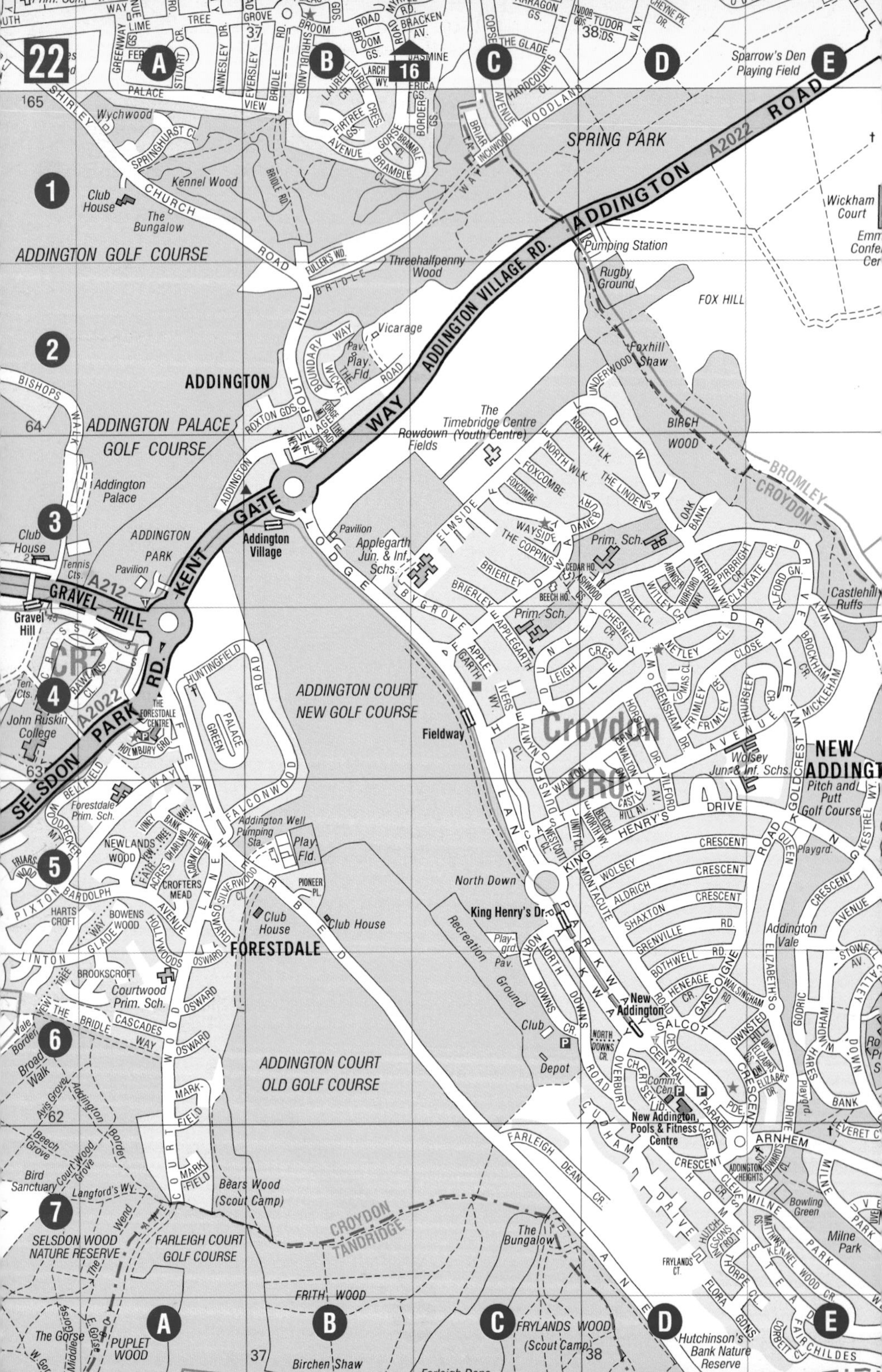
22
16
ADDINGTON GOLF COURSE
ADDINGTON PALACE GOLF COURSE
ADDINGTON
Addington Palace
ADDINGTON PARK
Gravel Hill
John Ruskin College
SPRING PARK
ADDINGTON ROAD
A2022
ADDINGTON VILLAGE RD.
WAY
KENT GATE
GRAVEL HILL
A212
SELSDON PARK RD.
Kennel Wood
Threehalfpenny Wood
Pumping Station
Rugby Ground
FOX HILL
Wickham Court
Sparrow's Den Playing Field
Foxhill Shaw
BIRCH WOOD
The Timebridge Centre (Youth Centre)
Rowdown Fields
Addington Village
Applegarth Jun. & Inf. Schs.
ADDINGTON COURT NEW GOLF COURSE
Fieldway
Croydon
CR0
CR2
NEW ADDINGTON
Wolsey Jun. & Inf. Schs.
Pitch and Putt Golf Course
Castlehill Ruffs
BROMLEY
CROYDON
Forestdale Prim. Sch.
FORESTDALE
Courtwood Prim. Sch.
Addington Well Pumping Sta.
North Down
King Henry's Dr.
Recreation Ground
New Addington
New Addington Pools & Fitness Centre
Addington Vale
ADDINGTON COURT OLD GOLF COURSE
Bears Wood (Scout Camp)
CROYDON
TANDRIDGE
SELSDON WOOD NATURE RESERVE
FARLEIGH COURT GOLF COURSE
FRITH WOOD
FRYLANDS WOOD (Scout Camp)
Hutchinson's Bank Nature Reserve
Milne Park
Bowling Green
PUPLET WOOD
Birchen Shaw
Farleigh Dene
The Gorse
Bird Sanctuary
The Bungalow

CROYDON ROAD
A232
17
23
CONEY HALL
West Wickham Common
HAYES COMMON
Colyers Wood
West Wickham
BR4
Coney Hall Rec. Grd.
Wickham Court Farm
Playing Field
School
Hast Hill
Baston Manor
Keston Court Riding School
Miry Grove
KESTON
Padmall Wood
Rouse Farm
Arlington Orchard
Well Wood
Elm Farm
Fox Hill Nursery
NASH
Nash
Nash Farm
Long Shaw
Cooper's Wood
North Pole Farm
Fuller's Wood
James's Wood
Waytes
Five Oaks
Baldwin Shaw
Bradmanshill Wood
Rushfield Shaw
Broomfieldbank Shaw
Metropolitan Police Dog Training Establishment
Keston
BR2
Jackass Shaw
Foxhill Fm.
Leafy Grove
Heathfield House
Keston Postmill (dis.)
Knightons
War Bank
The Temple (Roman Mausoleum)
Keston Court Farm
Milchden
Glebe Farm
24
Longlands Nurseries
Kimberley Poultry Farm
Vale Farm
Layham's Farm Cottage
Layham's Farm
Furze Bottom
VULCAN BUSINESS CENTRE
ADDINGTON BUSINESS CENTRE
MERIDIAN CENTRE
Sports Ground
Pav.
Greyhound Training Kennels
Ten. Cts.
West Wickham Res. (covered)
Hoppershatch Shaw
Highams Hill
Higham's Hill
LEAVES GREEN
Greenacres Riding Sch.
Bradmoor
High House Farm
Ashmore Farm
The Green
Milking Farm
ROSE COTTAGES
MAIN RD. A233
LEAVES GRN. RD.
WESTERHAM RD.
BASTON ROAD B265
HEATHFIELD
LAYHAMS ROAD
NASH LANE
JACKASS LANE
FOX LANE
BLACKNESS LANE
CHURCH LANE
ASHMORE LANE
Play. Fld.
28
540
41
F G H J K
1 2 3 4 5 6 7

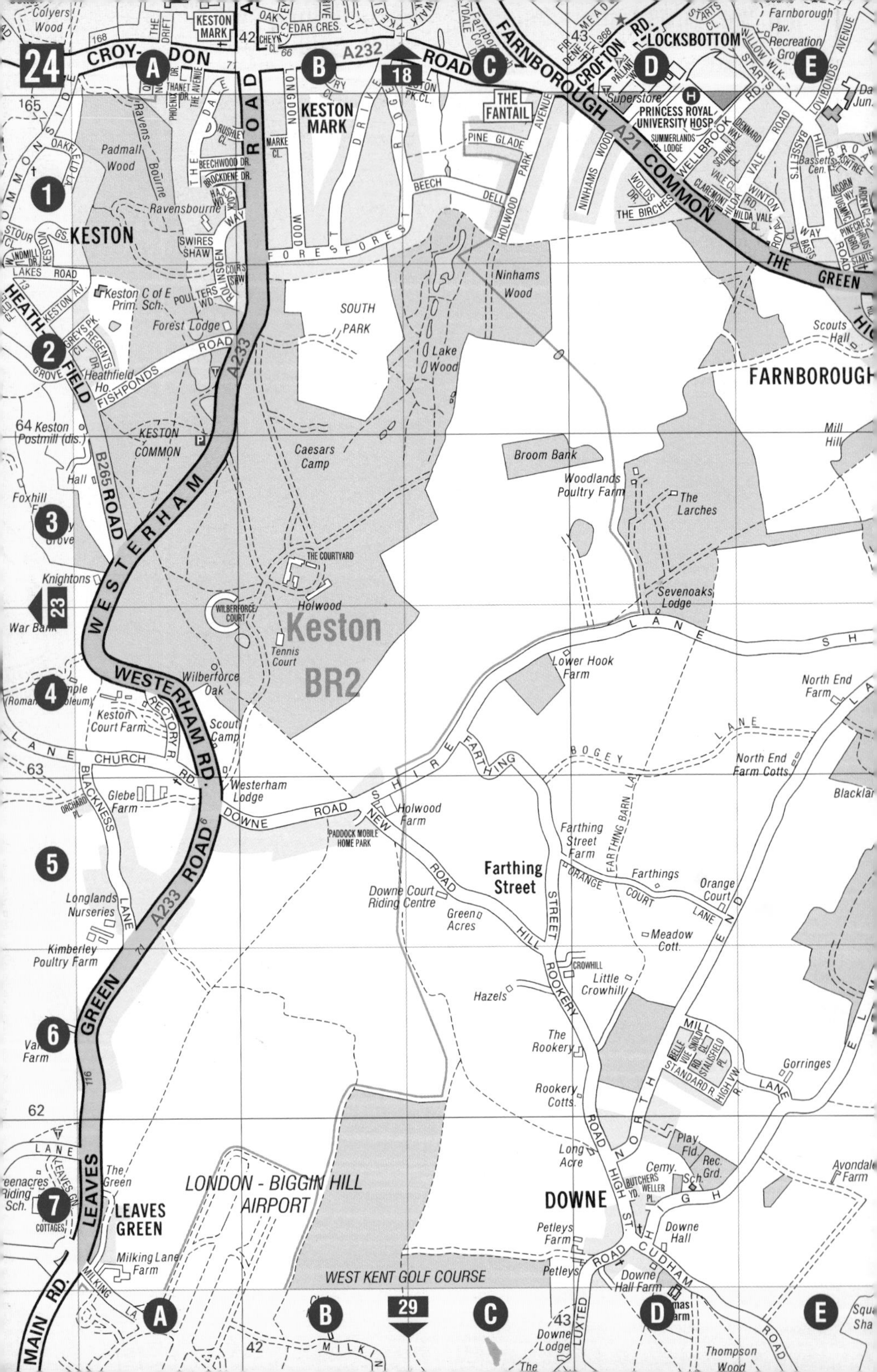

CROYDON ROAD
A232
18
KESTON MARK
FARNBOROUGH COMMON
A21
CROFTON RD.
LOCKSBOTTOM
Superstore
PRINCESS ROYAL UNIVERSITY HOSP
THE FANTAIL
PINE GLADE
KESTON
Padmall Wood
Ravensbourne
Keston C of E Prim. Sch.
Forest Lodge
FISHPONDS ROAD
Heathfield Ho.
HEATHFIELD
WESTERHAM ROAD
A233
KESTON COMMON
Keston Postmill (dis.)
Foxhill
Knightons
23
War Bank
SOUTH PARK
Lake Wood
Ninhams Wood
Caesars Camp
Broom Bank
Woodlands Poultry Farm
The Larches
FARNBOROUGH
Scouts Hall
Mill Hill
THE COURTYARD
Holwood
WILBERFORCE COURT
Keston
BR2
Tennis Court
Wilberforce Oak
Sevenoaks Lodge
Lower Hook Farm
SHIRE LANE
North End Farm
BOGEY LANE
North End Farm Cotts
Keston Court Farm
CHURCH RD.
Scout Camp
Westerham Lodge
Glebe Farm
DOWNE ROAD
Holwood Farm
PADDOCK MOBILE HOME PARK
FARTHING STREET
Farthing Street Farm
Farthing Street
FARTHING BARN LA.
ORANGE COURT LANE
Farthings
Orange Court
Downe Court Riding Centre
Green Acres
NEW ROAD HILL
Meadow Cott.
Longlands Nurseries
Kimberley Poultry Farm
BLACKNESS LANE
GREEN LANE
CROWHILL
Little Crowhill
Hazels
ROOKERY ROAD
The Rookery
Rookery Cotts.
MILL
STANDARD R.
HIGH VW.
Gorringes
LANE
NORTH END
HIGH ELMS
Long Acre
Play Fld.
Rec. Grd.
Cemy.
Sch.
Avondale Farm
BUTCHERS YD.
WELLER PL.
DOWNE
HIGH ST.
Downe Hall
Petleys Farm
Petleys
Downe Hall Farm
CUDHAM ROAD
LONDON - BIGGIN HILL AIRPORT
WEST KENT GOLF COURSE
LEAVES GREEN
The Green
Milking Lane Farm
MILKING LA.
MAIN RD.
LEAVES GREEN
COTTAGES
29
LUXTED
Downe Lodge
Thompson Wood

Orpington
BR6
GREEN STREET GREEN
FARNBOROUGH
STREET FARNBOROUGH
B2158
SEVENOAKS ROAD
A223
A21
SEVENOAKS WAY
HILL
HIGH ST.
ORPINGTON HOSPITAL
Hospice
Ontario Centre
Newstead Wood Sch. for Girls
Tubbenden Jun. & Inf. Schools
Playing Field
Farnborough Prim. Sch.
The Manse
Church Field Plantation
OLD ROAD
Ramus Wood
Cocksett Plantation
Cocksett Hill
The Lodge
High Elms Nature Cen.
Woodpiece
HIGH ELMS COUNTRY PARK
Whitelands Wood
Club House
The Rookery
High Elms Clockhouse
HIGH ELMS GOLF COURSE
CUCKOO WOOD
Burnt Gorse
Spinney Way Nurseries
Sevenoaks
TN14
HAZELWOOD
Hang Grove Fa
Hazel Wood
Endsleigh
The Shack
White Earth
Snag Farm
Southfields
Rose Cott.
The Oaks
CUDHAM PK. RD.
SNAG LANE
NORTH END LANE
Rec. Grd.
Great Mollums Wood
Little Mollums Wood
Foxberry Wood
Homefield Spring
Norsted Manor Farm
THE CHASE
Chelsfield Hall
Rounds Wood
Chelsfield Wood
Glentrammon Rec. Grd.
Prim. Sch.
High Beeches
Charmwood Farm
Charm Wood
A21 ROAD
F G H J K
1 2 3 4 5 6 7
19
26
30
45
46
545
62
63
64
65

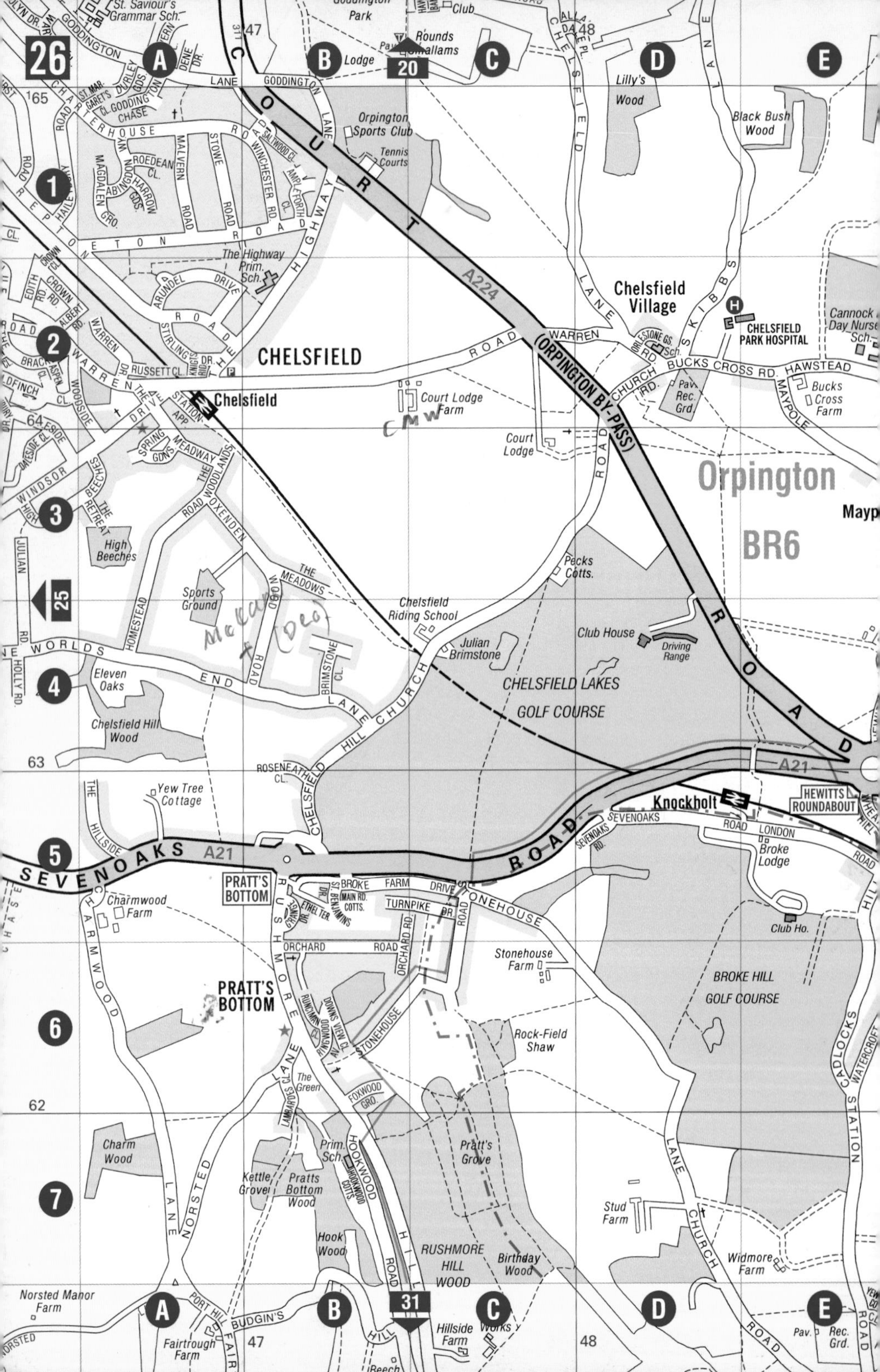
26
A
B
C
D
E
1
2
3
4
5
6
7
20
25
31
47
48
165
64
63
62
St. Saviour's Grammar Sch.
Goddington Park
Rounds Smallams
Lodge
Club
GODDINGTON LANE
CHARTERHOUSE ROAD
ST. MARGARET'S CL.
GODDINGTON CHASE
DURLEY GDS.
DENE DR.
ROEDEAN CL.
ABINGDON GDS.
HARROW GDS.
MAGDALEN GRO.
MALVERN ROAD
STOWE ROAD
WINCHESTER RD.
SALTWOOD CL.
AMPLEFORTH CL.
HAILEYBURY RD.
REPTON ROAD
ETON ROAD
THE HIGHWAY
The Highway Prim. Sch.
ARUNDEL DRIVE
STIRLING DR.
KNIGHTS RIDE
RUSSETT CL.
COURT ROAD
A224
(ORPINGTON BY-PASS)
Orpington Sports Club
Tennis Courts
Lilly's Wood
Black Bush Wood
CHELSFIELD LANE
SKIBBS LANE
Chelsfield Village
ORLESTONE GDS.
WARREN ROAD
CHURCH RD.
BUCKS CROSS RD.
HAWSTEAD
MAYPOLE
Rec. Grd.
CHELSFIELD PARK HOSPITAL
Cannock Day Nurse Sch.
Bucks Cross Farm
CHELSFIELD
Chelsfield
Court Lodge Farm
Court Lodge
STATION APP.
WARREN DR.
WOODSIDE
CROWN RD.
EDITH RD.
ALBERT RD.
SPRING GDNS.
MEADWAY
THE WOODLANDS
WINDSOR
DAVESIDE
BEECHES
THE RETREAT
High Beeches
JULIAN RD.
OXENDEN WOOD ROAD
THE MEADOWS
HOMESTEAD
Sports Ground
WORLDS END LANE
BRIMSTONE CL.
Eleven Oaks
Chelsfield Hill Wood
HOLLY RD.
Orpington
BR6
Mayp
Pecks Cotts.
Chelsfield Riding School
Julian Brimstone
Club House
Driving Range
CHELSFIELD LAKES GOLF COURSE
CHURCH HILL
ROSENEATH CL.
CHELSFIELD
A21
HEWITTS ROUNDABOUT
Knockholt
SEVENOAKS ROAD
SEVENOAKS RD.
LONDON ROAD
Broke Lodge
Club Ho.
BROKE HILL GOLF COURSE
Yew Tree Cottage
THE HILLSIDE
SEVENOAKS
PRATT'S BOTTOM
BROKE FARM DRIVE
ST. BENJAMINS DR.
ETHEL TER.
(MAIN RD. COTTS.)
TURNPIKE DR.
STONEHOUSE ROAD
Stonehouse Farm
ORCHARD ROAD
ORCHARD RD.
CHARMWOOD LANE
Charmwood Farm
RUSHMORE HILL
PRATT'S BOTTOM
RUNCIMAN CL.
RINGWOOD AV.
DOWNS VIEW CL.
STONEHOUSE
Rock-Field Shaw
The Green
LAMBARDES CL.
FOXWOOD GRO.
Prim. Sch.
HOOKWOOD COTTS.
HOOKWOOD ROAD
Pratt's Grove
Charm Wood
NORSTED LANE
Kettle Grove
Pratts Bottom Wood
Hook Wood
RUSHMORE HILL WOOD
Birthday Wood
Stud Farm
CHURCH ROAD
Widmore Farm
CADLOCKS
WATERCROFT
STATION
Norsted Manor Farm
PORT HILL
BUDGIN'S HILL
FAIRTROUGH
Fairtrough Farm
Hillside Farm
Works
Beech
Pav.
Rec. Grd.

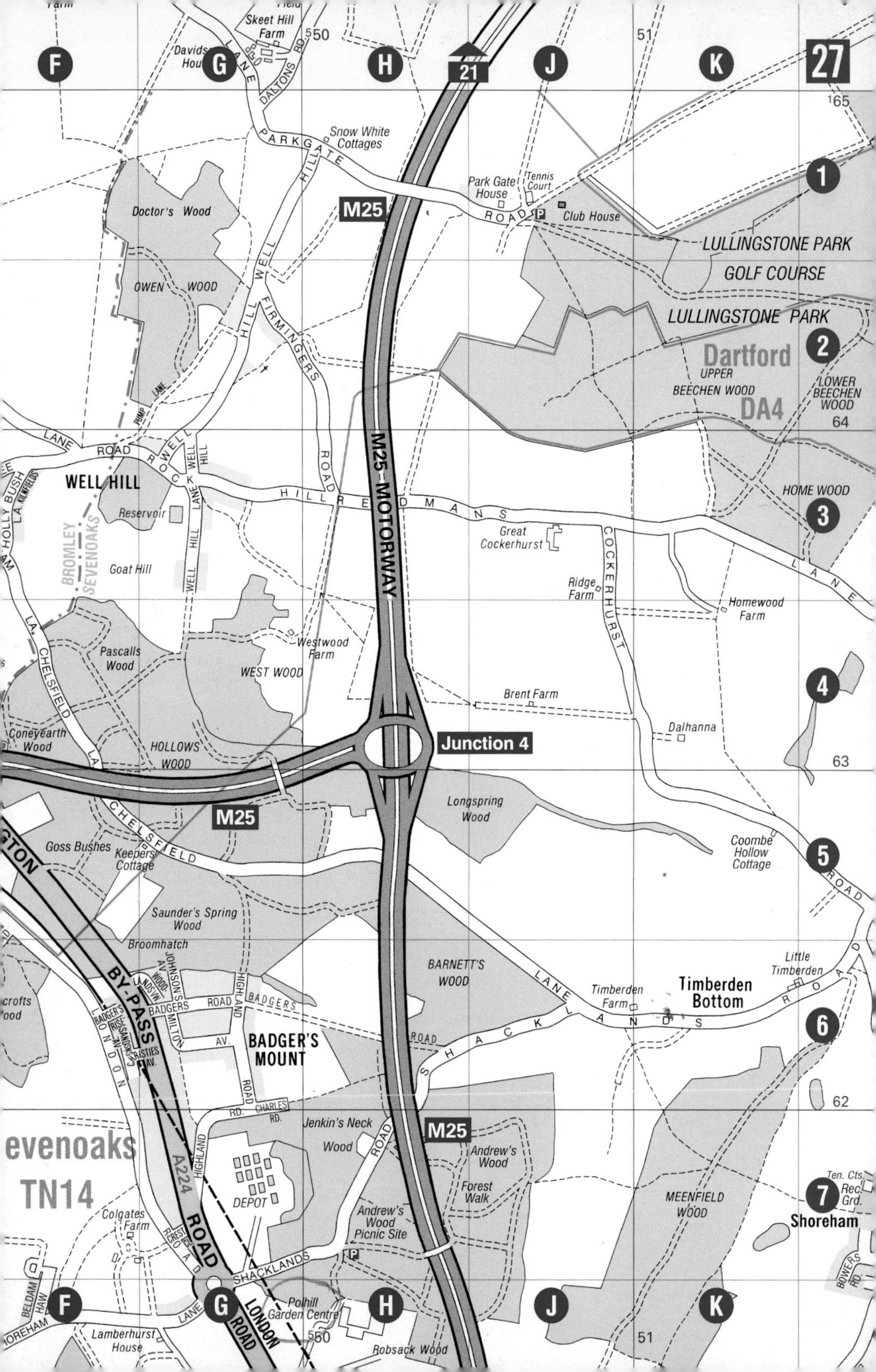
Skeet Hill Farm
550
51
F
G
H
J
K
21
165
1
2
3
4
5
6
7
Snow White Cottages
PARKGATE
M25
Park Gate House
Tennis Court
Club House
LULLINGSTONE PARK
GOLF COURSE
LULLINGSTONE PARK
Dartford
DA4
UPPER BEECHEN WOOD
LOWER BEECHEN WOOD
64
Doctor's Wood
OWEN WOOD
FIRMINGERS
M25 MOTORWAY
WELL HILL
Reservoir
BROMLEY
SEVENOAKS
Goat Hill
HOME WOOD
Great Cockerhurst
Ridge Farm
Homewood Farm
COCKERHURST
Pascalls Wood
Westwood Farm
WEST WOOD
Brent Farm
Coneyearth Wood
HOLLOWS WOOD
Dalhanna
Junction 4
63
Longspring Wood
Goss Bushes
Keepers Cottage
CHELSFIELD
Coombe Hollow Cottage
Saunder's Spring Wood
Broomhatch
BARNETT'S WOOD
Little Timberden
Timberden Farm
Timberden Bottom
SHACKLANDS ROAD
BY-PASS
BADGER'S MOUNT
BADGERS ROAD
MILTON AV.
HIGHLAND ROAD
CHARLES RD.
62
Jenkin's Neck Wood
Andrew's Wood
Forest Walk
MEENFIELD WOOD
evenoaks
TN14
DEPOT
Colgates Farm
Andrew's Wood Picnic Site
Ten. Cts.
Rec. Grd.
Shoreham
A224
LONDON ROAD
SHACKLANDS
Polhill Garden Centre
Lamberhurst House
Robsack Wood
BOWERS RD.
BELDAM HAW

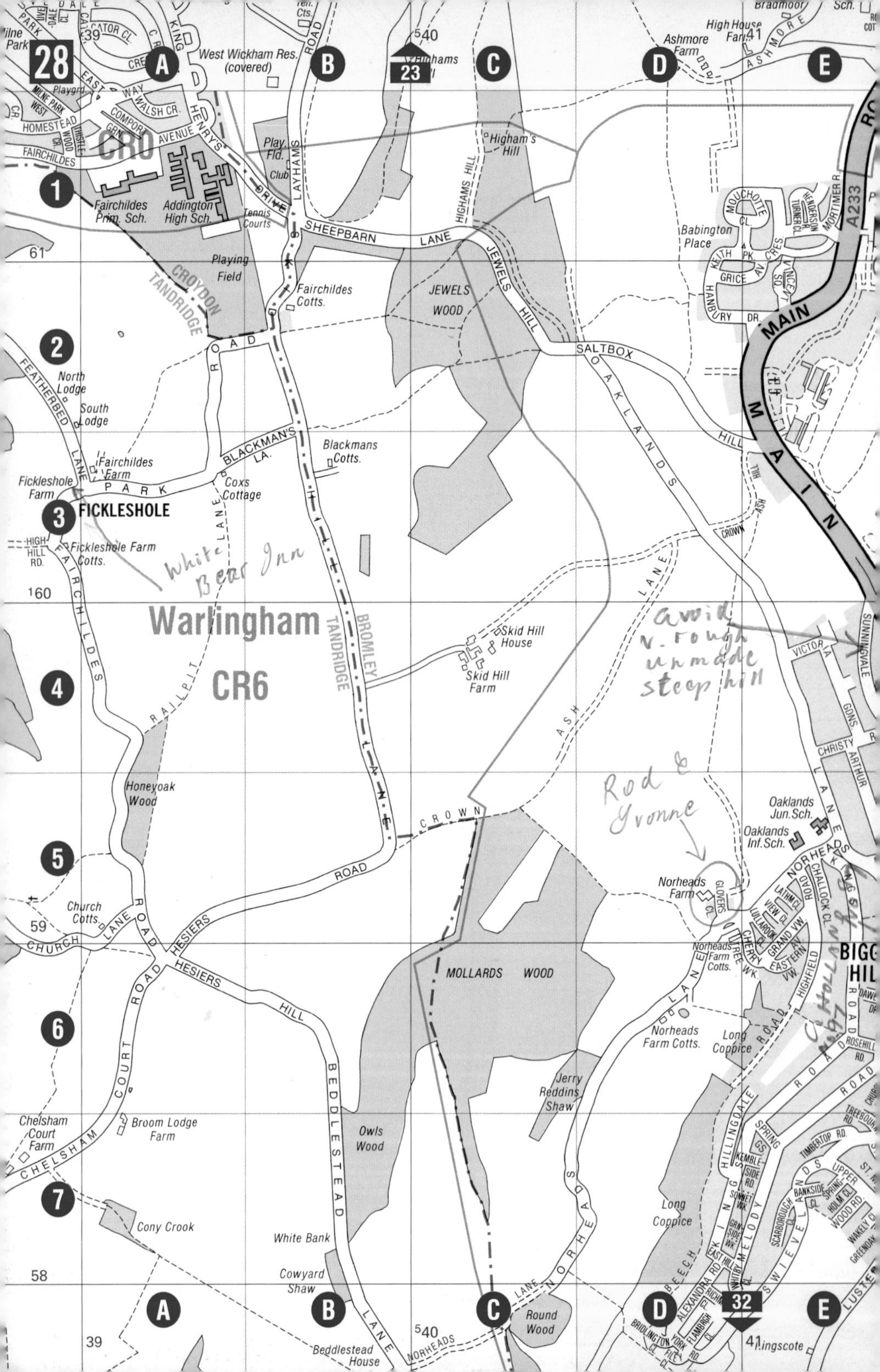

28
23
32
West Wickham Res. (covered)
Higham's Hill
Ashmore Farm
High House Farm
Fairchildes Prim. Sch.
Addington High Sch.
Playing Field
Fairchildes Cotts.
SHEEPBARN LANE
JEWELS WOOD
JEWELS HILL
SALTBOX
OAKLANDS
Babington Place
MAIN
A233
North Lodge
South Lodge
Fairchildes Farm
Fickleshole Farm
FICKLESHOLE
Fickleshole Farm Cotts.
Blackmans Cotts.
Coxs Cottage
BLACKMAN'S LA.
White Bear Inn
Warlingham
CR6
CR0
Skid Hill House
Skid Hill Farm
avoid v. rough unmade steep hill
ASH LANE
CROWN ROAD
Honeyoak Wood
Church Cotts.
HESIERS HILL
Rod & Yvonne
Norheads Farm
Oaklands Jun. Sch.
Oaklands Inf. Sch.
MOLLARDS WOOD
Norheads Farm Cotts.
Long Coppice
Jerry Reddins Shaw
Owls Wood
Chelsham Court Farm
Broom Lodge Farm
Cony Crook
White Bank
Cowyard Shaw
Round Wood
Beddlestead House
BEDDLESTEAD LANE
NORHEADS LANE
Lingscote

29
LEAVES GREEN
Keston
BR2
WEST KENT GOLF COURSE
Club House
MILKING LANE
GREEN HILL WEST
DOWNE
Downe Hall
Petleys Farm
Downe Hall Farm
Christmas Tree Farm
CUDHAM ROAD
Thompson Wood
Square Shaw
Downe Lodge
The Vicarage
Green Hill
LUXTED ROAD
Down House and Darwin Museum
Downe Court
Buckston Browne Research Farm
BIGGIN HILL AIRPORT
Downe Bank Nature Reserve
HANGROVE HILL
Cricket Grd.
Orpington
BR6
SOW WOOD
Snotsdale Wood
Hang Grove
Beechwood
The Boundary
Shaws Cott.
DOWNE ROAD
CHURCHILL WAY
Flora Nurseries
Spencers Grove
Luxted
Brownsea Hut (Boy Scouts)
Greenacres
Twenty Acre Shaw
Cudham Lodge Woods
South London Aero Club
Ladies Wood
Luxted Fm.
Downe Camp
Great Southfield Shaw
Leasons Wood
Clock Twr.
Bird House Wood
BIRDHOUSE LANE
Bromley Croft
SINGLE STREET
Single Street
Bottom Barn Farm
AIRPORT INDUSTRIAL ESTATE
BIGGIN HILL BUSINESS PARK
CONCORDE BUSINESS PK.
St. Julians Farm
Playing Fld.
Darwin Leisure Centre
Strakes Shaw
Costains Farm
Charles Darwin School
Barn Farm
Bertrey Cotts.
BERRY'S HILL
JAIL LANE
BLACKTHORN DRIVE
MAGNOLIA
ACER
SPRUCE RD.
Cemetery
Primrose Farm
Parkfield Fm.
Cudham C of E Prim. Sch.
BERRY'S LANE
Homeleigh Farm
RESTAVON CARAVAN SITE
BERRY'S GREEN
Blackbush Shaw
Golden Acres
Littlewood Farm
Biggin Hill Jun. & Inf. Schs.
Recreation Ground
Westerham
Grubb Grounds Farm
Brickyard Farm
OLD TYE AVENUE
TN16
Library
MAPLE LEAF CL.
CHURCH ROAD
APERFIELD ROAD
JUNIPER CL.
CHERRY LODGE GOLF COURSE
Oak Farm
Warren Farm
Foal Farm
Club House
Valley View
Pimlico Wood
Laurel Farm
APERFIELD
GREEN ROAD
MAIN ROAD
A233
Hall
DOUGLAS CT.
TUDOR CT.
MOSELLE RD
EDWARD RD
FOX-EARTH CL.
ST. WINIFRED'S RD
CLARENCE RD.
BELVEDERE CL.
WOODBURY CL.
GROVE
RICKETTS HILL RD.
Farley Kennels
Park Farm
Silver Beech Fm
BUCKHURST ROAD
Baverstock Farm
Withins Wood
Stud Farm
PAYNESFIELD
24
30
32
33
F G H J K
1 2 3 4 5 6 7
42 43 44
61 160 59 58
via Approach Lebanon Gdns & Stock Hill
traffic lights

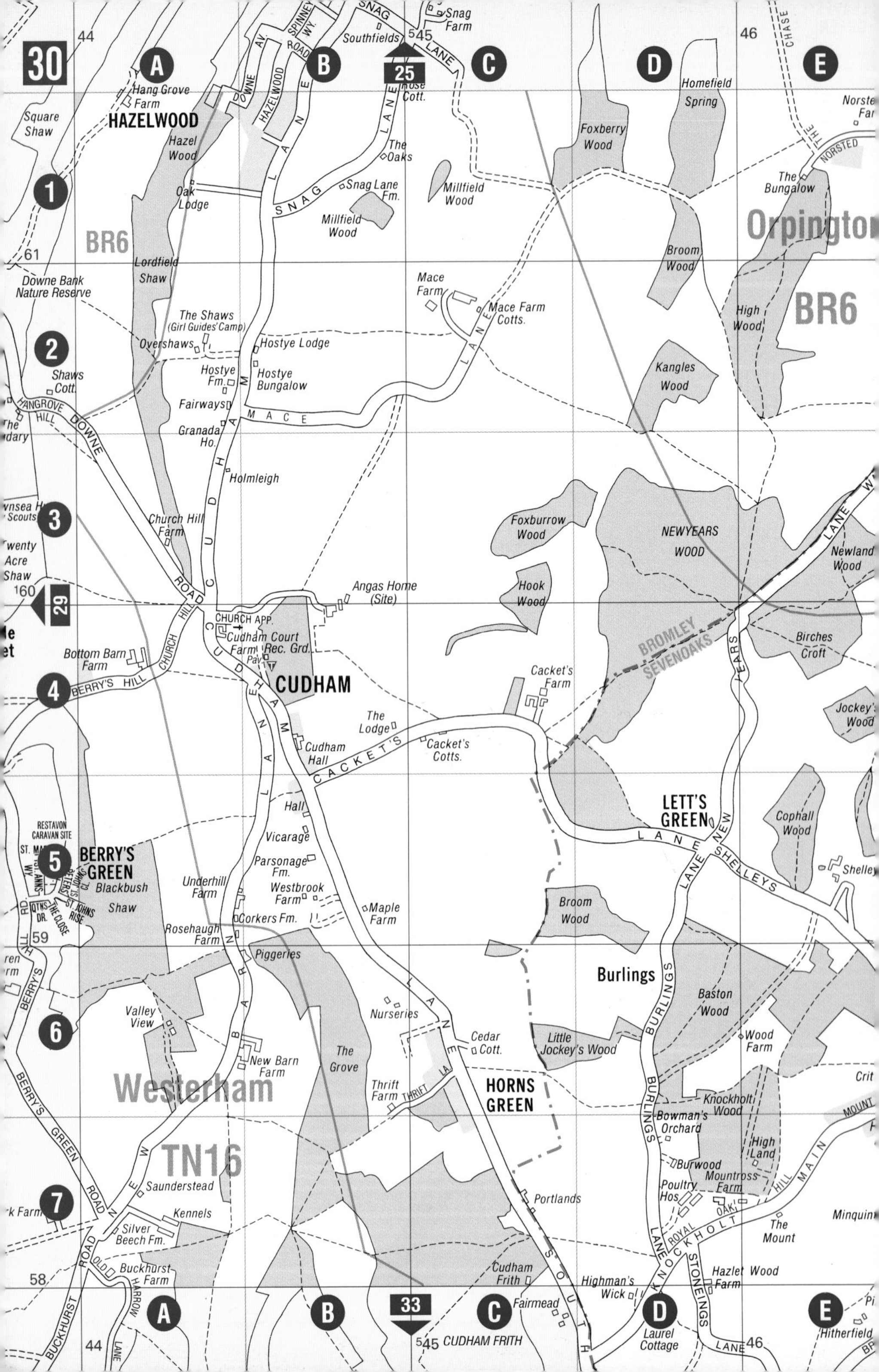
A
B
C
D
E
1
2
3
4
5
6
7
25
29
33
HAZELWOOD
Hazel Wood
Hang Grove Farm
Square Shaw
Oak Lodge
BR6
Lordfield Shaw
Downe Bank Nature Reserve
The Shaws (Girl Guides' Camp)
Overshaws
Shaws Cott.
Hostye Lodge
Hostye Fm.
Hostye Bungalow
Fairways
Granada Ho.
Holmleigh
Church Hill Farm
HANGROVE HILL
DOWNE ROAD
CUDHAM LANE
MACE LANE
SNAG LANE
Snag Lane Fm.
Snag Farm
Southfields
Rose Cott.
The Oaks
Millfield Wood
Mace Farm
Mace Farm Cotts.
Homefield Spring
Foxberry Wood
Broom Wood
Orpington
High Wood
Kangles Wood
The Bungalow
NORSTED
Foxburrow Wood
Hook Wood
NEWYEARS WOOD
Newland Wood
Birches Croft
Jockey's Wood
BROMLEY
SEVENOAKS
Angas Home (Site)
CHURCH APP.
Cudham Court Farm
Rec. Grd.
Pav.
CUDHAM
Bottom Barn Farm
BERRY'S HILL
CHURCH HILL
The Lodge
Cudham Hall
CACKET'S LANE
Cacket's Cotts.
Cacket's Farm
LETT'S GREEN
NEW YEARS LANE
SHELLEYS LANE
Cophall Wood
RESTAVON CARAVAN SITE
BERRY'S GREEN
Blackbush Shaw
Hall
Vicarage
Parsonage Fm.
Westbrook Farm
Underhill Farm
Maple Farm
Corkers Fm.
Rosehaugh Farm
Piggeries
Broom Wood
Burlings
Baston Wood
Wood Farm
Valley View
New Barn Farm
NEW BARN LANE
Nurseries
Cedar Cott.
The Grove
Thrift Farm
THRIFT LA.
HORNS GREEN
Little Jockey's Wood
Knockholt Wood
Bowman's Orchard
High Land
Burwood
Mountross Farm
Poultry Hos.
Westerham
TN16
Saunderstead
Kennels
Silver Beech Fm.
Buckhurst Farm
BERRY'S GREEN ROAD
Portlands
The Mount
KNOCKHOLT ROAD
MAIN ROAD
Minquin
Hazlet Wood Farm
Cudham Frith
Highman's Wick
Fairmead
Laurel Cottage
CUDHAM FRITH
STONEINGS LANE
BURLINGS LANE
SOUTH LANE
BUCKHURST ROAD
OLD HARROW LANE
Hitherfield
44
45
46
58
59
60
61

31
26
F
G
H
J
K
47
48
49
61
160
59
58
1
2
3
4
5
6
7
HALSTEAD
KNOCKHOLT POUND
CHEVENING
Sevenoaks
TN14
Rushmore Hill Wood
Hillside Farm
Works
Fairtrough Farm
Lower Brooms Wood
Upper Brooms Wood
Lattice Coppice
Beech Cott.
Garden Cen.
Widmore Farm
Stud Farm
Rec. Grd.
Pav.
Halstead Primary Sch.
Lower Randle's Wood
The Washneys
Perry Wood
Closeheath Wood
Deerleap Wood
Warren Court Farm
Park Farm
Piece Wood
New Stables Farm
Nursery
Curry Wood Farm
Curry Farm
Woodvale Cottage
Kangles Farm
Hawfield Wood
Singles Cross
Long Bottoms Shaw
Park Cnr.
Chapel Croft
Blueberry Farm
The Spinney Nurseries
Aldwyn Lodge
Garden Centre
Knockholt Village Centre
Play. Fields
Ivy Farm
Tennis Cts.
Mast
Chine Farm Place
Homefield
Lees Wood
Lodge
Ashfield Wood
Cooper's Wood
The Keyhole
Ash Platt
Lord Chatham's Ride
Minny Wood
Knockholt Beeches
Knockholt Lodge
St. Katherine's Knockholt C of E Prim. Sch.
WT Sta.
Masts
Sand Banks
Park House
Keepers Cottage
Summerhouse Wood
Coalhearth Cottage
The Spinney
Park Wood
Sundridge Hill Farm
Pilgrims' Way (course of)
Roughfields Wood
Hagbush Wood
Rushmore Road
Hookwood Road
Budgin's Hill
Port Hill
Fairtrough Road
Perrys La.
Stubbs Hill
Singles Cross La.
Randles Lane
Pound La. or Bond St.
Bond Cl.
Main Road
Harrow Rd.
London Road
Star Hill Road
Birchwood Lane
Blueberry Lane
Knockholt Road
Chevening Lane
Sundridge Lane
Sundridge Hill
Knockholt Lane
Halstead Hill
Old Road
Waylands Cl.
Knockholt La.
Deerleap Lane
Deerleap La.
Hunters Wlk.
Southdene
Parkside
The Meadows
Meadway
Kilnwood
Church Road
Station Road
Clarks La.
Yew Tree Cotts.
Shoreham Lane
Otford Road
Ivy La.
ockholt

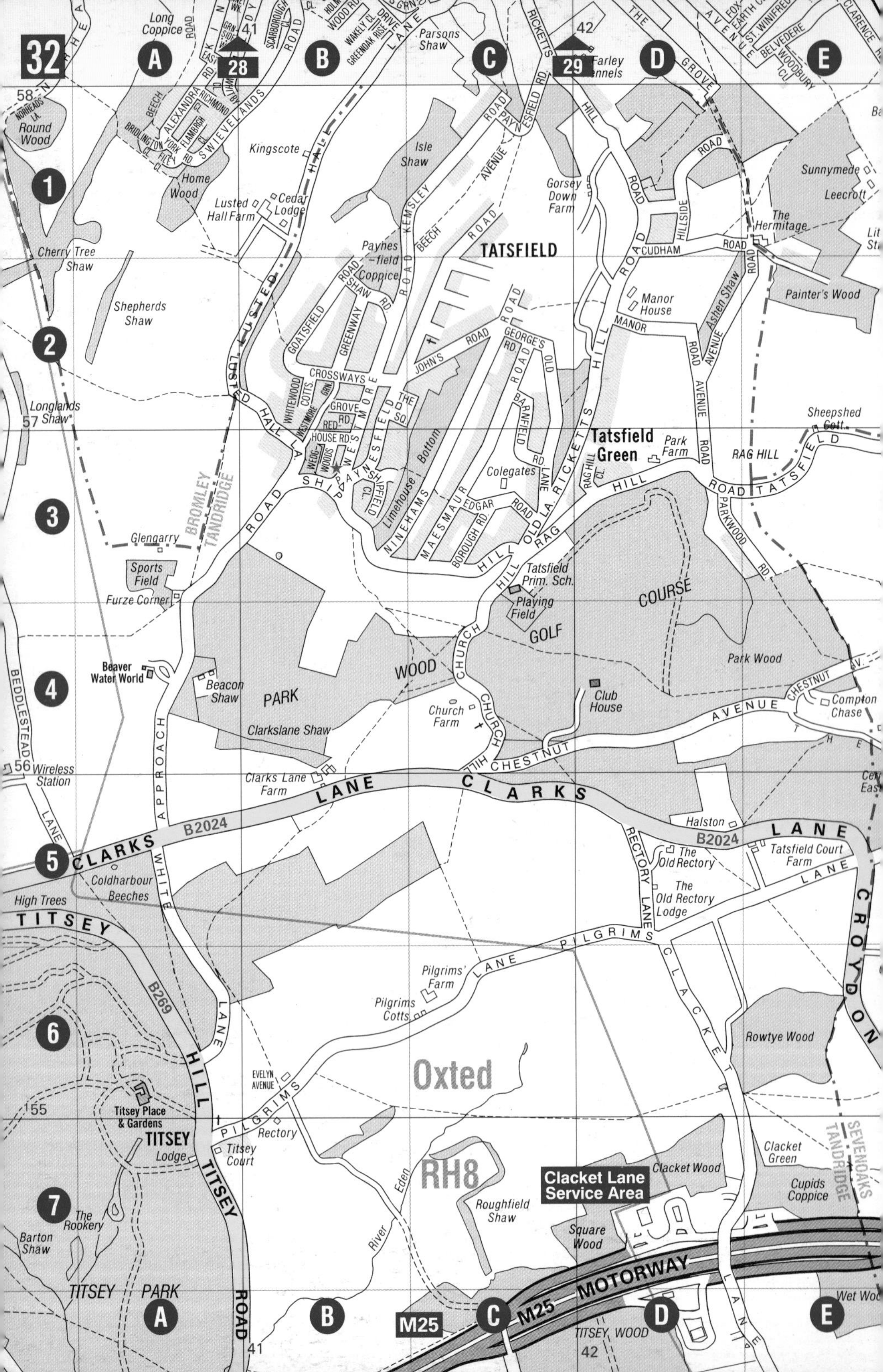

28
29
Long Coppice
Round Wood
Home Wood
Kingscote
Lusted Hall Farm
Cedar Lodge
Parsons Shaw
Farley Kennels
Isle Shaw
Gorsey Down Farm
Paynesfield Coppice
TATSFIELD
Cherry Tree Shaw
Shepherds Shaw
Manor House
Ashen Shaw
Sunnymede
Leecroft
The Hermitage
Painter's Wood
Longlands Shaw
Limehouse Bottom
Colegates
Tatsfield Green
Park Farm
RAG HILL
Sheepshed Cott.
BROMLEY
TANDRIDGE
Glengarry
Sports Field
Furze Corner
Tatsfield Prim. Sch.
Playing Field
GOLF COURSE
Park Wood
Beaver Water World
Beacon Shaw
PARK WOOD
Church Farm
Club House
Compton Chase
Clarkslane Shaw
Wireless Station
Clarks Lane Farm
CLARKS LANE
B2024
Halston
The Old Rectory
Tatsfield Court Farm
The Old Rectory Lodge
Coldharbour Beeches
High Trees
TITSEY HILL
B269
Pilgrims' Farm
Pilgrims Cotts
PILGRIMS LANE
Rowtye Wood
Oxted
RH8
Titsey Place & Gardens
TITSEY
Lodge
Rectory
Titsey Court
Clacket Green
SEVENOAKS
TANDRIDGE
Clacket Wood
Clacket Lane Service Area
Cupids Coppice
Roughfield Shaw
The Rookery
Barton Shaw
Square Wood
M25 MOTORWAY
TITSEY PARK
TITSEY ROAD
TITSEY WOOD
CLACKET LANE
CROYDON LANE
Wet Wood

33
F
G
H
J
K
29
30
1
2
3
4
5
6
7
TN14
TN16
WESTERHAM HILL
Westerham
WESTERHAM
Hawley's Corner
Force Green
Hill Park
BROMLEY
SEVENOAKS
M25
M25 MOTORWAY
A233
B2024
WESTERHAM ROAD
LONDON ROAD
HILL
GRAYS ROAD
SILVERSTEAD LANE
PILGRIMS WAY
BEGGARS LANE
CROYDON RD.
BRASTED A25 RD.
Park Farm
Kennels
Silver Beech Fm
Withins Wood
CUDHAM FRITH
Fairmead
Highman's Wick
Piggeries
Rosemary Farm
Bombers Lodge
Shellem Wood
Southwood Farm
Southwood
Buckhurst
Bombers Farm
Squirrel Wood
Cudham Frith Farm
Bombers Cott.
Woodlands
Cudham Grange
Joelands
Joeland's Wood
Westerham Riding School
Gray's Farm
Silversted
Blawan Orchard
Tor Croft
Broomcocks Wood
South Farm
Westerham Heights
Heights View
Fort Cotts.
Deepdale
Deepdale Cott.
Pilgrim House
Play. Fld.
Round Shaw
BETSOM'S HILL
Highfield
Lime Villa
Whitelands Shaw
Whitlands
Betsoms
Playing Field
Pav.
Betsomhill Farm
Weir
Force Green Farm Cottages
Force Green Farm
Green Leas
Hartley Wood
Charmans Farm
WESTERHAM WOOD
Gaysham Cottages
Tennis Court
Churchill C of E Prim. Sch.
Court Lodge
Green Croft Farm
King George's Field
Lodge
The Crown
Bowl Grn
CHURCHILL BUS. PK.
WESTERHAM TRADE CEN.
545
58
57
56
55
44

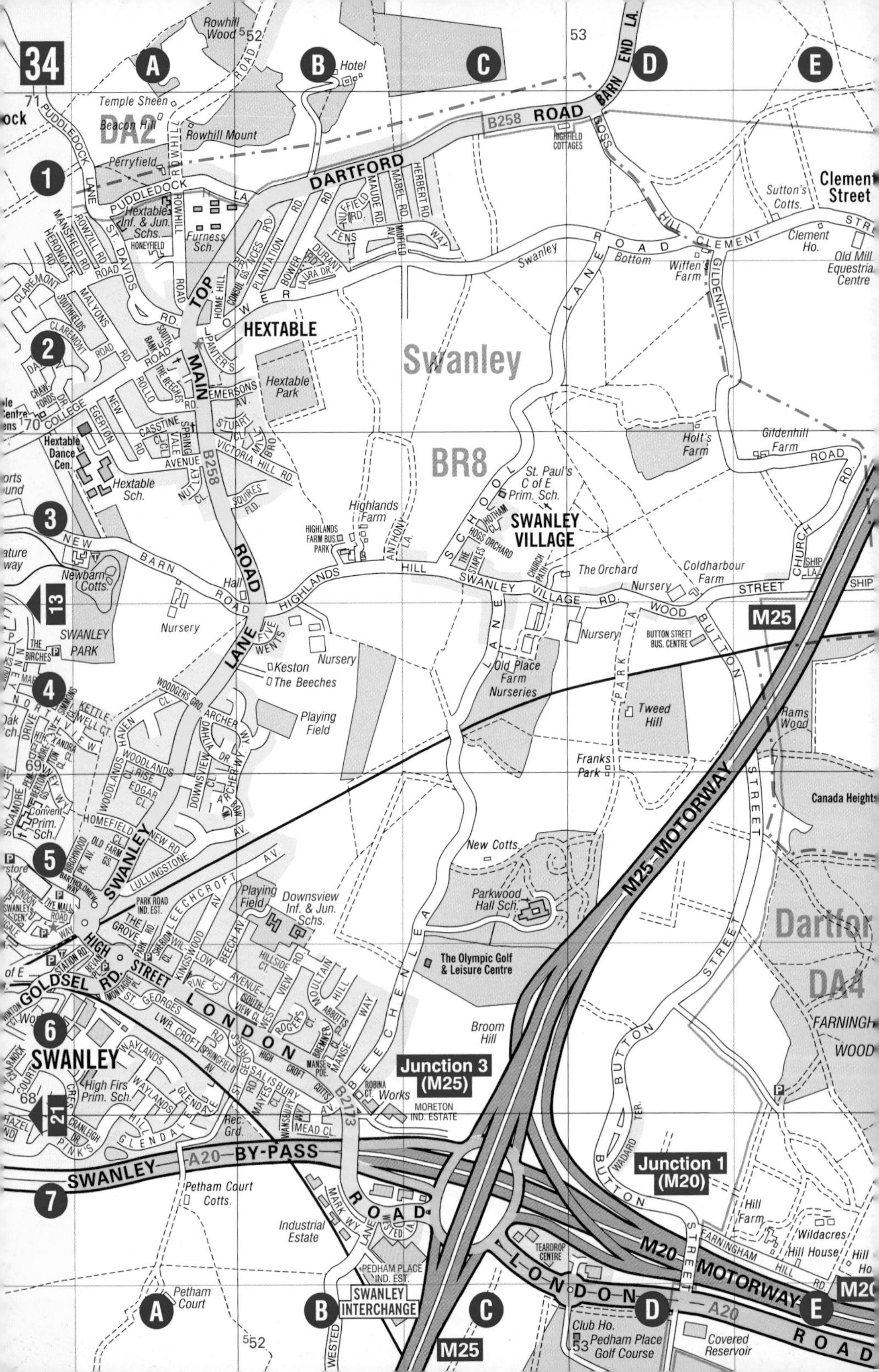
34
A
B
C
D
E
1
2
3
4
5
6
7
13
21
52
53
68
69
70
71
Rowhill Wood
Hotel
Temple Sheen
Beacon Hill
DA2
Rowhill Mount
Perryfield
B258 ROAD
BARN END LA.
HIGHFIELD COTTAGES
GOSS HILL
DARTFORD
PUDDLEDOCK LANE
PUDDLEDOCK LA
ROWHILL ROAD
Hextable Inf. & Jun. Schs.
Furness Sch.
HONEYFIELD
MANSFIELD RD.
ROWZILL RD.
HERONGATE RD.
ST. DAVIDS ROAD
CLAREMONT
MALYONS ROAD
SOUTHFIELDS
TOP
MAIN ROAD
HOME HILL
CONSUL GS.
PRINCES PL.
PLANTATION RD.
BOWER RD.
NUTFIELD RD.
MAUDE RD.
MABEL RD.
HERBERT RD.
MIDFIELD AV.
FENS WAY
DURANT RD.
LAURA DR.
LOWER ROAD
Swanley Bottom
Sutton's Cotts.
Clement Street
Clement Ho.
Old Mill Equestrian Centre
Wiffen's Farm
GILDENHILL
CLEMENT STREET
HEXTABLE
Swanley
PANTER'S
BANK RD.
THE BEECHES
ROLLO RD.
EMERSONS AV.
Hextable Park
COLLEGE
EGERTON
NEW RD.
CASSTINE CL.
SPRING VALE CL.
STUART CL.
MILL BRO.
VICTORIA HILL RD.
AVENUE
NUTLEY CL.
B258
SQUIRES FLD.
Hextable Dance Cen.
Hextable Sch.
BR8
Holt's Farm
Gildenhill Farm
ROAD
CHURCH RD.
St. Paul's C of E Prim. Sch.
SCHOOL LANE
HOTHAM CL.
HOGS ORCHARD
THE STAPLES
SWANLEY VILLAGE
CHURCH PATH
The Orchard
Coldharbour Farm
Highlands Farm
HIGHLANDS FARM BUS. PARK
ANTHONY LA.
NEW BARN ROAD
Newbarn Cotts.
HIGHLANDS HILL
SWANLEY VILLAGE RD
Nursery
WOOD
STREET
SHIP LA.
M25
Hall
SWANLEY PARK
THE BIRCHES
FIVE WENTS
Keston
The Beeches
Nursery
BUTTON STREET BUS. CENTRE
BUTTON STREET
Old Place Farm Nurseries
PARK LA.
Tweed Hill
Rams Wood
Playing Field
WOODGERS GRO.
ARCHER WY.
DAHLIA DR.
KETTLEWELL CT.
NORTHVIEW
HAVEN CL.
WOODLANDS RISE
EDGAR CL.
DOWNSVIEW CL.
ARCHER RD.
BOW AV.
Franks Park
Canada Heights
Convent Prim. Sch.
SYCAMORE
HOMEFIELD CL.
NEW RD.
OLD FARM GS.
BIRCHWOOD PK. AV.
SWANLEY
LULLINGSTONE AV.
New Cotts.
M25 MOTORWAY
LEECHCROFT AV.
PARK ROAD IND. EST.
Playing Field
Downsview Inf. & Jun. Schs.
Parkwood Hall Sch.
Dartford
DA4
THE GROVE
HIGH STREET
STATION RD.
GOLDSEL RD.
KINGSWOOD AV.
BEECH AV.
WILLOW AV.
HILLSIDE CT.
MOULTAIN HILL
PINE CL.
SOUTHVIEW CL.
WEST VIEW RD.
The Olympic Golf & Leisure Centre
BEECHENLEA
MONTAGUE PL.
ST. GEORGES RD.
LONDON
LWR. CROFT
ROGERS CT.
ABBOTTS CT.
MANSE WAY
FARNINGHAM WOOD
Broom Hill
SWANLEY
High Firs Prim. Sch.
WAYLANDS
GLENDALE
SPRINGFIELD AV.
SALISBURY AV.
HIGH CROFT
MANSE PDE.
COTTS.
Junction 3 (M25)
ROBINA CT.
Works
MORETON IND. ESTATE
B2173
MEAD CL.
Rec. Grd.
PINK'S HILL
SWANLEY A20 BY-PASS
Petham Court Cotts.
Industrial Estate
MARK WY.
ROAD
WESTED LA.
LANE
Junction 1 (M20)
WADARD TER.
BUTTON STREET
Hill Farm
Wildacres
Hill House
FARNINGHAM HILL RD.
M20 MOTORWAY
TEARDROP CENTRE
LONDON ROAD
A20
PEDHAM PLACE IND. EST.
SWANLEY INTERCHANGE
Petham Court
Club Ho.
Pedham Place Golf Course
Covered Reservoir
WESTED
M25

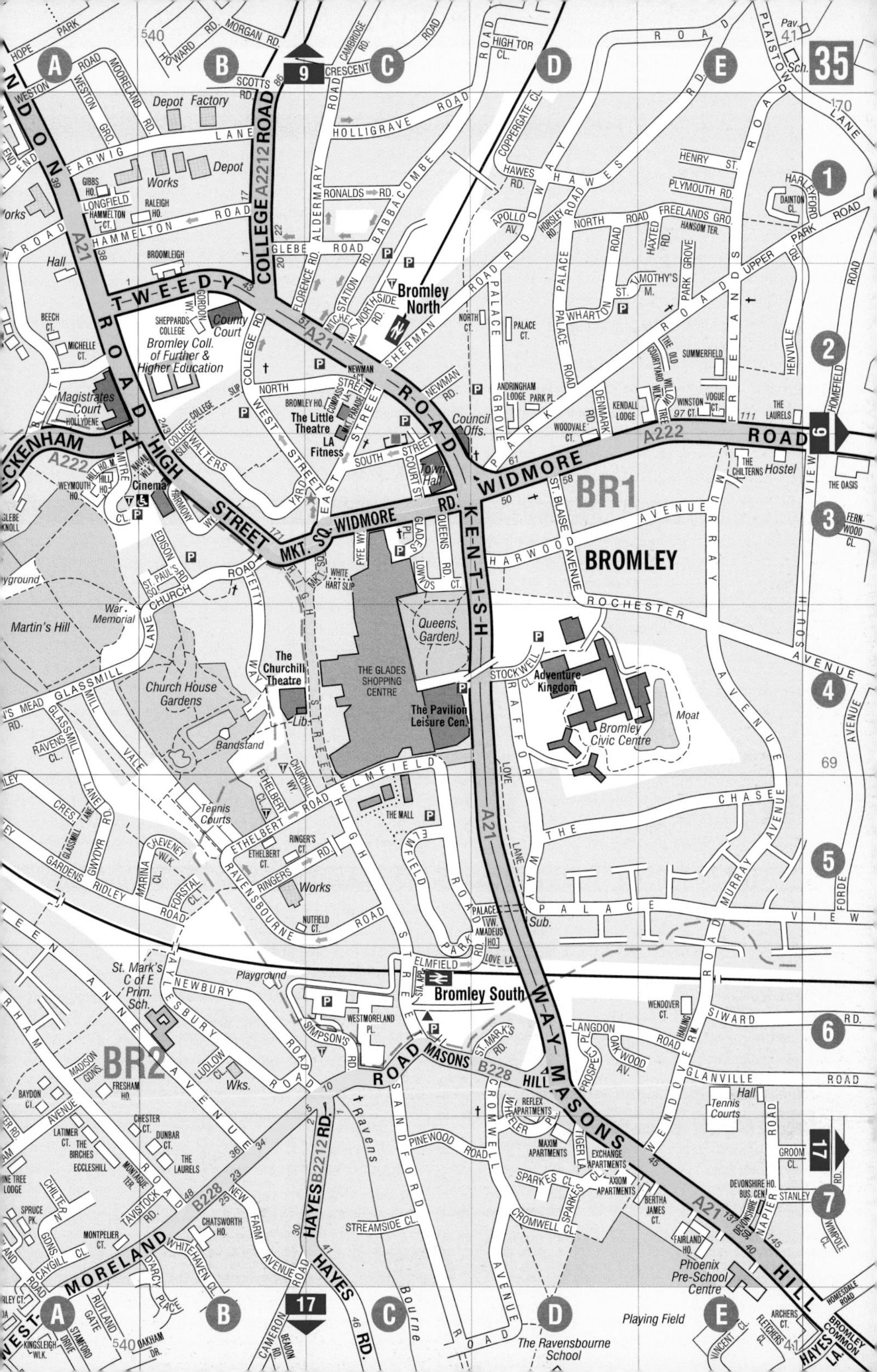

35
A
B
C
D
E
1
2
3
4
5
6
7
9
17
BR1
BR2
BROMLEY
Bromley North
Bromley South
Depot
Factory
Works
Depot
TWEEDY ROAD
LONDON ROAD
A21
A222
A2212
B228
B2212
COLLEGE ROAD
HOLLIGRAVE ROAD
RONALDS RD.
GLEBE ROAD
ALDERMARY RD.
BABBACOMBE RD.
FLORENCE RD.
STATION RD.
NORTHSIDE RD.
MITCHELL WAY
SHERMAN ROAD
HIGH TOR CL.
CAMBRIDGE RD.
CRESCENT
MORGAN RD.
HOWARD RD.
SCOTTS RD.
HOPE PARK
WESTON ROAD
WESTON GRO.
MOORELAND RD.
FARWIG LANE
GIBBS HO.
LONGFIELD
HAMMELTON CT.
HAMMELTON ROAD
RALEIGH HO.
BROOMLEIGH
Hall
BEECH CT.
MICHELLE CT.
Magistrates Court
HOLLYDENE
County Court
SHEPPARDS COLLEGE
Bromley Coll. of Further & Higher Education
GORDON WY.
NORTH ST.
WEST STREET
EAST STREET
BROMLEY HO.
COMPASS
MKT. PARADE
The Little Theatre
LA Fitness
NEWMAN CT.
NEWMAN RD.
ROAD
Council Offs.
Town Hall
SOUTH STREET
COURT ST.
WIDMORE RD.
MKT. SQ.
HIGH STREET
KENTISH WAY
WIDMORE ROAD
NORTH CT.
PALACE CT.
PALACE GROVE
PARK ROAD
ANDRINGHAM LODGE
PARK PL
WOODVALE CT.
DENMARK RD.
KENDALL LODGE
COPPERGATE CL.
HAWES RD.
HAWES ROAD
APOLLO AV.
HORSLEY RD.
NORTH ROAD
PALACE ROAD
WHARTON RD.
ST. TIMOTHY'S M.
HAXTED RD.
FREELANDS GRO.
HANSOM TER.
PARK GROVE
FREELANDS ROAD
HENRY ST.
PLYMOUTH RD.
PLAISTOW LANE
Pav.
Sch.
DAINTON CL.
HARLEYFORD
UPPER PARK ROAD
HENVILLE RD.
HOMEFIELD RD.
SUMMERFIELD
THE OLD COURTYARD
WILLOW TREE WLK.
WINSTON CT.
VOGUE CT.
THE LAURELS
THE CHILTERNS
Hostel
THE OASIS
FERNWOOD CL.
ST. BLAISE AVENUE
AVENUE
HARWOOD AVENUE
ROCHESTER AVENUE
MURRAY AVENUE
SOUTH VIEW
SOUTH AVENUE
THE CHASE
PALACE VIEW
MURRAY ROAD
Adventure Kingdom
Bromley Civic Centre
Moat
STOCKWELL CL.
RAFFORD WAY
LOVE LANE
THE GLADES SHOPPING CENTRE
The Pavilion Leisure Cen.
Queens Garden
GLADES PL.
QUEENS RD.
LOWNDS CT.
WHITE HART SLIP
FYFE WY.
The Churchill Theatre
Lib.
CHURCHILL WY.
ELMFIELD ROAD
ETHELBERT RD.
ETHELBERT CL.
ETHELBERT CT.
RINGER'S CT.
RINGERS RD.
THE MALL
Works
NUTFIELD CT.
RAVENSBOURNE ROAD
ELMFIELD PARK
PALACE VW.
AMADEUS HO.
Sub.
Church House Gardens
Bandstand
Tennis Courts
War Memorial
Martin's Hill
Playground
CHURCH LANE
ST. PAUL'S SQ.
EDISON RD.
TETTY WAY
GLASSMILL LANE
BLYTH RD.
BECKENHAM LA.
MITRE CL.
WEYMOUTH HO.
Cinema
HARMONY WY.
WALTERS
COLLEGE SLIP
GLEBE KNOLL
RAVENS MEAD RD.
RAVENSCL.
VALE
CRES.
GWYDYR RD.
GARDENS
RIDLEY ROAD
MARINA CL.
CHEVENEY WLK.
FORSTAL CL.
St. Mark's C of E Prim. Sch.
AYLESBURY ROAD
NEWBURY RD.
LUDLOW CL.
Wks.
ANNE AVENUE
MADISON GDNS.
FRESHAM HO.
BAYDON CT.
CHESTER CT.
DUNBAR CT.
LATIMER CT.
THE BIRCHES
ECCLESHILL
MONTAGUE TER.
THE LAURELS
TAVISTOCK RD.
CHILTERN GDNS.
SPRUCE PK.
MONTPELIER CT.
CAYGILL CL.
CHATSWORTH HO.
WHITEHAVEN CL.
D'ARCY PLACE
MORELAND ROAD
WEST-MORELAND
RUTLAND GATE
KINGSLEIGH WLK.
DRIVE
STAMFORD
OAKHAM DR.
NEW FARM AVENUE
HAYES RD.
CAMERON RD.
BEADON RD.
Ravens Bourne
SANDFORD ROAD
PINEWOOD ROAD
STREAMSIDE CL.
CROMWELL AVENUE
CROMWELL CL.
WESTMORELAND PL.
SIMPSON'S RD.
MASONS HILL
ST. MARK'S RD.
STN. APP.
Playground
MASONS HILL
REFLEX APARTMENTS
WHEELER PL.
MAXIM APARTMENTS
TIGER LA.
EXCHANGE APARTMENTS
AXIOM APARTMENTS
SPARKES CL.
LANGDON ROAD
PROSPECT PL.
OAKWOOD AV.
WENDOVER CT.
WENDOVER RD.
HAILING M.
SIWARD RD.
GLANVILLE ROAD
Hall
Tennis Courts
GROOM CL.
DEVONSHIRE HO. BUS. CEN.
DEVONSHIRE SQ.
STANLEY RD.
NAPIER RD.
WIMPOLE CL.
BERTHA JAMES CT.
FAIRLAND HO.
Phoenix Pre-School Centre
HOMESDALE ROAD
ARCHERS CT.
FLETCHERS CL.
VINCENT CL.
BROMLEY COMMON
HAYES LA.
Playing Field
The Ravensbourne School

INDEX

Including Streets, Places & Areas, Hospitals & Hospices, Industrial Estates,
Selected Flats & Walkways, Junction Names, Stations and Selected Places of Interest.

HOW TO USE THIS INDEX

1. Each street name is followed by its Postcode District and then by its Locality abbreviation(s) and then by its map reference; e.g. **Abbey La.** BR3: Beck . . . .4B **8** is in the BR3 Postcode District and the Beckenham Locality and is to be found in square 4B on page **8**. The page number is shown in bold type.

2. A strict alphabetical order is followed in which Av., Rd., St., etc. (though abbreviated) are read in full and as part of the street name; e.g. **Alder Way** appears after **Alderton Rd.** but before **Alderwood Rd.**

3. Streets and a selection of flats and walkways too small to be shown on the maps, appear in the index with the thoroughfare to which it is connected shown in brackets; e.g. **Abingdon Lodge** *BR2: Brom . . . .6G* ***9*** *(off Beckenham La.)*

4. Addresses that are in more than one part are referred to as not continuous.

5. Places and areas are shown in the index in **BLUE TYPE** and the map reference is to the actual map square in which the town centre or area is located and not to the place name shown on the map; e.g. **ADDINGTON 2B 22**

6. An example of a selected place of interest is Bromley Mus. 4A 20

7. An example of a station is **Addington Village Stop (CT) . . . .3B 22.** Included are Rail **(Rail)** and Croydon Tramlink **(CT)**

8. Junction names are shown in the index in **BOLD CAPITAL TYPE**; e.g. **CRITTALLS CORNER 4B 12**

9. An example of a hospital is BECKENHAM HOSPITAL 6A 8

10. Map references for entries that appear on large scale page **35** are shown first, with small scale map references shown in brackets; e.g. **Aldermary Rd.** BR1: Brom 1C **35** (5H **9**)

GENERAL ABBREVIATIONS

All. : Alley
App. : Approach
Av. : Avenue
Bri. : Bridge
Bus. : Business
Cvn. : Caravan
Cen. : Centre
Chu. : Church
Cir. : Circus
Cl. : Close
Coll. : College
Comn. : Common
Cnr. : Corner
Cott. : Cottage
Cotts. : Cottages
Ct. : Court
Cres. : Crescent
Cft. : Croft
Dr. : Drive
E. : East
Est. : Estate
Fld. : Field
Flds. : Fields
Gdn. : Garden
Gdns. : Gardens
Gth. : Garth
Ga. : Gate
Gt. : Great
Grn. : Green
Gro. : Grove
Hgts. : Heights
Ho. : House
Ho's. : Houses
Ind. : Industrial
Info. : Information
La. : Lane
Lit. : Little
Lwr. : Lower
Mnr. : Manor
Mans. : Mansions
Mkt. : Market
Mdw. : Meadow
Mdws. : Meadows
M. : Mews
Mt. : Mount
Mus. : Museum
Nth. : North
Pal. : Palace
Pde. : Parade
Pk. : Park
Pas. : Passage
Pl. : Place
Ri. : Rise
Rd. : Road
Rdbt. : Roundabout
Shop. : Shopping
Sth. : South
Sq. : Square
Sta. : Station
St. : Street
Ter. : Terrace
Twr. : Tower
Trad. : Trading
Up. : Upper
Va. : Vale
Vw. : View
Vs. : Villas
Vis. : Visitors
Wlk. : Walk
W. : West
Yd. : Yard

LOCALITY ABBREVIATIONS

Addtn : **Addington**
Beck : **Beckenham**
Bexl : **Bexley**
Big H : **Biggin Hill**
Bras : **Brasted**
Brom : **Bromley**
Chels : **Chelsfield**
Chst : **Chislehurst**
Crock : **Crockenhill**
Croy : **Croydon**
Cud : **Cudham**
Dart : **Dartford**
Downe : **Downe**
Dun G : **Dunton Green**
Farnb : **Farnborough**
Farn : **Farningham**
Hals : **Halstead**
Hayes : **Hayes**
Kes : **Keston**
Knock : **Knockholt**
Limp : **Limpsfield**
Lon : **London**
New Ad : **New Addington**
Orp : **Orpington**
Pet W : **Petts Wood**
Prat B : **Pratts Bottom**
St M Cry : **St Mary Cray**
St P : **St Pauls Cray**
Sels : **Selsdon**
S'ham : **Shoreham**
Sidc : **Sidcup**
Sund : **Sundridge**
Sutt H : **Sutton At Hone**
Swan : **Swanley**
Tats : **Tatsfield**
Thor H : **Thornton Heath**
T'sey : **Titsey**
Wadd : **Waddon**
Warl : **Warlingham**
Well : **Welling**
W W'ck : **West Wickham**
Westrm : **Westerham**

A

Abbey Gdns. BR7: Chst 5D **10**
Abbey La. BR3: Beck 4B **8**
Abbey Pk. BR3: Beck 4B **8**
Abbey Rd. CR0: Croy 7A **14**
Abbey Trad. Est. SE26 . . . .2A **8**
Abbotsbury Rd. BR2: Hayes 6G **17**
Abbots Cl. BR5: Farnb 5F **19**
Abbots Way BR3: Beck 2K **15**
Abbotts Cl. BR8: Swan 6B **34**
Aberdare Cl. BR4: W W'ck 6D **16**
Abergeldie Rd. SE12 . . . .3A **4**
Abingdon Ho. BR1: Brom 1E **35**
Abingdon Lodge *BR2: Brom 6G* ***9***
(off Beckenham La.)
Abingdon Way BR6: Chels 1A **26**
Abinger Cl. BR1: Brom 7B **10**
CR0: New Ad 3D **22**
Acacia Cl. BR5: Pet W 2G **19**
SE20 . . . .6F **7**
Acacia Gdns. BR4: W W'ck 6D **16**
Acacia Rd. BR3: Beck 7A **8**
Acacia Wlk. BR8: Swan 6J **13**
Academy Gdns. CR0: Croy 5E **14**
Acer Rd. TN16: Big H 5F **29**
Acers BR7: Chst 4B **10**
Acorn Cl. BR7: Chst 2F **11**
Acorn Gdns. SE19 . . . .5E **6**
Acorn Way BR3: Beck 2D **16**
BR6: Farnb 1E **24**
Adair Cl. SE25 . . . .7G **7**
Adam Cl. SE6 . . . .1A **8**
Adamson Way BR3: Beck 2D **16**
Adamsrill Rd. SE26 . . . .1J **7**
Adams Rd. BR3: Beck 2K **15**
Adams Way CR0: Croy 3E **14**
SE25 . . . .2G **15**
Adcock Wlk. BR6: Orp 1J **25**
Adderley Gdns. SE9 . . . .1D **10**
ADDINGTON 2B **22**
Addington Bus. Cen. CR0: New Ad 6F **23**
Addington Gro. SE26 . . . .1K **7**
Addington Hgts. CR0: New Ad 7D **22**

Addington Rd. BR4: W W'ck 1D 22
CR0: Croy 5A 14
Addington Village Rd. CR0: Addtn 3A 22
(not continuous)
Addington Village Stop (CT) 3B 22
ADDISCOMBE 5F 15
Addiscombe Av. CR0: Croy 5F 15
Addiscombe Ct. Rd. CR0: Croy 5D 14
Addiscombe Gro. CR0: Croy 6D 14
Addiscombe Rd. CR0: Croy 6D 14
Addiscombe Stop (CT) 5F 15
Addison Cl. BR5: Pet W 3F 19
Addison Dr. SE12 2A 4
Addison Pl. SE25 1F 15
Addison Rd. BR2: Brom 2K 17
SE25 1F 15
Addisons Cl. CR0: Croy 6A 16
Adelaide Ct. BR3: Beck 4A 8
Adelaide Rd. BR7: Chst 2E 10
Admiral Cl. BR5: St P 1C 20
Admiral Seymour Rd. SE9 1E 4
Adolf St. SE6 1C 8
Advance Rd. SE27 1B 6
Adventure Kingdom 4D 35 (6J 9)
Agaton Rd. SE9 6H 5
Ainsdale Cl. BR6: Orp 5G 19
Ainsworth Rd. CR0: Croy 5A 14
Airport Ind. Est. TN16: Big H 4F 29
Akabusi Cl. CR0: Croy 3F 15
Albany M. BR1: Brom 3H 9
Albany Rd. BR7: Chst 2E 10
Albemarle Pk. BR3: Beck 5C 8
Albemarle Rd. BR3: Beck 5C 8
Albert Mans. *CR0: Croy* *5C 14*
(off Lansdowne Rd.)
Albert Rd. BR2: Brom 2A 18
BR5: St M Cry 3A 20
BR6: Chels 2K 25
SE9 7D 4
SE20 3J 7
SE25 1F 15
Albert Yd. SE19 3D 6
Albion Pl. SE25 7F 7
Albion St. CR0: Croy 5A 14
Albyfield BR1: Brom 1C 18
Alden Ct. CR0: Croy 7D 14
Aldermary Rd. BR1: Brom 1C 35 (5H 9)
Alder Rd. DA14: Sidc 7K 5
Alders, The BR4: W W'ck 5C 16
Aldersgrove Av. SE9 7C 4
Aldersmead Av. CR0: Croy 3J 15
Aldersmead Rd. BR3: Beck 4K 7
Alderton Rd. CR0: Croy 4E 14
Alder Way BR8: Swan 6J 13
Alderwood Rd. SE9 3J 5
Aldrich Cres. CR0: New Ad 5D 22
Aldwick Cl. SE9 7J 5
Alexander Cl. BR2: Hayes 5H 17
DA15: Sidc 2K 5
Alexander Ct. BR3: Beck 5E 8
Alexander Rd. BR7: Chst 3E 10
Alexandra Cl. BR8: Swan 6K 13
Alexandra Cres. BR1: Brom 3G 9
Alexandra Dr. SE19 2D 6
Alexandra Pl. CR0: Croy 5D 14
SE25 2C 14
Alexandra Rd. CR0: Croy 5D 14
SE26 3J 7
TN16: Big H 1A 32
Alexandra Wlk. SE19 2D 6
Alfan La. DA2: Dart 2J 13
Alford Grn. CR0: New Ad 3E 22
Alfred Rd. SE25 2F 15
Alice Thompson Cl. SE12 6B 4
Alison Cl. CR0: Croy 5J 15
Alkham Twr. *BR5: St M Cry* *1B 20*
(off Bapchild Pl.)
Allandale Pl. BR6: Chels 7C 20
Allard Cl. BR5: Orp 4B 20
Allenby Rd. TN16: Big H 6G 29
Allendale Cl. SE26 2J 7
Allen Rd. BR3: Beck 6J 7
Allerford Rd. SE6 1C 8
Alleyn Pk. SE21 1D 6
Alleyn Rd. SE21 1D 6
Allington Rd. BR6: Orp 6G 19
Allwood Cl. SE26 1J 7
Alma Pl. CR7: Thor H 2A 14
SE19 4E 6
Alma Rd. BR5: Orp 6C 20
Almond Cl. BR2: Brom 4D 18
Almond Dr. BR8: Swan 6J 13
Almond Way BR2: Brom 4D 18
Alnwick Rd. SE12 3A 4
Alpha Rd. CR0: Croy 5D 14
Alpine Cl. CR0: Croy 7D 14
Alpine Copse BR1: Brom 6D 10
Altash Way SE9 6E 4
Alton Gdns. BR3: Beck 4B 8
Altyre Cl. BR3: Beck 2A 16
Altyre Rd. CR0: Croy 6C 14
Altyre Way BR3: Beck 2A 16
Alverstone Gdns. SE9 5H 5
Alverston Gdns. SE25 2D 14
Alwold Cres. SE12 3A 4
Alwyn Cl. CR0: New Ad 4C 22
Amadeus Ho. BR1: Brom 5D 35
Amberley Cl. BR6: Chels 2J 25
Amberley Ct. BR3: Beck 4A 8
DA14: Sidc 2B 12
Amberley Gro. CR0: Croy 4E 14
SE26 2G 7
Amblecote Cl. SE12 7A 4
Amblecote Mdws. SE12 7A 4
Amblecote Rd. SE12 7A 4
Ambleside BR1: Brom 3E 8
Ambleside Av. BR3: Beck 2K 15
Ambrose Cl. BR6: Orp 7J 19
Amersham Rd. CR0: Croy 3B 14
Amesbury Rd. BR1: Brom 7A 10
Amethyst Ct. *BR6: Chels* *2H 25*
(off Farnborough Hill)
Amherst Cl. BR5: St M Cry 1K 19
Amherst Dr. BR5: St M Cry 1J 19
Amida Leisure Cen. 2A 16
Ampleforth Cl. BR6: Chels 1B 26
Ancaster M. BR3: Beck 7J 7
Ancaster Rd. BR3: Beck 7J 7
Andace Pk. Gdns. BR1: Brom 6K 9
Andorra Ct. BR1: Brom 5K 9
Andover Rd. BR6: Orp 5G 19
Andreck Ct. *BR3: Beck* *6D 8*
(off Crescent Rd.)
Andrew's Cl. BR5: St P 6C 12
Andrews Pl. SE9 3G 5
Andringham Lodge BR1: Brom 2D 35
ANERLEY 6G 7
Anerley Gro. SE19 4E 6
Anerley Hill SE19 3E 6
Anerley Pk. SE20 4F 7
Anerley Pk. Rd. SE20 4G 7
Anerley Rd. SE19 4F 7
SE20 4F 7
Anerley Station (Rail) 5G 7
Anerley Sta. Rd. SE20 5G 7
Anerley Va. SE19 4E 6
Angelica Gdns. CR0: Croy 5J 15
Anglesea Rd. BR5: St M Cry 3B 20
Annandale Rd. CR0: Croy 6F 15
DA15: Sidc 4K 5
Anne Boleyn Ct. SE9 3H 5
Anne of Cleeves Ct. SE9 3J 5
Annesley Dr. CR0: Croy 7A 16
Anne Sutherland Ho.
BR3: Beck 4K 7
Annsworthy Av. CR7: Thor H 7C 6
Annsworthy Cres. SE25 6C 6
Anselm Cl. CR0: Croy 7E 14
Ansford Rd. BR1: Brom 2D 8
Anstridge Path SE9 3J 5
Anstridge Rd. SE9 3J 5
Anthony La. BR8: Swan 3B 34
Anthony Rd. SE25 3F 15
Antigua Wlk. SE19 2C 6
APERFIELD 6G 29
Aperfield Rd. TN16: Big H 6G 29
Aperfields TN16: Big H 6G 29
Apex Cl. BR3: Beck 5C 8
Apollo Av. BR1: Brom 1D 35 (5J 9)
Apostle Way CR7: Thor H 6A 6
Appleby Cl. BR5: Pet W 4H 19
Appledore Cl. BR2: Brom 2G 17
Appledore Cres. DA14: Sidc 7K 5
Applegarth CR0: New Ad 4C 22
(not continuous)
Apple Orchard BR8: Swan 1J 21
Appleton Rd. SE9 1D 4
Appletree Cl. SE20 5G 7
Approach, The BR6: Orp 6J 19
Approach Rd. TN16: Tats 5A 32
April Cl. BR6: Chels 2J 25
April Glen SE23 1J 7
Apsley Ct. BR5: St M Cry 3A 20
Apsley Rd. SE25 1G 15
Aragon Cl. BR2: Brom 5C 18
CR0: New Ad 6F 23
Arbor Cl. BR3: Beck 6C 8
Arbrook Cl. BR5: St P 7K 11
Arbury Ter. SE26 1F 7
Arcade CR0: Croy 6B 14
Arcade, The *CR0: Croy* *7B 14*
(off High St.)
SE9 *3F 5*
(off High St.)
Arcade Chambers SE9 3F 5
Archer Rd. BR5: St M Cry 2K 19
SE25 1G 15
Archers Ct. BR2: Brom 7E 35 (1J 17)
Archer Way BR8: Swan 4A 34
Archery Rd. SE9 2E 4
Arcus Rd. BR1: Brom 3F 9
Arden Gro. BR6: Farnb 1E 24
Ardent Cl. SE25 7D 6
Ardingly Cl. CR0: Croy 7J 15
Ardley Cl. SE6 1K 7
Arena Stop (CT) 2H 15
Arkell Gro. SE19 4A 6
Arkindale Rd. SE6 1D 8
Arlington Cl. DA15: Sidc 4K 5
Armistice Gdns. SE25 7F 7
Armstrong Cl. BR1: Brom 7B 10
Arne Gro. BR6: Orp 7J 19
Arnhem Dr. CR0: New Ad 7E 22
Arnulf St. SE6 1C 8
Arnulls Rd. SW16 3A 6
Arpley Sq. *SE20* *4H 7*
(off High St.)
Arragon Gdns. BR4: W W'ck 7C 16
Arrol Rd. BR3: Beck 7H 7
Arsenal Rd. SE9 1E 4
Arthur Ct. *CR0: Croy* *7D 14*
(off Fairfield Path)
Arthur Rd. TN16: Big H 4E 28
Artington Cl. BR6: Farnb 1F 25
Arun Ct. SE25 2F 15
Arundel Cl. CR0: Wadd 7A 14
Arundel Ct. BR2: Brom 6F 9
Arundel Dr. BR6: Chels 2A 26
Arundel Rd. CR0: Croy 3C 14
Aschurch Rd. CR0: Croy 4E 14
Ascot Rd. BR5: St M Cry 1J 19
Ashbourne Ri. BR6: Orp 1H 25
Ashburnham Ct. BR3: Beck 6D 8
Ashburton Av. CR0: Croy 5G 15
Ashburton Cl. CR0: Croy 5F 15
Ashburton Gdns. CR0: Croy 6F 15
Ashburton Memorial Homes CR0: Croy 4G 15
Ashburton Rd. CR0: Croy 6F 15
Ashby Wlk. CR0: Croy 3B 14
Ash Cl. BR5: Pet W 2G 19
BR8: Swan 6H 13
DA14: Sidc 1A 12
SE20 6H 7
Ashcroft Theatre *7C 14*
(in Fairfield Halls)
Ashdale Rd. SE12 5A 4
Ashdown Cl. BR3: Beck 6C 8
Ashfield Cl. BR3: Beck 4B 8
Ashfield La. BR7: Chst 3E 10
(not continuous)
Ash Gro. BR4: W W'ck 6D 16
SE20 6H 7
Ashgrove Rd. BR1: Brom 3E 8
Ashleigh Point SE23 1J 7
Ashleigh Rd. SE20 7G 7
Ashley Gdns. BR6: Orp 2H 25
Ashling Rd. CR0: Croy 5F 15
Ashmead Ga. BR1: Brom 5K 9
Ashmere Av. BR3: Beck 6E 8
Ashmore La. BR2: Kes 7K 23
Ash Rd. BR6: Chels 4J 25
CR0: Croy 6B 16
TN16: Westrm 7J 33
Ash Row BR2: Brom 4D 18
Ash Tree Cl. CR0: Croy 3K 15
Ashtree Cl. BR6: Farnb 1E 24
Ash Tree Way CR0: Croy 2J 15
Ashurst Cl. SE20 5G 7
Ashurst Wlk. CR0: Croy 6G 15
Ashwater Rd. SE12 5A 4
Ashwood Gdns. CR0: New Ad 3D 22
Aspen Cl. BR6: Chels 2K 25
BR8: Swan 5J 13
Aspen Copse BR1: Brom 6C 10
Asprey M. BR3: Beck 2A 16
Asprey Pl. BR1: Brom 6B 10

Aston Cl. DA14: Sidc 1K **11**
Aston Pl. SW16 . . . . 3A **6**
Athelstan Way BR5: St P 5K **11**
Atkins Dr. BR4: W W'ck 6E **16**
Atkinson Cl. BR6: Chels 2K **25**
Atterbury Cl. TN16: Westrm 7J **33**
Attlee Cl. CR7: Thor H 2B **14**
Aubyn Hill SE27 . . . . 1B **6**
Auckland Cl. SE19 . . . . 5E **6**
Auckland Gdns. SE19 . . . . 5D **6**
Auckland Hill SE27 . . . . 1B **6**
Auckland Ri. SE19 . . . . 5D **6**
Auckland Rd. SE19 . . . . 5E **6**
Audley Wlk. BR5: St M Cry 3B **20**
Audrey Cl. BR3: Beck 3C **16**
Augustine Rd. BR5: St P 7C **12**
Augustus La. BR6: Orp 6K **19**
Austin Av. BR2: Brom 2B **18**
Austin Rd. BR5: St M Cry 3K **19**
Autumn Gro. BR1: Brom 3J **9**
Avalon Cl. BR6: Chels 7C **20**
Avalon Rd. BR6: Chels 6A **20**
Avard Gdns. BR6: Farnb 1F **25**
Avebury Rd. BR6: Orp 7G **19**
Avenue, The BR1: Brom 7A **10**
BR2: Kes 1A **24**
BR3: Beck 5C **8**
(not continuous)
BR4: W W'ck 4D **16**
BR5: St P 4A **12**
BR6: Orp 6J **19**
CR0: Croy 7D **14**
TN16: Tats 4E **32**
Avenue Gdns. SE25 . . . . 6F **7**
Avenue Rd. BR3: Beck 6J **7**
SE20 . . . . 5H **7**
SE25 . . . . 6E **6**
TN16: Tats 2D **32**
Avenue Road Stop (CT) 6J **7**
Averil Gro. SW16 . . . . 3A **6**
AVERY HILL 3J **5**
Avery Hill Rd. SE9 . . . . 3J **5**
Aviemore Cl. BR3: Beck 2A **16**
Aviemore Way BR3: Beck 2K **15**
Avington Gro. SE20 . . . . 4H **7**
Avondale Rd. BR1: Brom 3F **9**
SE9 . . . . 6D **4**
Avonstowe Cl. BR6: Farnb 7F **19**
Axiom Apartments BR2: Brom 7D **35**
Axtaine Rd. BR5: St M Cry 4C **20**
Aycliffe Cl. BR1: Brom 1C **18**
Aylesbury Rd. BR2: Brom 6B **35** (7H **9**)
Aylesford Av. BR3: Beck 2K **15**
Aylesham Rd. BR6: Orp 4J **19**
Aylett Rd. SE25 . . . . 1G **15**
Aynscombe Angle BR6: Orp 4K **19**
Azalea Dr. BR8: Swan 1J **21**

B

Babbacombe Rd. BR1: Brom 1C **35** (5H **9**)
Backley Gdns. SE25 . . . . 3F **15**
Back Rd. DA14: Sidc 1K **11**
Badgers Copse BR6: Orp 6J **19**
Badgers Cft. SE9 . . . . 7F **5**
Badgers Hole CR0: Croy 7J **15**
BADGER'S MOUNT 6G **27**
Badger's Ri. TN14: Hals 6F **27**
Badgers Rd.
TN14: Hals, S'ham 6G **27**
(not continuous)
Bailey Pl. SE26 . . . . 3J **7**
Baird Gdns. SE19 . . . . 1D **6**
Bakers Ct. SE25 . . . . 7D **6**
Bakers M. BR6: Chels 3J **25**
Balcaskie Rd. SE9 . . . . 2E **4**
Balder Ri. SE12 . . . . 6A **4**
Balfour Rd. BR2: Brom 2A **18**
SE25 . . . . 2F **15**
Balgowan Rd. BR3: Beck 7K **7**
Ballamore Rd. BR1: Brom . . . . 7A **4** & 1H **9**
Balmoral Av. BR3: Beck 1K **15**
Balmoral Ct. *BR3: Beck 5D 8*
(off The Avenue)
SE12 . . . . 1J **9**
SE27 . . . . 1B **6**
Bamford Rd. BR1: Brom 2D **8**
Bampton Rd. SE23 . . . . 1J **7**
Banavie Gdns. BR3: Beck 5D **8**
Bancroft Gdns. BR6: Orp 5J **19**
Bankfoot Rd. BR1: Brom 1F **9**
Bankside Cl. DA5: Bexl 1J **13**
TN16: Big H 7E **28**
Bankside Way SE19 . . . . 3D **6**
Bannatyne's Health Club
Grove Park 6A **4**
Bannister Gdns. BR5: St P 7B **12**
Bapchild Pl. BR5: St M Cry 1B **20**
Barclay Rd. CR0: Croy 7C **14**
Barcombe Cl. BR5: St P 7J **11**
Bardolph Av. CR0: Sels 5A **22**
Bardsley Cl. CR0: Croy 7E **14**
Barfield Rd. BR1: Brom 7D **10**
Barfreston Way SE20 . . . . 5G **7**
Bargrove Cl. SE20 . . . . 4F **7**
Barham Cl. BR2: Brom 5B **18**
BR7: Chst 2E **10**
Barham Rd. BR7: Chst 2E **10**
Baring Cl. SE12 . . . . 6A **4**
Baring Rd. CR0: Croy 5F **15**
SE12 . . . . 6A **4**
Bark Hart Rd. BR6: Orp 5A **20**
Barmouth Rd. CR0: Croy 6J **15**
Barnard Cl. BR7: Chst 5G **11**
Barn End La. DA2: Dart, Swan 1D **34**
Barnesdale Cres. BR5: St M Cry 3K **19**
Barnet Dr. BR2: Brom 6B **18**
Barnet Wood Rd. BR2: Brom 6K **17**
Barnfield Av. CR0: Croy 6H **15**
Barnfield Cl. BR8: Crock 4H **21**
Barnfield Rd. BR5: St P 7C **12**
TN16: Tats 2C **32**
Barnfield Wood Cl. BR3: Beck 3E **16**
Barnfield Wood Rd. BR3: Beck 3E **16**
Barnhill Av. BR2: Brom 2G **17**
Barnmead Rd. BR3: Beck 5J **7**
Baron's Wlk. CR0: Croy 3K **15**
Barrington Wlk. SE19 . . . . 3D **6**
Barry Cl. BR6: Orp 7H **19**
Barson Cl. SE20 . . . . 4H **7**
Bartholomew Way BR8: Swan 7K **13**
Barton Rd. DA14: Sidc 3D **12**
Barts Cl. BR3: Beck 2B **16**
Barwood Av. BR4: W W'ck 5C **16**
Basil Gdns. CR0: Croy 5J **15**
SE27 . . . . 2B **6**
Basket Gdns. SE9 . . . . 2D **4**
Bassett's Cl. BR6: Farnb 1E **24**
Bassett's Way BR6: Farnb 1E **24**
Baston Mnr. Rd. BR2: Hayes, Kes 7J **17**
Baston Rd. BR2: Hayes 6J **17**
Batchwood Grn. BR5: St P 7K **11**
Bath Ct. *SE26 . . . . 1F 7*
(off Droitwich Cl.)
Baths Rd. BR2: Brom 1A **18**
Battenberg Wlk. SE19 . . . . 3D **6**
Baugh Rd. DA14: Sidc 2B **12**
Baxter Cl. BR1: Brom 7E **10**
Baydon Ct. BR2: Brom 6A **35** (7G **9**)
Bayes Cl. SE26 . . . . 2H **7**
Bayfield Rd. SE9 . . . . 1C **4**
Bay Tree Cl. BR1: Brom 5A **10**
Beachborough Rd. BR1: Brom 1D **8**
Beaconsfield Pde. SE9 . . . . 1B **10**
Beaconsfield Rd. BR1: Brom 7A **10**
CR0: Croy 3C **14**
SE9 . . . . 6D **4**
Beadman Pl. SE27 . . . . 1A **6**
Beadman St. SE27 . . . . 1A **6**
Beadon Rd. BR2: Brom 7B **35** (1H **17**)
Beagles Cl. BR5: Orp 6C **20**
Beamish Rd. BR5: Orp 4B **20**
Beanshaw SE9 . . . . 1D **10**
Beardell St. SE19 . . . . 3E **6**
Bearsted Ter. BR3: Beck 5B **8**
Beauchamp Rd. SE19 . . . . 5C **6**
Beaulieu Av. SE26 . . . . 1G **7**
Beaumanor Gdns. SE9 . . . . 1D **10**
Beaumont Rd. BR5: Pet W 3G **19**
SE19 . . . . 3B **6**
Beaverbank Rd. SE9 . . . . 5J **5**
Beaver Cl. SE20 . . . . 4F **7**
Beaver Ct. BR3: Beck 4C **8**
Beavers Lodge DA14: Sidc 1J **11**
Beaver Water World 4A **32**
Beaverwood Rd. BR7: Chst 2H **11**
Beblets Cl. BR6: Chels 2J **25**
Beck Ct. BR3: Beck 7J **7**
BECKENHAM 5B **8**
Beckenham Bus. Cen. BR3: Beck 3K **7**
Beckenham Crematorium BR3: Beck 7H **7**
Beckenham Gro. BR2: Brom 6E **8**
Beckenham Hill Est. BR3: Beck 2C **8**
Beckenham Hill Rd. BR3: Beck 3C **8**
SE6 . . . . 3C **8**
Beckenham Hill Station (Rail) 2D **8**
BECKENHAM HOSPITAL 6A **8**
Beckenham Junction Station (Rail & CT) 5B **8**
Beckenham La. BR2: Brom 3A **35** (6F **9**)
Beckenham Pl. Pk. BR3: Beck 4C **8**
Beckenham Rd. BR3: Beck 5J **7**
BR4: W W'ck 4C **16**
Beckenham Road Stop (CT) 5K **7**
Beckenham Theatre Cen., The 6C **8**
Becket Cl. SE25 . . . . 3F **15**
Becketts Cl. BR6: Orp 7J **19**
Beckett Wlk. BR3: Beck 3K **7**
Beckford Dr. BR5: Orp 4G **19**
Beckford Rd. CR0: Croy 3E **14**
Beck La. BR3: Beck 7J **7**
Beck River Pk. BR3: Beck 5B **8**
Beck Way BR3: Beck 7A **8**
Becondale Rd. SE19 . . . . 2D **6**
Beddington Grn. BR5: St P 5J **11**
Beddington Path BR5: St P 5J **11**
Beddington Rd. BR5: St P 6H **11**
Beddlestead La. CR6: Warl . . . . 6B **28** & 4A **32**
Bedens Rd. DA14: Sidc 3D **12**
Bedford Ct. *CR0: Croy 5B 14*
(off Tavistock Rd.)
Bedford Pk. CR0: Croy 5B **14**
Bedford Pl. CR0: Croy 5C **14**
Bedford Rd. BR6: Orp 6A **20**
DA15: Sidc 7K **5**
Bedgebury Rd. SE9 . . . . 1C **4**
Bedser Cl. CR7: Thor H 7B **6**
Bedwardine Rd. SE19 . . . . 4D **6**
Beech Av. BR8: Swan 6A **34**
TN16: Tats 1C **32**
Beech Copse BR1: Brom 5C **10**
Beech Ct. BR1: Brom 2A **35**
BR3: Beck 4A **8**
Beechcroft BR7: Chst 4D **10**
Beechcroft Cl. BR6: Orp 1G **25**
Beechcroft Rd. BR6: Orp 1G **25**
Beech Dell BR2: Kes 1C **24**
Beechenlea La. BR8: Swan 6B **34**
Beeches, The BR8: Swan 2A **34**
Beeches Cl. SE20 . . . . 5H **7**
Beechfield Cotts. BR1: Brom 5K **9**
Beechfield Rd. BR1: Brom 6K **9**
Beechhill Rd. SE9 . . . . 2F **5**
Beech Ho. CR0: New Ad 3C **22**
Beech Ho. Rd. CR0: Croy 7C **14**
Beechmont Cl. BR1: Brom 2F **9**
Beech Rd. BR6: Chels 4K **25**
TN16: Big H 1A **32**
Beechwood Av. BR6: Chels 2H **25**
CR7: Thor H 1A **14**
Beechwood Dr. BR2: Kes 1A **24**
Beechwood Ri. BR7: Chst 1E **10**
Beechwoods Ct. SE19 . . . . 2E **6**
Beeken Dene BR6: Farnb 1F **25**
Beggars La. TN16: Westrm 7J **33**
Bekesbourne Twr. *BR5: Orp 5C 20*
(off Wichling Cl.)
Belcroft Cl. BR1: Brom 4G **9**
Beldam Haw TN14: Hals 7F **27**
Belfast Rd. SE25 . . . . 1G **15**
Belfry Cl. BR1: Brom 1E **18**
Belgrave Cl. BR5: St M Cry 1B **20**
Belgrave Rd. SE25 . . . . 1E **14**
Belgravia Gdns. BR1: Brom 3F **9**
Bellefield Rd. BR5: St M Cry 2A **20**
Bellevue Pk. CR7: Thor H 7B **6**
Belle Vue Rd. BR6: Downe 6D **24**
Bellfield CR0: Sels 5A **22**
Bell Gdns. BR5: St M Cry 2B **20**
BELL GREEN 1K **7**
Bell Grn. SE26 . . . . 1A **8**
Bell Grn. La. SE26 . . . . 2A **8**
Bell Hill CR0: Croy 6B **14**
BELLINGHAM 1B **8**
Bellingham Grn. SE6 . . . . 1B **8**
Bell Mdw. SE19 . . . . 2D **6**
Belmont La. BR7: Chst 2F **11**
(not continuous)
Belmont Pde. BR7: Chst 2F **11**
Belmont Rd. BR3: Beck 6K **7**
BR7: Chst 2E **10**
SE25 . . . . 2G **15**
Belton Rd. DA14: Sidc 1K **11**
Belvedere Rd. SE19 . . . . 4E **6**
TN16: Big H 7H **29**
Belvoir Cl. SE9 . . . . 7D **4**

Benbury Cl. BR1: Brom 2D **8**
Bencurtis Pk. BR4: W W'ck 7E **16**
Benedict Cl. BR6: Orp 7H **19**
Benenden Grn. BR2: Brom 2H **17**
Bennetts Av. CR0: Croy 6K **15**
Bennetts Copse BR7: Chst 3B **10**
Bennetts Way CR0: Croy 6K **15**
Bensham Cl. CR7: Thor H 1B **14**
Bensham Gro. CR7: Thor H 6B **6**
Bensham La. CR0: Croy 4A **14**
CR7: Thor H 2A **14**
Bensham Mnr. Rd. CR7: Thor H 1B **14**
Bensham Mnr. Rd. Pas. CR7: Thor H 1B **14**
Benson Rd. CR0: Wadd 7A **14**
Bentfield Gdns. SE9 7C **4**
Bentons La. SE27 1B **6**
Benton's Ri. SE27 2C **6**
Bercta Rd. SE9 6H **5**
Berens Ct. DA14: Sidc 1J **11**
Berens Rd. BR5: St M Cry 2C **20**
Berens Way BR7: Chst 7J **11**
Beresford Dr. BR1: Brom 7B **10**
Berger Cl. BR5: Pet W 3G **19**
Berkeley Cl. BR5: Pet W 4H **19**
Berkeley Ct. BR8: Swan 7K **13**
*CR0: Croy 7C **14***
(off Coombe Rd.)
Berkshire Ho. SE6 1B **8**
Bernel Dr. CR0: Croy 7A **16**
Berne Rd. CR7: Thor H 2B **14**
Berney Ho. BR3: Beck 2K **15**
Berney Rd. CR0: Croy 4C **14**
Berridge Rd. SE19 2C **6**
Berryfield Cl. BR1: Brom 5B **10**
Berryhill SE9 1G **5**
Berryhill Gdns. SE9 1G **5**
Berrylands BR6: Chels 7B **20**
Berry La. SE21 1C **6**
Berryman's La. SE26 1J **7**
BERRY'S GREEN 5K **29**
Berry's Grn. Rd. TN16: Big H 5K **29**
Berry's Hill TN16: Big H 5K **29**
Bertha Hollamby Ct. *DA14: Sidc 2B **12***
(off Sidcup Hill)
Bertha James Ct. BR2: Brom 7E **35** (1J **17**)
Bertie Rd. SE26 3J **7**
Bert Rd. CR7: Thor H 2B **14**
Berwick Cres. DA15: Sidc 4K **5**
Berwick Way BR6: Orp 5K **19**
Best Ter. BR8: Crock 3H **21**
Betchworth Way CR0: New Ad 5D **22**
Bethersden Cl. BR3: Beck 4A **8**
BETHLEM ROYAL HOSPITAL, THE 4B **16**
Betony Cl. CR0: Croy 5J **15**
Betts Cl. BR3: Beck 6K **7**
Betts Way SE20 5G **7**
Beulah Av. CR7: Thor H 6B **6**
Beulah Cres. CR7: Thor H 6B **6**
Beulah Gro. CR0: Croy 3B **14**
Beulah Hill SE19 3A **6**
Beulah Rd. CR7: Thor H 7B **6**
Bevan Pl. BR8: Swan 6A **34**
Beverley Av. DA15: Sidc 4K **5**
Beverley Ho. *BR1: Brom 2E **8***
(off Brangbourne Rd.)
Beverley Hyrst CR0: Croy 6E **14**
Beverley Rd. BR2: Brom 6B **18**
SE20 6G **7**
Beverstone Rd. CR7: Thor H 1A **14**
Bevill Cl. SE25 7F **7**
Bevington Rd. BR3: Beck 6C **8**
Bewlys Rd. SE27 2A **6**
Bexley La. DA14: Sidc 1B **12**
Bexley Music & Dance Cen. *1K **11***
(off Station Rd.)
Bexley Rd. SE9 2G **5**
BICKLEY 7B **10**
Bickley Cres. BR1: Brom 1B **18**
Bickley Pk. Rd. BR1: Brom 7B **10**
Bickley Rd. BR1: Brom 6A **10**
Bickley Station (Rail) 7B **10**
Bicknor Rd. BR6: Orp 4H **19**
Bidborough Cl. BR2: Brom 2G **17**
Biddenden Way SE9 1D **10**
BIGGIN HILL 6F **29**
Biggin Hill SE19 5A **6**
BIGGIN HILL AIRPORT 1E **28**
Biggin Hill Bus. Pk.
TN16: Big H 4F **29**
Biggin Way SE19 4A **6**
Bigginwood Rd. SW16 4A **6**
Bill Hamling Cl. SE9 6E **4**
Billinton Hill CR0: Croy 6C **14**
Bilsby Gro. SE9 1A **10**
Bingham Rd. CR0: Croy 5F **15**
Binnington Twr. BR2: Brom 3B **18**
Birbetts Rd. SE9 6E **4**
Birchanger Rd. SE25 2F **15**
Birches, The BR2: Brom 7A **35**
BR6: Farnb 1D **24**
BR8: Swan 6K **13**
Birchington Cl. BR5: Orp 5B **20**
Birchmead BR6: Farnb 6D **18**
Birch Row BR2: Brom 4D **18**
Birch Tree Av. BR4: W W'ck 2G **23**
Birch Tree Way CR0: Croy 6G **15**
Birchwood Av. BR3: Beck 1A **16**
DA14: Sidc 1A **12**
Birchwood Dr. DA2: Dart 1K **13**
Birchwood La. TN14: Dun G 4K **31**
Birchwood Pde. DA2: Dart 1K **13**
Birchwood Pk. Av. BR8: Swan 7K **13**
Birchwood Rd. BR5: Pet W 1G **19**
BR8: Swan 5H **13**
DA2: Dart 2J **13**
Birdbrook Rd. SE3 1B **4**
Birdham Cl. BR1: Brom 2B **18**
Birdhouse La. BR6: Downe 4J **29**
Bird in Hand La. BR1: Brom 6A **10**
Bird in Hand Path *CR0: Croy 4C **14***
(off Sydenham Rd.)
Birkbeck Rd. BR3: Beck 6H **7**
DA14: Sidc 1K **11**
Birkbeck Station (Rail & CT) 7H **7**
Birkdale Cl. BR6: Orp 4G **19**
Birkdale Gdns. CR0: Croy 7J **15**
Bisenden Rd. CR0: Croy 6D **14**
Bishop Butt Cl. BR6: Orp 7J **19**
Bishops Av. BR1: Brom 6K **9**
Bishop's Cl. SE9 6H **5**
Bishops Ct. CR0: Croy 6E **14**
Bishops Grn. *BR1: Brom 5K **9***
(off Up. Park Rd.)
Bishop's Rd. CR0: Croy 4A **14**
Bishopsthorpe Rd. SE26 1J **7**
Bishops Wlk. BR7: Chst 5F **11**
CR0: Addtn 2A **22**
Blackberry Fld. BR5: St P 5K **11**
Blackbrook La. BR1: Brom 2C **18**
BR2: Brom 2D **18**
BLACKFEN 5K **5**
Blackfen Rd. DA15: Sidc 2K **5**
Blackhorse La. CR0: Croy 4F **15**
Blackhorse Lane Stop (CT) 4F **15**
Blackhorse Rd. DA14: Sidc 1K **11**
Blacklands Rd. SE6 1D **8**
Blackman's La. CR6: Warl 3A **28**
Blackness La. BR2: Kes 5A **24**
Blacksmith's La. BR5: St M Cry 2B **20**
Blackthorne Av. CR0: Croy 5H **15**
Blackthorn Rd. TN16: Big H 5F **29**
Blair Cl. DA15: Sidc 2K **5**
Blair Ct. BR3: Beck 5C **8**
Blakeney Av. BR3: Beck 5A **8**
Blakeney Rd. BR3: Beck 4A **8**
Blake Rd. CR0: Croy 6D **14**
Blake's Grn. BR4: W W'ck 5D **16**
Blakewood Ct. *SE20 4G **7***
(off Anerley Pk.)
Blanchard Cl. SE9 7D **4**
Blandford Av. BR3: Beck 6K **7**
Blandford Rd. BR3: Beck 6H **7**
Bland St. SE9 1C **4**
Blanmerle Rd. SE9 5G **5**
Blann Cl. SE9 3C **4**
Blean Gro. SE20 4H **7**
Blendon Path BR1: Brom 4G **9**
Blenheim Cl. SE12 5A **4**
Blenheim Ct. BR2: Brom 1G **17**
DA14: Sidc 7J **5**
Blenheim Rd. BR1: Brom 1B **18**
BR6: Orp 6B **20**
SE20 4H **7**
Blenheim Shop. Cen. SE20 4H **7**
Bletchingley Cl. CR7: Thor H 1A **14**
Bloomfield Rd. BR2: Brom 2A **18**
Bloomfield Ter. TN16: Westrm 7J **33**
Bloom Gro. SE27 1A **6**
Bloomhall Rd. SE19 2C **6**
Bloxam Gdns. SE9 2D **4**
Bluebell Cl. BR6: Farnb 6F **19**
SE26 1E **6**
Blueberry La. TN14: Knock 5G **31**
Blue Riband Ind. Est. CR0: Croy 6A **14**
Blunts Rd. SE9 2F **5**
Blyth Ct. BR1: Brom 2A **35**
Blythe Hill BR5: St P 5J **11**
Blyth Rd. BR1: Brom 2A **35** (5G **9**)
Blyth Wood Pk. BR1: Brom 2A **35** (5G **9**)
Bob Hope Theatre, The 3E **4**
Bodmin Cl. BR5: Orp 5B **20**
Bogey La. BR6: Downe 4D **24**
Bolderwood Way BR4: W W'ck 6C **16**
Boleyn Gdns. BR4: W W'ck 6C **16**
Boleyn Gro. BR4: W W'ck 6D **16**
Bolton Cl. SE20 6F **7**
Bolton Gdns. BR1: Brom 3G **9**
Bombers La. TN16: Westrm 1J **33**
Bonar Pl. BR7: Chst 4B **10**
Bonchester Cl. BR7: Chst 4D **10**
Bond Cl. TN14: Knock 4H **31**
Bond St. TN14: Knock 4H **31**
Bon Marche Ter. M. *SE27 1D **6***
(off Gypsy Rd.)
Bonney Way BR8: Swan 6K **13**
Bonville Rd. BR1: Brom 2G **9**
Booth Rd. CR0: Croy 6A **14**
Border Cres. SE26 2G **7**
Border Gdns. CR0: Croy 1C **22**
Border Rd. SE26 2G **7**
Borkwood Pk. BR6: Orp 1J **25**
Borkwood Way BR6: Orp 1H **25**
Borough Hill CR0: Wadd 7A **14**
Borough Rd. TN16: Tats 3C **32**
Bosbury Rd. SE6 1D **8**
Boscobel Cl. BR1: Brom 6C **10**
Bosco Cl. BR6: Orp 1J **25**
Boscombe Ho. *CR0: Croy 5C **14***
(off Sydenham Rd.)
Bostall Rd. BR5: St P 4A **12**
Boswell Cl. BR5: Orp 3B **20**
Boswell Rd. CR7: Thor H 1B **14**
Botany Bay La. BR7: Chst 7F **11**
Bothwell Rd. CR0: New Ad 6D **22**
Boughton Av. BR2: Hayes 4G **17**
Boulogne Rd. CR0: Croy 3B **14**
Boulter Cl. BR1: Brom 7D **10**
Boundary Cl. SE20 6F **7**
Boundary Rd. DA15: Sidc 2K **5**
Boundary Way CR0: Addtn 2B **22**
Bourbon Ho. SE6 2D **8**
Bourdon Rd. SE20 6H **7**
Bourne Rd. BR2: Brom 1A **18**
Bourneside Gdns. SE6 2D **8**
Bourne St. CR0: Croy 6A **14**
Bourne Va. BR2: Hayes 5G **17**
Bourne Way BR2: Hayes 6G **17**
BR8: Swan 7H **13**
Bournewood Rd. BR5: Orp 4B **20**
Bowen Dr. SE21 1D **6**
Bowens Wood CR0: Sels 5A **22**
Bower Rd. BR8: Swan 2B **34**
Bowers Rd. TN14: S'ham 7K **27**
Bowley Cl. SE19 3E **6**
Bowley La. SE19 2E **6**
Bowmead SE9 6E **4**
Box Tree Wlk. BR5: Orp 5C **20**
Boyland Rd. BR1: Brom 2G **9**
Brabourne Cl. SE19 2D **6**
Brabourne Ri. BR3: Beck 2D **16**
Bracewood Gdns. CR0: Croy 7E **14**
Bracken Av. CR0: Croy 7B **16**
Brackendene DA2: Dart 1K **13**
Bracken Hill Cl. BR1: Brom 2A **35** (5G **9**)
Bracken Hill La. BR1: Brom 5G **9**
Brackens BR3: Beck 4B **8**
Brackens, The BR6: Chels 2K **25**
Brackley Rd. BR3: Beck 4A **8**
Bradford Cl. BR2: Brom 5C **18**
SE26 1G **7**
Bradley Rd. SE19 3B **6**
Bradshaws Cl. SE25 7F **7**
Brady Dr. BR1: Brom 7D **10**
Braemar Av. CR7: Thor H 7A **6**
Braemar Gdns. BR4: W W'ck 5D **16**
DA15: Sidc 7J **5**
Braeside BR3: Beck 2B **8**
Brafferton Rd. CR0: Croy 7B **14**
Bramble Cl. BR3: Beck 2D **16**
CR0: Croy 1B **22**
Brambledown Cl. BR4: W W'ck 2F **17**
Bramerton Rd. BR3: Beck 7A **8**
Bramley Cl. BR6: Farnb 5E **18**
BR8: Swan 1K **21**
Bramley Way BR4: W W'ck 6C **16**
Brampton Rd. CR0: Croy 4E **14**

Brandon Ho. *BR3: Beck* .2C **8**
(off Beckenham Hill Rd.)
Brangbourne Rd. BR1: Brom .2D **8**
Branscombe Ct. BR2: Brom .2G **17**
Bransell Cl. BR8: Crock .3H **21**
Branston Cres. BR5: Pet W .5G **19**
Brantwood Way BR5: St P .7B **12**
Branxholme Ct. *BR1: Brom* .5G **9**
(off Highland Rd.)
Brasted Cl. BR6: Orp .6K **19**
SE26 .1H **7**
Brasted La. TN14: Knock .7E **30**
Brasted Lodge BR3: Beck .4B **8**
Brasted Rd. TN16: Westrm .7K **33**
Bratten Ct. CR0: Croy .3C **14**
Braundton Av. DA15: Sidc .5K **5**
Braybrooke Gdns. SE19 .4D **6**
Braywood Rd. SE9 .1J **5**
Breakspears Dr. BR5: St P .5K **11**
Breckonmead BR1: Brom .6K **9**
Bredhurst Cl. SE20 .3H **7**
Bredon Rd. CR0: Croy .4E **14**
Bremner Cl. BR8: Swan .6B **34**
Brenchley Cl. BR2: Brom .3G **17**
BR7: Chst .5D **10**
Brenchley Rd. BR5: St P .6J **11**
Brendon Rd. SE9 .6J **5**
Brenley Gdns. SE9 .1C **4**
Brentwood Cl. SE9 .5H **5**
Brewery Rd. BR2: Brom .5B **18**
Briar Gdns. BR2: Hayes .5G **17**
Briar La. CR0: Addtn .1C **22**
Briar Rd. DA5: Bexl .1J **13**
Briarswood Way BR6: Chels .2J **25**
Briary Ct. DA14: Sidc .2A **12**
Briary Gdns. BR1: Brom .2J **9**
Briary Lodge BR3: Beck .5D **8**
Brickfield Cotts. BR7: Chst .2D **10**
Brickfield Farm Gdns.
BR6: Farnb .1F **25**
Brickfield Rd. CR7: Thor H .5A **6**
Brickwood Rd. CR0: Croy .6D **14**
Bridgelands Cl. BR3: Beck .4A **8**
Bridge Leisure Cen., The .1A **8**
Bridge Pl. CR0: Croy .5C **14**
Bridge Rd. BR3: Beck .4A **8**
BR5: St M Cry .3A **20**
Bridge Row CR0: Croy .5C **14**
Bridgetown Cl. SE19 .2D **6**
Bridgewater Cl. BR7: Chst .7H **11**
Bridgewood Cl. SE20 .4G **7**
Bridle Rd. CR0: Croy .7B **16**
(not continuous)
Bridle Way BR6: Farnb .1F **25**
CR0: Croy .2B **22**
Bridle Way, The CR0: Sels .6A **22**
Bridlington Cl. TN16: Big H .1A **32**
Bridport Rd. CR7: Thor H .7A **6**
Brierley CR0: New Ad .3C **22**
(not continuous)
Brierley Cl. SE25 .1F **15**
Brightwell Cl. CR0: Croy .5A **14**
Brigstock Rd. CR7: Thor H .2A **14**
Brimstone Cl. BR6: Chels .4B **26**
Brindle Ga. DA15: Sidc .5K **5**
Brindley Way BR1: Brom .2H **9**
Briset Rd. SE9 .1C **4**
Bristow Rd. SE19 .2D **6**
BRITISH HOME .2A **6**
Brittain Ho. SE9 .5D **4**
Brittenden Cl. BR6: Chels .3J **25**
Brittenden Pde. BR6: Chels .3J **25**
Broadcroft Rd. BR5: Pet W .4G **19**
BROAD GREEN .4A **14**
Broad Grn. Av. CR0: Croy .4A **14**
Broadheath Dr. BR7: Chst .2C **10**
Broadlands Rd. BR1: Brom .1J **9**
Broad Lawn SE9 .6F **5**
Broad Oak Cl. BR5: St P .6K **11**
Broadoaks Way BR2: Brom .2G **17**
Broad Wlk. BR6: Chels .7C **20**
Broadwater Gdns. BR6: Farnb .1E **24**
Broadway BR8: Crock .3H **21**
Broadway Av. CR0: Croy .2C **14**
Broadway Ct. BR3: Beck .7D **8**
Broadway Ho. *BR1: Brom* .2E **8**
(off Bromley Rd.)
Brockdene Dr. BR2: Kes .1A **24**
Brockenhurst Rd. CR0: Croy .4G **15**
Brockham Cres. CR0: New Ad .4E **22**
Brocklesby Rd. SE25 .1G **15**
Brockman Ri. BR1: Brom .1E **8**
Brockwell Av. BR3: Beck .2C **16**
Brockwell Cl. BR5: St M Cry .2J **19**
Brograve Gdns. BR3: Beck .6C **8**
Broke Farm Dr. BR6: Prat B .5B **26**
Brome Rd. SE9 .1E **4**
Bromhedge SE9 .7E **4**
BROMLEY .6H **9**
Bromley Av. BR1: Brom .4F **9**
BROMLEY COMMON .5B **18**
Bromley Comn. BR2: Brom .7E **35** (1K **17**)
Bromley Cres. BR2: Brom .5A **35** (7G **9**)
Bromley Gdns. BR2: Brom .5A **35** (7G **9**)
Bromley Gro. BR2: Brom .6E **8**
Bromley Hill BR1: Brom .3F **9**
Bromley Ho. BR1: Brom .2B **35**
Bromley Indoor Bowls Cen. .5B **20**
Bromley Ind. Cen. BR1: Brom .7A **10**
Bromley La. BR7: Chst .4F **11**
Bromley Mus. .4A **20**
Bromley North Station (Rail) .2C **35** (5H **9**)
BROMLEY PARK .5F **9**
Bromley Pk. BR1: Brom .1A **35** (5G **9**)
Bromley Rd. BR1: Brom .1D **8**
BR2: Brom .6C **8**
BR3: Beck .5C **8**
BR7: Chst .5E **10**
SE6 .1D **8**
Bromley Ski Cen. .5D **12**
Bromley South Station (Rail) .6C **35** (7H **9**)
Bromley Valley Gymnastics Cen. .6K **11**
Brompton Cl. SE20 .6F **7**
Brook Ct. BR3: Beck .5A **8**
SE12 .7B **4**
Brookend Rd. DA15: Sidc .5K **5**
Brook Ind. Pk. BR5: St M Cry .1B **20**
Brooklands Av. DA15: Sidc .6J **5**
Brooklands Pk. SE3 .1A **4**
Brook La. BR1: Brom .3H **9**
Brooklyn SE20 .4F **7**
Brooklyn Av. SE25 .1G **15**
Brooklyn Gro. SE25 .1G **15**
Brooklyn Rd. BR2: Brom .2A **18**
SE25 .1G **15**
Brookmead Av. BR1: Brom .2C **18**
Brookmead Cl. BR5: St M Cry .4A **20**
Brookmead Way
BR5: St M Cry .3A **20**
Brook Rd. BR8: Swan .7J **13**
CR7: Thor H .1B **14**
Brooks Cl. SE9 .6F **5**
Brookscroft CR0: Sels .6A **22**
Brookside BR6: Orp .4J **19**
Brookside Way CR0: Croy .3J **15**
Brooks Way BR5: St P .6B **12**
Brookwood Cl. BR2: Brom .1G **17**
Broom Av. BR5: St P .6A **12**
Broom Cl. BR2: Brom .3B **18**
Broomfield Rd. BR3: Beck .7K **7**
Broom Gdns. CR0: Croy .7B **16**
BROOM HILL .4J **19**
Broomhill Rd. BR6: Orp .4K **19**
Broomleigh BR1: Brom .1B **35**
Broom Rd. CR0: Croy .7B **16**
Broomsleigh Bus. Pk.
SE26 .2A **8**
Broomwood Cl. CR0: Croy .2J **15**
Broomwood Rd. BR5: St P .6A **12**
Broseley Gro. SE26 .2K **7**
Broster Gdns. SE25 .7E **6**
Broughton Rd. BR6: Orp .6G **19**
Brow Cl. BR5: Orp .4C **20**
Brow Cres. BR5: Orp .5B **20**
Brownlow Rd. CR0: Croy .7D **14**
Brownspring Dr. SE9 .1E **10**
Broxbourne Rd. BR6: Orp .5J **19**
Bruce Ct. DA15: Sidc .1J **11**
Bruce Gro. BR6: Orp .5K **19**
Bruce Rd. SE25 .1C **14**
Brunel Cl. SE19 .3E **6**
Brunner Ho. SE6 .1D **8**
Brunswick Pl. SE19 .4F **7**
Brunswick Ter. BR3: Beck .5C **8**
Bruton Cl. BR7: Chst .4C **10**
Bryden Cl. SE26 .2K **7**
Buckhurst Rd. TN16: Westrm .3F **33**
Buckingham Av. CR7: Thor H .5A **6**
DA16: Well .1K **5**
Buckingham Cl. BR5: Pet W .4H **19**
Buckingham Dr. BR7: Chst .1F **11**
Buckingham Gdns.
CR7: Thor H .6A **6**
Buckland Rd. BR6: Orp .1H **25**
Buckleigh Way SE19 .4E **6**
Buckler Gdns. SE9 .7E **4**
Bucknall Way BR3: Beck .1C **16**
Bucks Cross Rd. BR6: Chels .2D **26**
Budgin's Hill BR6: Prat B .1G **31**
Bulganak Rd. CR7: Thor H .1B **14**
Buller Rd. CR7: Thor H .6C **6**
Bullers Cl. DA14: Sidc .2D **12**
Bullers Wood Dr. BR7: Chst .4C **10**
Bull La. BR7: Chst .4G **11**
Bullrush Cl. CR0: Croy .3D **14**
Bungalow Rd. SE25 .1D **14**
Bunkers Hill DA14: Sidc .1E **12**
Burdett Cl. DA14: Sidc .2D **12**
Burdett Rd. CR0: Croy .3C **14**
Burdock Cl. CR0: Croy .5J **15**
Burford Rd. BR1: Brom .1B **18**
Burford Way CR0: New Ad .3D **22**
Burghill Rd. SE26 .1K **7**
Burgoyne Rd. SE25 .1E **14**
Burham Cl. SE20 .4H **7**
BURLINGS .6D **30**
Burlings La. TN14: Knock .6D **30**
Burlington Cl. BR6: Farnb .6E **18**
Burlington Rd. CR7: Thor H .6B **6**
Burmarsh Ct. SE20 .5H **7**
Burma Ter. SE19 .2D **6**
Burnham Gdns. CR0: Croy .4E **14**
Burnham Way SE26 .2A **8**
Burnhill Rd. BR3: Beck .6B **8**
Burnt Ash Hgts. BR1: Brom .2J **9**
Burnt Ash Hill SE12 .5A **4**
Burnt Ash La. BR1: Brom .4H **9**
Burntwood Vw. SE19 .2E **6**
Burrell Cl. CR0: Croy .3K **15**
Burrell Row BR3: Beck .6B **8**
Burrfield Dr. BR5: St M Cry .2C **20**
Burton Cl. CR7: Thor H .7C **6**
Burton Ct. SE20 .6H **7**
Burtwell La. SE27 .1C **6**
Burwash Ct. BR5: St M Cry .2B **20**
Burwood Av. BR2: Hayes .6J **17**
Bushell Way BR7: Chst .2D **10**
Bushey Av. BR5: Pet W .4G **19**
Bushey Rd. CR0: Croy .6B **16**
Bushey Way BR3: Beck .3E **16**
Bushy Lees DA15: Sidc .3K **5**
Butchers Yd. *BR6: Downe* .7D **24**
(off High St.)
Bute Rd. CR0: Croy .5A **14**
Butterfly La. SE9 .3G **5**
Buttermere Rd. BR5: St P .1C **20**
Button St. BR8: Swan .4D **34**
Button St. Bus. Cen.
BR8: Swan .4D **34**
Butts Rd. BR1: Brom .2F **9**
Buxton Rd. CR7: Thor H .2A **14**
Bycroft St. SE20: .4J **7**
Bygrove CR0: New Ad .3C **22**
Byne Rd. SE26 .3H **7**
Byron Cl. SE20 .7G **7**
SE26 .1K **7**
Bywood Av. CR0: Croy .3H **15**

C

Cacket's La. TN14: Cud .4B **30**
Cadlocks Hill TN14: Hals .6E **26**
Cadogan Cl. BR3: Beck .5E **8**
Cadwallon Rd. SE9 .6G **5**
Caerleon Cl. DA14: Sidc .2B **12**
Cairndale Cl. BR1: Brom .4G **9**
Cairo New Rd. CR0: Croy .6A **14**
Caithness Gdns. DA15: Sidc .3K **5**
Calcott Wlk. SE9 .1B **10**
Calley Down Cres. CR0: New Ad .6E **22**
Calmont Rd. BR1: Brom .3E **8**
Calverley Cl. BR3: Beck .3C **8**
Calvert Cl. DA14: Sidc .3D **12**
Calvin Cl. BR5: St P .7C **12**
Cambert Way SE3 .1A **4**
Camborne Rd.
CR0: Croy .4F **15**
DA14: Sidc .1B **12**
Cambray Rd. BR6: Orp .4J **19**
Cambria Cl. DA15: Sidc .5J **5**
Cambria Ho. *SE26* .1F **7**
(off High Level Dr.)
Cambridge Av. DA16: Well .1K **5**
Cambridge Grn. SE9 .5G **5**
Cambridge Gro. SE20 .5G **7**

Cambridge Rd. BR1: Brom . . . 1C **35** (4H **9**)
DA14: Sidc . . . 1H **11**
SE20 . . . 7G **7**
Camden Cl. BR7: Chst . . . 5F **11**
Camden Gdns. CR7: Thor H . . . 7A **6**
Camden Gro. BR7: Chst . . . 3E **10**
Camden Hill Rd. SE19 . . . 3D **6**
Camden Pk. Rd. BR7: Chst . . . 4C **10**
Camden Way BR7: Chst . . . 4C **10**
CR7: Thor H . . . 7A **6**
Camelot Cl. TN16: Big H . . . 5E **28**
Cameron Rd. BR2: Brom . . . 7B **35** (2H **17**)
CR0: Croy . . . 3A **14**
Cameron Ter. SE12 . . . 7A **4**
Camille Cl. SE25 . . . 7F **7**
Camlan Rd. BR1: Brom . . . 1G **9**
Campbell Rd. CR0: Croy . . . 4A **14**
Campfield Rd. SE9 . . . 4C **4**
Camrose Cl. CR0: Croy . . . 4K **15**
Canada Heights . . . 5E **34**
Canal Wlk. CR0 . . . 3D **14**
SE26 . . . 2H **7**
Canbury M. SE26 . . . 1F **7**
Canbury Path BR5: St M Cry . . . 1K **19**
Canham Rd. SE25 . . . 7D **6**
Canning Rd. CR0: Croy . . . 6E **14**
Canon Rd. BR1: Brom . . . 7K **9**
Canon's Wlk. CR0: Croy . . . 7J **15**
Canterbury Cl. BR3: Beck . . . 5C **8**
Canterbury Ct. SE12 . . . 7A **4**
Canterbury Gro. SE27 . . . 1A **6**
Canterbury Ho. *CR0: Croy . . . 5C 14*
(off Sydenham Rd.)
Canterbury Rd. CR0: Croy . . . 4A **14**
Cantley Gdns. SE19 . . . 5E **6**
Capel Cl. BR2: Brom . . . 5B **18**
Capel Ct. SE20 . . . 5H **7**
Capri Rd. CR0: Croy . . . 5E **14**
Capstone Rd. BR1: Brom . . . 1G **9**
Carberry Rd. SE19 . . . 3D **6**
Cardinal Cl. BR7: Chst . . . 5G **11**
Cardinham Rd. BR6: Chels . . . 1J **25**
Carew Rd. CR7: Thor H . . . 1A **14**
Carew Way BR5: Orp . . . 5B **20**
Cargreen Pl. SE25 . . . 1E **14**
Cargreen Rd. SE25 . . . 1E **14**
Carisbrooke Rd. BR2: Brom . . . 1K **17**
Carlton Ct. SE20 . . . 5G **7**
Carlton Grn. DA14: Sidc . . . 1J **11**
Carlton Pde. BR6: St M Cry . . . 4A **20**
Carlton Rd. DA14: Sidc . . . 2J **11**
Carlton Ter. SE26 . . . 1H **7**
Carlyle Av. BR1: Brom . . . 7A **10**
Carlyle Rd. CR0: Croy . . . 6F **15**
Carlys Cl. BR3: Beck . . . 6J **7**
Carmichael Rd. SE25 . . . 2E **14**
Carmine Ct. BR1: Brom . . . 4G **9**
Carnac St. SE27 . . . 1C **6**
Carnecke Gdns. SE9 . . . 2D **4**
Carolina Rd. CR7: Thor H . . . 6A **6**
Caroline Cl. CR0: Croy . . . 7D **14**
Caroline Ct. SE6 . . . 1E **8**
Carolyn Dr. BR6: Chels . . . 7K **19**
Carpenters Arms Path SE9 . . . 3E **4**
Carrington Cl. CR0: Croy . . . 4K **15**
Carstairs Rd. SE6 . . . 1D **8**
Carters Hill Cl. SE9 . . . 5B **4**
Cascade Cl. BR5: St P . . . 7B **12**
Cascades CR0: Sels . . . 6A **22**
Casewick Rd. SE27 . . . 2A **6**
Cassland Rd. CR7: Thor H . . . 1C **14**
Casstine Cl. BR8: Swan . . . 2A **34**
Casterbridge Rd. SE3 . . . 1A **4**
Castle Cl. BR2: Brom . . . 7F **9**
Castlecombe Rd. SE9 . . . 1B **10**
Castle Ct. SE26 . . . 1K **7**
Castledine Rd. SE20 . . . 4G **7**
Castleford Av. SE9 . . . 5G **5**
Castle Hill Av. CR0: New Ad . . . 5C **22**
Castleton Cl. CR0: Croy . . . 3K **15**
Castleton Rd. SE9 . . . 1A **10**
Cathcart Dr. BR6: Orp . . . 6H **19**
Catherine Howard Ct. SE9 . . . 3J **5**
Catherine of Aragon Ct. SE9 . . . 3H **5**
Catherine Parr Ct. SE9 . . . 3J **5**
Catling Cl. SE23 . . . 1H **7**
Cator Cl. CR0: New Ad . . . 7F **23**
Cator Cres. CR0: New Ad . . . 7F **23**
Cator La. BR3: Beck . . . 5A **8**
Cator Rd. SE26 . . . 3J **7**
Cattistock Rd. SE9 . . . 2B **10**
Cavendish Rd. CR0: Croy . . . 5A **14**
Cavendish Way BR4: W W'ck . . . 5C **16**
Caveside Cl. BR7: Chst . . . 5D **10**
Cawnpore St. SE19 . . . 2D **6**
Caygill Cl. BR2: Brom . . . 7A **35** (1G **17**)
Cecil Way BR2: Hayes . . . 5H **17**
Cedar Cl. BR2: Brom . . . 7B **18**
BR8: Swan . . . 6H **13**
Cedar Copse BR1: Brom . . . 6C **10**
Cedar Cres. BR2: Brom . . . 7B **18**
Cedarhurst BR1: Brom . . . 4F **9**
Cedarhurst Dr. SE9 . . . 2B **4**
Cedar Mt. SE9 . . . 5C **4**
Cedar Rd. BR1: Brom . . . 6K **9**
CR0: Croy . . . 6C **14**
Cedars Rd. BR3: Beck . . . 6K **7**
Cedar Tree Gro. SE27 . . . 2A **6**
Cedric Rd. SE9 . . . 7H **5**
Celtic Av. BR2: Brom . . . 7F **9**
Centrale Shop. Cen. CR0: Croy . . . 6B **14**
Central Hill SE19 . . . 2B **6**
Central Pde. CR0: New Ad . . . 6D **22**
SE20 . . . 4J 7
(off High St.)
Central Pl. SE25 . . . 2F **15**
Central Ter. BR3: Beck . . . 7J **7**
Centre Comn. Rd. BR7: Chst . . . 3F **11**
Chadd Dr. BR1: Brom . . . 7B **10**
Chaffinch Av. CR0: Croy . . . 3J **15**
Chaffinch Bus. Pk. BR3: Beck . . . 1J **15**
Chaffinch Cl. CR0: Croy . . . 2J **15**
Chaffinch Rd. BR3: Beck . . . 5K **7**
Chaldon Ct. SE19 . . . 5C **6**
Chaldon Path CR7: Thor H . . . 1A **14**
Chalet Cl. DA5: Bexl . . . 1J **13**
Chalet Ct. CR7: Thor H . . . 2B **14**
Chalfont Rd. SE25 . . . 7E **6**
Chalford Rd. SE21 . . . 1C **6**
Chalkenden Cl. SE20 . . . 4G **7**
Chalk Pit Av. BR5: St P . . . 7B **12**
Challin St. SE20 . . . 5H **7**
Challock Cl. TN16: Big H . . . 5E **28**
Chamberlain Cres. BR4: W W'ck . . . 5C **16**
Champion Cres. SE26 . . . 1K **7**
Champion Rd. SE26 . . . 1K **7**
Champness Cl. SE27 . . . 1C **6**
Chancery La. BR3: Beck . . . 6C **8**
Chanctonbury Cl. SE9 . . . 7G **5**
Chandaria Ct. *CR0: Croy . . . 6B 14*
(off Church Rd.)
Chandlers Ct. SE12 . . . 5A **4**
Chantry Cl. DA14: Sidc . . . 2D **12**
Chantry La. BR2: Brom . . . 2A **18**
Chapel Farm Rd. SE9 . . . 7E **4**
Chapel Rd. SE27 . . . 1A **6**
Chapel Wlk. CR0: Croy . . . 6B **14**
Chapman's La. BR5: St P . . . 6C **12**
Charing Cl. BR6: Orp . . . 1J **25**
Charing Ct. BR2: Brom . . . 6F **9**
Charldane Rd. SE9 . . . 7G **5**
Charles Cl. DA14: Sidc . . . 1A **12**
Charlesfield SE9 . . . 7B **4**
Charles Rd. TN14: Hals . . . 6G **27**
Charles St. CR0: Croy . . . 7B **14**
Charleville Cir. SE26 . . . 2F **7**
Charlotte Pk. Av. BR1: Brom . . . 7B **10**
Charlton Dr. TN16: Big H . . . 6F **29**
Charlwood CR0: Sels . . . 5A **22**
Charminster Rd. SE9 . . . 1A **10**
Charmwood La. BR6: Prat B . . . 5A **26**
Charnock BR8: Swan . . . 1K **21**
(not continuous)
Charnwood Rd. SE25 . . . 2C **14**
Charrington Rd. CR0: Croy . . . 6B **14**
Chart Cl. BR2: Brom . . . 5F **9**
CR0: Croy . . . 3H **15**
Charterhouse Rd. BR6: Chels . . . 7K **19**
Charters Cl. SE19 . . . 2D **6**
Chartham Gro. SE27 . . . 1A **6**
Chartham Rd. SE25 . . . 7G **7**
Chartwell Bus. Cen. BR1: Brom . . . 7A **10**
Chartwell Cl. CR0: Croy . . . 5C **14**
SE9 . . . 6J **5**
Chartwell Dr. BR6: Farnb . . . 2G **25**
Chartwell Lodge BR3: Beck . . . 4B **8**
Chartwell Way SE20 . . . 5G **7**
Chase, The BR1: Brom . . . 5D **35** (7J **9**)
BR6: Prat B . . . 1E **30**
Chatfield Rd. CR0: Croy . . . 5A **14**
Chatham Av. BR2: Hayes . . . 4G **17**
Chatsworth Av. BR1: Brom . . . 1J **9**
Chatsworth Cl. BR4: W W'ck . . . 6G **17**
Chatsworth Ho. BR2: Brom . . . 7B **35**
Chatsworth Pde. BR5: Pet W . . . 2F **19**
Chatsworth Rd. CR0: Croy . . . 7C **14**
Chatterton Rd. BR2: Brom . . . 1A **18**
Chaucer Grn. CR0: Croy . . . 4G **15**
Chaundrye Cl. SE9 . . . 3E **4**
Chelford Rd. BR1: Brom . . . 2E **8**
Chelsea Ct. *BR1: Brom . . . 7B 10*
(off Holmdene Ct.)
CHELSFIELD . . . **2A 26**
Chelsfield Gdns. SE26 . . . 1H **7**
Chelsfield Hill BR6: Chels . . . 5B **26**
Chelsfield La. BR5: Orp . . . 4C **20**
BR6: Chels, Orp . . . 6C **20**
BR6: Orp, Chels . . . 4F **27**
TN14: Hals, S'ham . . . 5F **27**
CHELSFIELD PARK HOSPITAL . . . 2D **26**
Chelsfield Rd. BR5: St M Cry . . . 3B **20**
Chelsfield Station (Rail) . . . 2A **26**
CHELSFIELD VILLAGE . . . **2D 26**
Chelsham Ct. Rd. CR6: Warl . . . 7A **28**
Chelsiter Ct. DA14: Sidc . . . 1J **11**
Cheltenham Rd. BR6: Chels . . . 7K **19**
Chenies, The BR6: Pet W . . . 3H **19**
DA2: Dart . . . 1K **13**
Chepstow Ri. CR0: Croy . . . 7D **14**
Chepstow Rd. CR0: Croy . . . 7D **14**
Chequers Cl. BR5: St P . . . 1J **19**
Chequers Pde. *SE9 . . . 3E 4*
(off Eltham High St.)
Cheriton Av. BR2: Brom . . . 2G **17**
Cheriton Ct. SE12 . . . 4A **4**
Cherry Av. BR8: Swan . . . 1J **21**
Cherrycot Hill BR6: Farnb . . . 1F **25**
Cherrycot Ri. BR6: Farnb . . . 1F **25**
Cherry Orchard Cl. BR5: St M Cry . . . 2B **20**
Cherry Orchard Gdns. CR0: Croy . . . 5C **14**
Cherry Orchard Rd. BR2: Brom . . . 6B **18**
CR0: Croy . . . 6C **14**
Cherry Tree Wlk. BR3: Beck . . . 1A **16**
BR4: W W'ck . . . 1G **23**
TN16: Big H . . . 6E **28**
Cherry Wlk. BR2: Hayes . . . 5H **17**
Chertsey Cres. CR0: New Ad . . . 6D **22**
Chesham Av. BR5: Pet W . . . 3E **18**
Chesham Cres. SE20 . . . 5H **7**
Chesham Rd. SE20 . . . 6H **7**
Chesney Cres. CR0: New Ad . . . 4D **22**
Chessell Cl. CR7: Thor H . . . 1A **14**
Chessington Way BR4: W W'ck . . . 6C **16**
Chester Ct. BR2: Brom . . . 7B **35**
Chesterfield Cl. BR5: St M Cry . . . 1D **20**
Chester Rd. DA15: Sidc . . . 2K **5**
(not continuous)
Chestnut Av. BR4: W W'ck . . . 2F **23**
TN16: Tats, Westrm . . . 4C **32**
Chestnut Cl. BR6: Chels . . . 2K **25**
SE6 . . . 2D **8**
Chestnut Gro. DA2: Dart . . . 1J **13**
SE20 . . . 4G **7**
Chestnut Pl. SE26 . . . 1E **6**
Cheston Av. CR0: Croy . . . 6K **15**
Cheveney Wlk. BR2: Brom . . . 5B **35** (7H **9**)
CHEVENING . . . **7K 31**
Chevening La. TN14: Knock . . . 4J **31**
Chevening Rd. SE19 . . . 3C **6**
Cheviot Gdns. SE27 . . . 1A **6**
Cheviot Rd. SE27 . . . 2A **6**
Cheyne Cl. BR2: Brom . . . 7B **18**
Cheyne Pk. Dr. BR4: W W'ck . . . 7D **16**
Cheyne Wlk. CR0: Croy . . . 6F **15**
Chichele Gdns. CR0: Croy . . . 7D **14**
Chichester M. SE27 . . . 1A **6**
Chichester Rd. CR0: Croy . . . 7D **14**
Child's La. SE19 . . . 3D **6**
Chilham Rd. SE9 . . . 1B **10**
Chilham Way BR2: Hayes . . . 4H **17**
Chiltern Cl. CR0: Croy . . . 7D **14**
Chiltern Gdns. BR2: Brom . . . 7A **35** (1G **17**)
Chilterns, The BR1: Brom . . . 3E **35**
Chinbrook Cres. SE12 . . . 7A **4**
Chinbrook Rd. SE12 . . . 7A **4**
Chine Farm Pl. TN14: Knock . . . 5H **31**
Chingley Cl. BR1: Brom . . . 3F **9**
Chipperfield Rd. BR5: St P . . . 5K **11**
(not continuous)
Chipstead Av. CR7: Thor H . . . 1A **14**
Chipstead Cl. SE19 . . . 4E **6**
Chisholm Rd. CR0: Croy . . . 6D **14**
CHISLEHURST . . . **3E 10**
Chislehurst Caves . . . 5D **10**
Chislehurst Rd. BR1: Brom . . . 6A **10**
BR5: Orp, St M Cry, Pet W . . . 1H **19**

Chislehurst Rd. BR6: Orp 4J **19**
BR7: Chst 6A **10**
DA14: Sidc 2K **11**
Chislehurst Station (Rail) 6D **10**
CHISLEHURST WEST 2D **10**
Chislet Cl. BR3: Beck 4B **8**
Chorleywood Cres. BR5: St P 6J **11**
Christ Church Rd. BR3: Beck 6B **8**
Christchurch Rd. DA15: Sidc 1J **11**
Christian Flds. SW16 4A **6**
Christie Dr. CR0: Croy 2F **15**
Christies Av. TN14: Hals 6F **27**
Christmas Tree Farm 1J **29**
Christy Rd. TN16: Big H 4E **28**
Chudleigh DA14: Sidc 1A **12**
Chulsa Rd. SE26 2G **7**
Church All. CR0: Croy 5A **14**
Church App. SE21 1C **6**
TN14: Cud 4A **30**
Church Av. BR3: Beck 5B **8**
DA14: Sidc 2K **11**
Churchbury Rd. SE9 4C **4**
Churchdown BR1: Brom 1F **9**
Church Dr. BR4: W W'ck 7F **17**
Church Farm Cl. BR8: Crock 3H **21**
Churchfields Rd. BR3: Beck 6J **7**
Church Hill BR6: Orp 4K **19**
TN14: Big H 4A **30**
TN16: Tats 4C **32**
Church Hill Wood BR5: St M Cry 2J **19**
Churchill Bus. Pk. TN16: Westrm 7K **33**
Churchill Ct. BR6: Farnb 2F **25**
TN16: Westrm 7J **33**
Churchill Theatre & Library 4B **35** (6H **9**)
Churchill Way BR1: Brom 4B **35** (6H **9**)
TN16: Big H, Downe 2G **29**
Church La. BR2: Brom 5B **18**
BR7: Chst 5F **11**
CR6: Warl 6A **28**
TN16: Tats 4C **32**
Churchley Rd. SE26 1G **7**
Church Path BR8: Swan 3C **34**
CR0: Croy 6B **14**
Church Rd. BR2: Brom 3B **35** (6H **9**)
(Glassmill La.)
BR2: Brom 7F **9**
(Shortlands Rd.)
BR2: Kes 4A **24**
BR6: Chels 4B **26**
BR6: Farnb 2F **25**
BR8: Crock 4J **21**
BR8: Swan 3E **34**
CR0: Croy 7B **14**
(not continuous)
DA14: Sidc 1K **11**
SE19 5D **6**
TN14: Hals 7D **26**
TN16: Big H 6F **29**
Church Row BR7: Chst 5F **11**
Church Row M. BR7: Chst 4F **11**
Churchside Cl. TN16: Big H 6E **28**
Church St. CR0: Croy 7A **14**
Church Street Stop (CT) 6B **14**
Church Vw. BR8: Swan 7J **13**
Cinderford Way BR1: Brom 1F **9**
Cintra Pk. SE19 4E **6**
Cissbury Ho. SE26 1F **7**
Clacket La. TN16: Westrm 6D **32**
Clairville Point *SE23* *1J 7*
(off Dacres Rd.)
Clare Cnr. SE9 4G **5**
Claremont Cl. BR6: Farnb 1D **24**
Claremont Rd. BR1: Brom 1B **18**
BR8: Swan 4K **13**
CR0: Croy 5F **15**
Clarence Av. BR1: Brom 1B **18**
Clarence Cres. DA14: Sidc 1A **12**
Clarence Rd. BR1: Brom 7A **10**
CR0: Croy 4C **14**
DA14: Sidc 1A **12**
SE9 6D **4**
TN16: Big H 7H **29**
Clarenden Pl. DA2: Dart 2K **13**
Clarendon Cl. BR5: St P 7K **11**
Clarendon Ct. *BR3: Beck* *5C 8*
(off Blair Ct.)
BR3: Beck 5E **8**
(West Oak)
Clarendon Grn. BR5: St P 1K **19**
Clarendon Gro. BR5: St P 1K **19**
Clarendon Path BR5: St P 1K **19**
(not continuous)
Clarendon Rd. CR0: Croy 6A **14**
Clarendon Way BR5: St P 7J **11**
BR7: Chst 7J **11**
Claret Gdns. SE25 7D **6**
Clareville Rd. BR5: Farnb 6F **19**
Clarks La. TN14: Hals 1K **31**
TN16: Tats 5A **32**
Claybourne M. SE19 4D **6**
Claybridge Rd. SE12 1K **9**
Clay Farm Rd. SE9 6H **5**
Claygate Cres. CR0: New Ad 3D **22**
Clayhill Cres. SE9 1A **10**
Clay Wood Cl. BR6: Orp 4H **19**
Cleave Av. BR6: Chels 3H **25**
Cleaverholme Cl. SE25 3G **15**
Clegg Ho. SE3 1A **4**
Clement Rd. BR3: Beck 6J **7**
CLEMENT STREET 1E **34**
Clement St. BR8: Swan, Dart 1E **34**
Clevedon Rd. SE20 5J **7**
Cleve Rd. DA14: Sidc 1C **12**
Cleves Cres. CR0: New Ad 7D **22**
Clifford Av. BR7: Chst 3C **10**
Clifford Ho. *BR3: Beck* *3C 8*
(off Calverley Cl.)
Clifford Rd. SE25 1F **15**
Clifton Cl. BR6: Farnb 2F **25**
Clifton Ct. BR3: Beck 5C **8**
Clifton M. SE25 1D **14**
Clifton Rd. DA14: Sidc 1H **11**
SE25 1D **14**
Cliftonville Ct. SE12 5A **4**
Clive Pas. SE21 1C **6**
Clive Rd. SE21 1C **6**
Clockhouse Ct. BR3: Beck 6K **7**
Clock Ho. Rd. BR3: Beck 7K **7**
Clock House Station (Rail) 5K **7**
Cloister Gdns. SE25 3G **15**
Cloisters Av. BR2: Brom 2C **18**
Cloonmore Av. BR6: Chels 1J **25**
Close, The BR3: Beck 1K **15**
BR5: Pet W 3H **19**
DA14: Sidc 1A **12**
SE25 3F **15**
TN16: Big H 5K **29**
Clovelly Gdns. SE19 5E **6**
Clovelly Way BR6: St M Cry 3J **19**
Cloverdale Gdns. DA15: Sidc 3K **5**
Club Gdns. Rd. BR2: Hayes 4H **17**
Clyde Rd. CR0: Croy 6E **14**
Coach Ho. M. SE20 4G **7**
Coal Port Cl. BR6: Chels 3J **25**
Coates Cl. CR7: Thor H 7B **6**
Coates Hill Rd. BR1: Brom 6D **10**
Cobbett Rd. SE9 1D **4**
Cobblestone Pl. CR0: Croy 5B **14**
Cobbsthorpe Vs. SE26 1J **7**
Cobden Ct. BR2: Brom 1K **17**
Cobden M. SE26 2G **7**
Cobden Rd. BR6: Farnb 1G **25**
SE25 2F **15**
Cobham Cl. BR2: Brom 4B **18**
Cobland Rd. SE12 1K **9**
Cockerhurst Rd. TN14: S'ham 3J **27**
Cockmannings La. BR5: St M Cry 5C **20**
Cockmannings Rd. BR5: St M Cry 4C **20**
Cocksett Av. BR6: Chels 3H **25**
Cocksure La. DA14: Sidc 1F **13**
Coe Av. SE25 3F **15**
Colbalt Cl. BR3: Beck 1J **15**
Colby M. SE19 2D **6**
Colby Rd. SE19 2D **6**
Coldharbour Crest SE9 7F **5**
Coldharbour Leisure Cen. 6E **4**
Colebrooke Ct. DA14: Sidc 1A **12**
Colebrooke Ri. BR2: Brom 6F **9**
Coleman Cl. SE25 6F **7**
Colemans Heath SE9 7F **5**
Colepits Wood Rd. SE9 2J **5**
Coleridge Rd. CR0: Croy 4H **15**
Coleridge Way BR6: St M Cry 3K **19**
Colesburg Rd. BR3: Beck 7A **8**
Colin Cl. BR4: W W'ck 7G **17**
CR0: Croy 7A **16**
College Grn. SE19 4D **6**
College Rd. BR1: Brom 2B **35** (5H **9**)
BR8: Swan 5K **13**
CR0: Croy 6C **14**
SE19 2E **6**
SE21 1E **6**
College Slip BR1: Brom 3B **35** (5H **9**)
College Vw. SE9 5C **4**
Colliers Ct. *CR0: Croy* *7C 14*
(off St Peter's Rd.)
Colliers Shaw BR2: Kes 2A **24**
Colliers Water La. CR7: Thor H 2A **14**
Collingtree Rd. SE26 1H **7**
Collingwood Cl. SE20 5G **7**
Colson Rd. CR0: Croy 6D **14**
Colview Ct. SE9 5C **4**
Colvin Cl. SE26 2H **7**
Colworth Rd. CR0: Croy 5F **15**
Colyer Cl. SE9 6G **5**
Combe Dene *BR2: Brom* *1G 17*
(off Cumberland Rd.)
Commonside BR2: Kes 1K **23**
Compass La. BR1: Brom 2C **35**
Comport Grn. CR0: New Ad 1A **28**
Compton Ct. SE19 3D **6**
Compton Rd. CR0: Croy 5G **15**
Concorde Bus. Pk. TN16: Big H 4F **29**
CONEY HALL 7F **17**
Coney Hall Pde. BR4: W W'ck 7F **17**
Coney Hill Rd. BR4: W W'ck 6F **17**
Congreve Rd. SE9 1E **4**
Conifer Cl. BR6: Orp 1G **25**
Conifer Way BR8: Swan 5H **13**
Coniffe Ct. SE9 2G **5**
Conisborough Cres. SE6 1D **8**
Coniscliffe Cl. BR7: Chst 5D **10**
Coniston Av. DA16: Well 1K **5**
Coniston Rd. BR1: Brom 3F **9**
CR0: Croy 4F **15**
Constance Cres. BR2: Hayes 4G **17**
Constance Rd. CR0: Croy 4A **14**
Consul Gdns. BR8: Swan 2A **34**
Contessa Cl. BR6: Farnb 2H **25**
Convent Cl. BR3: Beck 4D **8**
Convent Hill SE19 3B **6**
Cooden Cl. BR1: Brom 4J **9**
Cookham Dene Cl. BR7: Chst 5G **11**
Cookham Hill BR5: Orp 7F **21**
Cookham Rd. BR8: Swan 5F **13**
Coombe Ct. *CR0: Croy* *7C 14*
(off St Peter's Rd.)
Coombe Lea BR1: Brom 7B **10**
Coombe Rd. CR0: Croy 7C **14**
SE26 1G **7**
Cooper's La. SE12 6A **4**
Coopers M. BR3: Beck 6B **8**
Cooper's Yd. SE19 3D **6**
Copeman Cl. SE26 2H **7**
Copers Cope Rd. BR3: Beck 4A **8**
Copley Dene BR1: Brom 5A **10**
Copper Beech Cl. BR5: St M Cry 2B **20**
Copper Cl. SE19 4E **6**
Copperfields BR3: Beck 5D **8**
Copperfield Way BR7: Chst 3F **11**
Coppergate Cl. BR1: Brom 1D **35** (5J **9**)
Coppice Cl. BR3: Beck 1C **16**
Coppins, The CR0: New Ad 3C **22**
Copse Av. BR4: W W'ck 6C **16**
Copsewood Cl. DA15: Sidc 3K **5**
Copthorne Av. BR2: Brom 6C **18**
Corbett Cl. CR0: New Ad 7E **22**
Corbett Ct. SE26 1A **8**
Corbylands Rd. DA15: Sidc 4K **5**
Corkscrew Hill BR4: W W'ck 6D **16**
Cork Tree Ho. *SE27* *2A 6*
(off Lakeview Rd.)
Cornell Cl. DA14: Sidc 3D **12**
Cornerstone Ho. CR0: Croy 4B **14**
Cornflower La. CR0: Croy 5J **15**
Cornford Cl. BR2: Brom 2H **17**
Cornish Gro. SE20 5G **7**
Corn Mill Dr. BR6: Orp 4K **19**
Cornwall Av. DA16: Well 1K **5**
Cornwall Dr. BR5: St P 4B **12**
Cornwall Gdns. SE25 1E **14**
Cornwallis Av. SE9 6J **5**
Cornwall Rd. CR0: Croy 6A **14**
Corona Rd. SE12 4A **4**
Cotelands CR0: Croy 7D **14**
Cotford Rd. CR7: Thor H 1B **14**
Cotmandene Cres. BR5: St P 6K **11**
Cotswold Ri. BR6: St M Cry 3J **19**
Cotswold St. SE27 1A **6**
Cottage Av. BR2: Brom 5B **18**
Cottingham Rd. SE20 4J **7**
Cottongrass Cl. CR0: Croy 5J **15**
Cotton Hill BR1: Brom 1D **8**
County Ga. SE9 7H **5**
County Rd. CR7: Thor H 6A **6**
Course, The SE9 7F **5**

Court Cres. BR8: Swan . . . 1K 21
Court Downs Rd. BR3: Beck . . . 6C 8
Courtenay Dr. BR3: Beck . . . 6E 8
Courtenay Rd. SE20 . . . 3J 7
Court Farm Rd. SE9 . . . 6C 4
Courtfield Ri. BR4: W W'ck . . . 7E 16
Courtlands Av. BR2: Hayes . . . 5F 17
SE12 . . . 2A 4
Courtney Cl. SE19 . . . 3D 6
Courtney Rd. CR0: Wadd . . . 7A 14
Court Rd. BR6: Chels, Orp . . . 4A 20
SE9 . . . 3E 4
SE25 . . . 6E 6
Court St. BR1: Brom . . . 3C 35 (6H 9)
Court Wood La. CR0: Sels . . . 7A 22
Court Yd. SE9 . . . 3E 4
Courtyard, The BR2: Kes . . . 3B 24
Courtyard M. BR5: St P . . . 4K 11
Coventry Rd. SE25 . . . 1F 15
Coverack Cl. CR0: Croy . . . 4K 15
Coverdale Gdns. CR0: Croy . . . 7E 14
Covert, The BR6: Pet W . . . 3H 19
SE19 . . . 4E 6
(off Fox Hill)
Covet Wood Cl. BR5: St M Cry . . . 3J 19
Covington Gdns. SW16 . . . 4A 6
Covington Way SW16 . . . 4A 6
(not continuous)
Cowden Rd. BR6: Orp . . . 4J 19
Cowden St. SE6 . . . 1B 8
Cowper Cl. BR2: Brom . . . 1A 18
Cowper Rd. BR2: Brom . . . 1A 18
Coxwell Rd. SE19 . . . 4D 6
Crabbs Cft. Cl. BR6: Farnb . . . 2F 25
Crab Hill BR3: Beck . . . 4E 8
Crabtree Wlk. CR0: Croy . . . 5F 15
Cradley Rd. SE9 . . . 5J 5
Craigen Av. CR0: Croy . . . 5G 15
Craigton Rd. SE9 . . . 1E 4
Crampton Rd. SE20 . . . 3H 7
Cranbrook Cl. BR2: Hayes . . . 3H 17
Cranbrook Rd. CR7: Thor H . . . 6B 6
Cranfield Cl. SE27 . . . 1B 6
Cranleigh Cl. BR6: Chels . . . 7K 19
SE20 . . . 6G 7
Cranleigh Dr. BR8: Swan . . . 1K 21
Cranleigh Gdns. SE25 . . . 7D 6
Cranley Pde. *SE9 . . . 1B 10*
(off Beaconsfield Rd.)
Cranmer Rd. CR0: Croy . . . 7A 14
Cranmore Rd. BR1: Brom . . . 1G 9
BR7: Chst . . . 2C 10
Crathie Rd. SE12 . . . 3A 4
Craven Rd. BR6: Chels . . . 7C 20
CR0: Croy . . . 5G 15
Crawfords BR8: Swan . . . 4K 13
Cray Av. BR5: St M Cry . . . 3A 20
Craybrooke Rd. DA14: Sidc . . . 1A 12
Craybury End SE9 . . . 6H 5
Crayfields Bus. Pk. BR5: St P . . . 5B 12
Crayfields Ind. Pk. BR5: St P . . . 6B 12
Craylands BR5: St P . . . 7B 12
Crayleigh Ter. DA14: Sidc . . . 3B 12
Cray Rd. BR8: Crock . . . 3G 21
DA14: Sidc . . . 3B 12
Crays Pde., The BR5: St P . . . 6B 12
Cray Valley Rd. BR5: St M Cry . . . 2K 19
Credenhall Dr. BR2: Brom . . . 5C 18
Crescent, The BR3: Beck . . . 5B 8
BR4: W W'ck . . . 3F 17
CR0: Croy . . . 2C 14
DA14: Sidc . . . 1J 11
Crescent Dr. BR5: Pet W . . . 2E 18
Crescent Gdns. BR8: Swan . . . 6H 13
Crescent Rd. BR1: Brom . . . 1C 35 (4H 9)
BR3: Beck . . . 6C 8
Crescent Way BR6: Orp . . . 2H 25
Crescent Wood Rd. SE26 . . . 1F 7
Cress M. BR1: Brom . . . 2E 8
Cresswell Rd. SE25 . . . 1F 15
Crest Cl. TN14: Hals . . . 7G 27
Crest Rd. BR2: Hayes . . . 4G 17
Crest Vw. Dr. BR5: Pet W . . . 2E 18
Creswell Dr. BR3: Beck . . . 2C 16
Crichton Ho. DA14: Sidc . . . 3C 12
Cricketers Wlk. SE26 . . . 2H 7
Cricket Ground Rd. BR7: Chst . . . 5E 10
Cricket La. BR3: Beck . . . 3K 7
CRITTALLS CORNER . . . 4B 12
CROCKENHILL . . . 3J 21
Crockenhill Rd. BR5: St M Cry . . . 2C 20
BR8: Crock . . . 2C 20
Crockham Way SE9 . . . 1D 10
Crocus Cl. CR0: Croy . . . 5J 15
Croft, The BR8: Swan . . . 7H 13
Croft Av. BR4: W W'ck . . . 5D 16
Croft Cl. BR7: Chst . . . 2C 10
Crofters Mead CR0: Sels . . . 5A 22
CROFTON . . . 6G 19
Crofton Av. BR6: Farnb . . . 6F 19
Crofton La. BR5: Farnb, Pet W . . . 6G 19
BR6: Pet W . . . 4G 19
Crofton Rd. BR6: Farnb, Orp . . . 7D 18
Crofton Roman Villa . . . 6H 19
Croft Rd. BR1: Brom . . . 3H 9
SW16 . . . 5A 6
Croftside, The SE25 . . . 7F 7
Croft Way DA15: Sidc . . . 7K 5
Crombie Rd. DA15: Sidc . . . 5J 5
Cromer Pl. BR6: Orp . . . 5H 19
Cromer Rd. SE25 . . . 7G 7
Cromford Cl. BR6: Orp . . . 7H 19
Cromlix Cl. BR7: Chst . . . 6E 10
Cromwell Av. BR2: Brom . . . 6D 35 (1J 17)
Cromwell Cl. BR2: Brom . . . 7D 35 (1J 17)
Cromwell Ho. CR0: Croy . . . 7A 14
Cromwell Rd. BR3: Beck . . . 6K 7
CR0: Croy . . . 4C 14
Crossland Rd. CR7: Thor H . . . 3A 14
Crossley Cl. TN16: Big H . . . 4F 29
Crossmead SE9 . . . 5E 4
Cross Rd. BR2: Brom . . . 6B 18
BR5: St M Cry . . . 2A 20
CR0: Croy . . . 5C 14
DA14: Sidc . . . 1A 12
Crossway BR5: Pet W . . . 1G 19
Crossway, The SE9 . . . 6C 4
Crossways CR2: Sels . . . 4A 22
TN16: Tats . . . 2B 32
Crossways Rd. BR3: Beck . . . 1B 16
Crouch Cl. BR3: Beck . . . 3B 8
Crouch Cft. SE9 . . . 7F 5
Crouchman's Cl. SE26 . . . 1E 6
Crowhill BR6: Downe . . . 6D 24
Crowhurst Way BR5: St M Cry . . . 2B 20
Crowland Rd. CR7: Thor H . . . 1C 14
Crown, The TN16: Westrm . . . 7J 33
Crown All. SE9 . . . 3E 4
Crown Ash Hill TN16: Big H . . . 3D 28
Crown Ash La. CR6: Warl . . . 5C 28
TN16: Big H, Warl . . . 5C 28
Crown Cl. BR6: Chels . . . 2K 25
Crown Ct. SE12 . . . 3A 4
Crown Dale SE19 . . . 3A 6
Crown Hill CR0: Croy . . . 6B 14
Crown La. BR2: Brom . . . 2A 18
BR7: Chst . . . 5F 11
Crown La. Gdns. SW16 . . . 2A 6
Crown La. Spur BR2: Brom . . . 3A 18
Crown Point SE19 . . . 3A 6
Crown Rd. BR6: Chels . . . 2K 25
Crown Woods Way SE9 . . . 2J 5
Crowther Rd. SE25 . . . 2F 15
Croxley Cl. BR5: St P . . . 6A 12
Croxley Grn. BR5: St P . . . 5A 12
Croyde Cl. DA15: Sidc . . . 4J 5
CROYDON . . . 7B 14
Croydon Clocktower . . . *7B 14*
(off Katherine St.)
Croydon Flyover, The CR0: Croy . . . 7A 14
Croydon Gro. CR0: Croy . . . 5A 14
Croydon Rd. BR2: Hayes, Kes . . . 7F 17
BR3: Beck . . . 1J 15
BR4: Hayes, W W'ck . . . 7F 17
SE20 . . . 6G 7
TN16: Westrm . . . 5E 32
Croydon Rd. Ind. Est. BR3: Beck . . . 1J 15
Croydon Sports Arena . . . 2H 15
Crundale Twr. *BR5: Orp . . . 5B 20*
(off Tintagel Rd.)
Crusader Gdns. CR0: Croy . . . 7D 14
CRYSTAL PALACE . . . 3E 6
Crystal Palace Athletics Stadium . . . 3F 7
Crystal Palace FC . . . 1D 14
Crystal Palace Indoor Bowling Club . . . *5G 7*
(off Ashurst Cl.)
Crystal Palace Mus. . . . 3E 6
Crystal Palace National Sports Cen. . . . 3F 7
Crystal Pal. Pde. SE19 . . . 3E 6
Crystal Pal. Pk. Rd. SE26 . . . 2F 7
Crystal Palace Station (Rail) . . . 3F 7
Crystal Pal. Sta. Rd. SE19 . . . 3F 7
Crystal Ter. SE19 . . . 3C 6
Crystal Vw. Ct. BR1: Brom . . . 1E 8
CUDHAM . . . 4B 30
Cudham Dr. CR0: New Ad . . . 6D 22
Cudham La. Nth. BR6: Downe . . . 3A 30
TN14: Cud . . . 3A 30
Cudham La. Sth.
TN14: Cud, Knock . . . 4A 30
Cudham Pk. Rd. TN14: Cud . . . 6H 25
Cudham Rd. BR6: Downe . . . 7D 24
TN16: Tats . . . 1D 32
Cuff Cres. SE9 . . . 3C 4
Culverstone Cl. BR2: Brom . . . 3G 17
Cumberland Av. DA16: Well . . . 1K 5
Cumberland Ct. CR0: Croy . . . 5C 14
Cumberland Rd. BR2: Brom . . . 7A 35 (1F 17)
SE25 . . . 3G 15
Cumberlow Av. SE25 . . . 7E 6
Cunningham Cl. BR4: W W'ck . . . 6C 16
Cupola Cl. BR1: Brom . . . 2J 9
Curnick's La. SE27 . . . 1B 6
Curtismill Cl. BR5: St P . . . 7A 12
Curtismill Way BR5: St P . . . 7A 12
Curzon Cl. BR6: Orp . . . 1G 25
Cuthbert Gdns. SE25 . . . 7D 6
Cuthbert Rd. CR0: Croy . . . 6A 14
Cuxton BR5: Pet W . . . 2F 19
Cyclamen Rd. BR8: Swan . . . 1J 21
Cypress Rd. SE25 . . . 6D 6
Cyril Lodge DA14: Sidc . . . 1K 11
Cyril Rd. BR6: Orp . . . 4K 19

D

Dacres Est. SE23 . . . 1J 7
Dacres Rd. SE23 . . . 1J 7
Daerwood Cl. BR2: Brom . . . 5C 18
Daffodil Cl. CR0: Croy . . . 5J 15
Dagmar Rd. SE25 . . . 2D 14
Dagnall Pk. SE25 . . . 3D 14
Dagnall Rd. SE25 . . . 2D 14
Dagonet Gdns. BR1: Brom . . . 1H 9
Dagonet Rd. BR1: Brom . . . 1H 9
Dahlia Dr. BR8: Swan . . . 4A 34
Dainford Cl. BR1: Brom . . . 2E 8
Dainton Cl. BR1: Brom . . . 1E 35 (5J 9)
Dairsie Ct. BR1: Brom . . . 5K 9
Dairsie Rd. SE9 . . . 1F 5
Dairy Cl. BR1: Brom . . . 4J 9
CR7: Thor H . . . 6B 6
Daisy Cl. CR0: Croy . . . 5J 15
Dale, The BR2: Kes . . . 1A 24
Dale Pk. Rd. SE19 . . . 5B 6
Dale Rd. BR8: Swan . . . 6H 13
Daleside BR6: Chels . . . 2K 25
Daleside Cl. BR6: Chels . . . 3K 25
Dale Wood Rd. BR6: Orp . . . 4H 19
Dallas Rd. SE26 . . . 1G 7
Dalmally Rd. CR0: Croy . . . 4E 14
Dalmany Pas. CR0: Croy . . . 4E 14
Dalmeny Av. SW16 . . . 6A 6
Dalton Cl. BR6: Orp . . . 7H 19
Daltons Rd. BR6: Crock, Orp . . . 7G 21
BR8: Crock . . . 7G 21
Daly Dr. BR1: Brom . . . 7D 10
Damson Ct. BR8: Swan . . . 1J 21
Dando Cres. SE3 . . . 1A 4
Danebury CR0: New Ad . . . 3D 22
Dane Cl. BR6: Farnb . . . 2G 25
Danecourt Gdns. CR0: Croy . . . 7E 14
Danehill Wlk. DA14: Sidc . . . 1K 11
Danescombe SE12 . . . 5A 4
Daneswood Av. SE6 . . . 1D 8
D'Arcy Pl. BR2: Brom . . . 7B 35 (1H 17)
Darent Ho. BR1: Brom . . . 2E 8
Dargate Cl. SE19 . . . 4E 6
Darley Cl. CR0: Croy . . . 3K 15
Darlington Rd. SE27 . . . 2A 6
Darns Hill BR8: Crock . . . 4H 21
Darrick Wood Rd. BR6: Orp . . . 6G 19
Darrick Wood School Sports Cen. . . . 7F 19
Darrick Wood School Sports Cen.
Swimming Pool . . . 7F 19
Dartmouth Rd. BR2: Hayes . . . 4H 17
SE26 . . . 1G 7
Dartnell Rd. CR0: Croy . . . 4E 14
Darwin Cl. BR6: Farnb . . . 2G 25
Darwin Leisure Cen. . . . 4H 29
Dassett Rd. SE27 . . . 2A 6
Davema Cl. BR7: Chst . . . 5D 10
Davenant Rd. CR0: Croy . . . 7A 14
David Ho. DA15: Sidc . . . 1K 11

David Lean Cinema 7B 14
(off Katherine St.)
David Lloyd Leisure
Kidbrooke 1A 4
Sidcup 2B 12
Davidson Rd. CR0: Croy 5D 14
Davies Cl. CR0: Croy 3F 15
Dawell Dr. TN16: Big H 6E 28
Dawson Av. BR5: St P 6A 12
Dawson Dr. BR8: Swan 4K 13
Days La. DA15: Sidc 4K 5
Deacons Leas BR6: Orp 1G 25
Deakins Ter. BR6: Orp 4K 19
Deans Cl. CR0: Croy 7E 14
Deans Ga. Cl. SE23 1J 7
Decimus Cl. CR7: Thor H 1C 14
Deepdale Av. BR2: Brom 1G 17
Deepdene Av. CR0: Croy 7E 14
Deepdene Ct. BR2: Brom 7F 9
Deepdene Point SE23 1J 7
Deerleap La. TN14: Knock 2J 31
Deer Pk. Way BR4: W W'ck 6G 17
De Frene Rd. SE26 1J 7
Degema Rd. BR7: Chst 2E 10
Delamare Cres. CR0: Croy 3H 15
De Lapre Cl. BR5: St M Cry 4C 20
Dell, The SE19 5E 6
Dellfield Cl. BR3: Beck 5D 8
Delmey Cl. CR0: Croy 7E 14
Delta Point CR0: Croy 5B 14
(off Wellesley Rd.)
Denberry Dr. DA14: Sidc 1A 12
Denbigh Cl. BR7: Chst 3C 10
Denbridge Rd. BR1: Brom 6C 10
Den Cl. BR3: Beck 7E 8
Dene, The CR0: Croy 7J 15
Dene Cl. BR2: Hayes 5G 17
DA2: Dart 1K 13
Dene Dr. BR6: Chels 7A 20
Denham Ct. SE26 1G 7
(off Kirkdale)
Denmark Path SE25 2G 15
Denmark Rd. BR1: Brom 2D 35 (5J 9)
SE25 2F 15
Denmark Wlk. SE27 1B 6
Denmead Rd. CR0: Croy 5A 14
Dennard Way BR6: Farnb 1E 24
Dennett Rd. CR0: Croy 5A 14
Den Rd. BR2: Brom 7E 8
Densole Cl. BR3: Beck 5K 7
Denton Ct. BR2: Brom 4D 18
Denver Cl. BR6: Pet W 3H 19
Derby Rd. CR0: Croy 5A 14
Derrick Rd. BR3: Beck 7A 8
DERRY DOWNS 3B 20
Derry Downs BR5: St M Cry 3B 20
Derwent Dr. BR5: Pet W 4G 19
Derwent Ho. SE20 6G 7
(off Derwent Rd.)
Derwent Rd. SE20 6F 7
Detling Rd. BR1: Brom 2H 9
Deveraux Cl. BR3: Beck 2D 16
Devonshire Ho. Bus. Cen.
BR2: Brom 7E 35
Devonshire Rd. BR6: Orp 4K 19
CR0: Croy 4C 14
SE9 6D 4
Devonshire Sq. BR2: Brom 7E 35 (1J 17)
Devonshire Way CR0: Croy 6K 15
Diameter Rd. BR5: Pet W 4E 18
Dickens Dr. BR7: Chst 3F 11
Dickensons La. SE25 2F 15
(not continuous)
Dickensons Pl. SE25 3F 15
Dickenswood Cl. SE19 4A 6
Dickson Rd. SE9 1D 4
Digby Pl. CR0: Croy 7E 14
Dilhorne Cl. SE12 7A 4
Dillwyn Cl. SE26 1K 7
Dingwall Av. CR0: Croy 6B 14
Dingwall Rd. CR0: Croy 5C 14
Dinsdale Gdns. SE25 2D 14
Dittisham Rd. SE9 1B 10
Ditton Pl. SE20 5G 7
Dixon Pl. BR4: W W'ck 5C 16
Dixon Rd. SE25 7D 6
Dobell Rd. SE9 2E 4
Doctors Cl. SE26 2H 7
Dodbrooke Rd. SE27 1A 6
Dome Hill Pk. SE26 1E 6
Dominion Rd. CR0: Croy 4E 14
Domonic Dr. SE9 1E 10
Dorado Gdns. BR6: Chels 7C 20
Dorchester Cl. BR5: St P 4A 12
Dorney Ri. BR5: St M Cry 1J 19
Dorrington Ct. SE25 6D 6
Dorrington Way BR3: Beck 2D 16
Dorrit Way BR7: Chst 3F 11
Dorryn Ct. SE26 2J 7
Dorset Av. DA16: Well 1K 5
Dorset Rd. BR3: Beck 7J 7
SE9 6D 4
Douglas Ct. TN16: Big H 6G 29
Douglas Dr. CR0: Croy 7B 16
Doveney Cl. BR5: St P 7B 12
Dovercourt Av. CR7: Thor H 1A 14
Dover Rd. SE19 3C 6
Doves Cl. BR2: Brom 6B 18
Dowding Rd. TN16: Big H 4F 29
Dowlerville Rd. BR6: Chels 3J 25
Downderry Rd. BR1: Brom 1E 8
DOWNE 7D 24
Downe Av. TN14: Cud 1B 30
Downe Bank Nature Reserve 2K 29
Downe Rd. BR2: Kes 5A 24
TN14: Cud 2A 30
DOWNHAM 2E 8
Downham La. BR1: Brom 2E 8
Downham Way BR1: Brom 2E 8
Down House and Darwin Mus. 1J 29
Downleys Cl. SE9 6D 4
Downman Rd. SE9 1D 4
Downs Av. BR7: Chst 2C 10
Downsbridge Rd. BR3: Beck 5E 8
Downs Hill BR3: Beck 4E 8
Downs Rd. BR3: Beck 6C 8
(not continuous)
CR7: Thor H 5B 6
Downs Vw. Cl. BR6: Prat B 6B 26
Downsview Cl. BR8: Swan 5A 34
Downsview Gdns. SE19 4A 6
Downsview Rd. SE19 4B 6
Downsway BR6: Orp 2H 25
Doyle Rd. SE25 1F 15
Dragons Health Club
St Paul's Cray 5C 12
Drake M. BR2: Brom 1K 17
Draper Ct. BR1: Brom 1B 18
Draven Cl. BR2: Hayes 4G 17
Drayton Av. BR6: Farnb 5E 18
Drayton Rd. CR0: Croy 6A 14
Drift, The BR2: Brom 7A 18
Drive, The BR3: Beck 6B 8
BR4: W W'ck 4E 16
BR6: Orp 6J 19
BR7: Chst 7J 11
CR7: Thor H 1C 14
DA14: Sidc 1A 12
Droitwich Cl. SE26 1F 7
Druids Way BR2: Brom 1E 16
Drummond Rd. CR0: Croy 6B 14
(not continuous)
Dryden Way BR6: Orp 5K 19
Dryland Av. BR6: Orp 1J 25
Duddington Cl. SE9 1A 10
Dudsbury Rd. DA14: Sidc 3A 12
Duggan Dr. BR7: Chst 3B 10
Dukesthorpe Rd. SE26 1J 7
Dukes Way BR4: W W'ck 7F 17
Dulverton Rd. SE9 6H 5
Dulwich Upper Wood Nature Pk. 2E 6
Dulwich Wood Av. SE19 1D 6
Dulwich Wood Pk. SE19 1D 6
Dumbreck Rd. SE9 1E 4
Dunbar Av. BR3: Beck 1K 15
Dunbar Ct. BR2: Brom 7B 35
Dunbar St. SE27 1B 6
Dundee Rd. SE25 2G 15
Dunelm Gro. SE27 1B 6
Dunfield Gdns. SE6 2C 8
Dunfield Rd. SE6 2C 8
(not continuous)
Dunheved Rd. Nth.
CR7: Thor H 3A 14
Dunheved Rd. Sth. CR7: Thor H 3A 14
Dunkeld Rd. SE25 1C 14
Dunkery Rd. SE9 1A 10
Dunkirk St. SE27 1B 6
Dunley Dr. CR0: New Ad 4C 22
Dunoran Home BR1: Brom 5B 10
Dunsfold Way CR0: New Ad 5C 22
Dunstan Glade BR5: Pet W 3G 19
Dunster Ho. SE6 1D 8
Dunvegan Rd. SE9 1E 4
Duppas Ct. CR0: Croy 7A 14
(off Duppas Hill Ter.)
Duppas Hill La. CR0: Croy 7A 14
Duppas Hill Rd. CR0: Wadd 7A 14
Duppas Hill Ter. CR0: Croy 7A 14
Duppas Rd. CR0: Wadd 7A 14
Duraden Cl. BR3: Beck 4C 8
Durant Rd. BR8: Swan 1B 34
Durban Rd. BR3: Beck 6A 8
SE27 1B 6
Durham Av. BR2: Brom 7A 35 (1G 17)
Durham Hill BR1: Brom 1G 9
Durham Ho. BR2: Brom 1F 17
Durham Rd. BR2: Brom 6A 35 (7G 9)
DA14: Sidc 2A 12
Durley Gdns. BR6: Chels 7A 20
Durnford Ho. SE6 1D 8
Durning Rd. SE19 2C 6
Durrant Way BR6: Farnb 2G 25
Duxberry Cl. BR2: Brom 2B 18
Dyke Dr. BR5: Orp 5B 20
Dykes Way BR2: Brom 7G 9
Dymchurch Cl. BR6: Orp 1H 25
Dyneley Rd. SE12 7B 4

E

Eagle Hill SE19 3C 6
Eagles Dr. TN16: Tats 7F 29
Ealdham Sq. SE9 1B 4
Earlshall Rd. SE9 1E 4
Earlsthorpe Rd. SE26 1J 7
Earls Way BR6: Orp 6K 19
Earlswood Av. CR7: Thor H 2A 14
Eastbury Rd. BR5: Pet W 3G 19
Eastcote BR6: Orp 5J 19
East Croydon Station (Rail & CT) 6C 14
East Dr. BR5: St M Cry 3A 20
Eastern Vw. TN16: Big H 6E 28
E. Hall Rd. BR5: St M Cry 4D 20
East Hill TN16: Big H 7D 28
E. India Way CR0: Croy 5E 14
Eastmead Cl. BR1: Brom 6B 10
Eastney Rd. CR0: Croy 5A 14
Eastnor Rd. SE9 5H 5
East Pl. SE27 1B 6
E. Rochester Way
DA15: Bexl, Sidc 1K 5
Eastry Av. BR2: Hayes 3G 17
East St. BR1: Brom 3C 35 (6H 9)
East Ter. DA15: Sidc 5K 5
East Way BR2: Hayes 4H 17
CR0: Croy 6K 15
Eastwell Cl. BR3: Beck 4K 7
Ebdon Way SE3 1A 4
Ebury Cl. BR2: Kes 7B 18
Ecclesbourne Rd. CR7: Thor H 2B 14
Eccleshill BR2: Brom 7A 35
Eccleston Cl. BR6: Orp 5G 19
Edar Ho. CR0: New Ad 3C 22
Eddisbury Ho. SE26 1F 7
Edenbridge Cl. BR5: St M Cry 1C 20
Eden Cl. DA5: Bexl 1J 13
EDEN PARK 2B 16
Eden Pk. Av. BR3: Beck 1K 15
(not continuous)
Eden Park Station (Rail) 2B 16
Eden Rd. BR3: Beck 1K 15
CR0: Croy 7C 14
DA5: Bexl 1H 13
SE27 1A 6
Eden Way BR3: Beck 2A 16
Ederline Av. SW16 6A 6
Edgar Cl. BR8: Swan 5A 34
Edgar Rd. TN16: Tats 3C 32
Edgeborough Way BR1: Brom 4A 10
Edgebury BR7: Chst 1E 10
Edgebury Wlk. BR7: Chst 1F 11
Edge Hill Ct. DA14: Sidc 1J 11
Edgehill Rd. BR7: Chst 7H 5
Edgepoint Cl. SE27 2A 6
Edgewood Dr. BR6: Chels 2J 25
Edgewood Grn. CR0: Croy 5J 15
Edgeworth Rd. SE9 1B 4
Edgington Way DA14: Sidc 4B 12
Edison Rd. BR2: Brom 3B 35 (6H 9)
Edith Rd. BR6: Chels 2K 25
SE25 2C 14
Edmund Rd. BR5: St M Cry 3B 20
Edmunds Av. BR5: St P 7C 12
Edridge Rd. CR0: Croy 7B 14

Edward Rd. BR1: Brom 4J 9
BR7: Chst 2E 10
CR0: Croy 4D 14
SE20 4J 7
TN16: Big H 7G 29
Edwards Gdns. BR8: Swan 1J 21
Edward Tyler Rd. SE12 6B 4
Edwin Arnold Ct.
DA14: Sidc 1J 11
Edwin Pl. *CR0: Croy* *5D 14*
(off Leslie Gro.)
Egerton Av. BR8: Swan 2A 34
Egerton Rd. SE25 7D 6
Egremont Rd. SE27 1A 6
Eileen Rd. SE25 2C 14
Eland Pl. CR0: Wadd 7A 14
Eland Rd. CR0: Wadd 7A 14
Elborough Rd. SE25 2F 15
Elderberry Gro. SE27 1B 6
Elder Gdns. SE27 2B 6
Elder Oak Cl. SE20 5G 7
Elder Oak Ct. *SE20* *5G 7*
(off Anerley Ct.)
Elder Rd. SE27 1B 6
Elderslie Cl. BR3: Beck 2B 16
Elderslie Rd. SE9 2F 5
Elderton Rd. SE26 1K 7
Elderwood Pl. SE27 2B 6
Eldon Av. CR0: Croy 6H 15
Eldon Pk. SE25 1G 15
Eldred Dr. BR5: Orp 5B 20
Elford Cl. SE3 1A 4
Elfrida Cres. SE6 1B 8
Elgal Cl. BR6: Farnb 2E 24
Elgin Rd. CR0: Croy 6E 14
Elham Cl. BR1: Brom 4A 10
Elibank Rd. SE9 1E 4
Elis David Almshouses
CR0: Croy 7A 14
Elizabeth Ct. *BR1: Brom* *5G 9*
(off Highland Rd.)
Elizabeth Ter. SE9 3E 4
Elizabeth Way BR5: St M Cry 2B 20
SE19 4C 6
Ella Cl. BR3: Beck 6B 8
Ellenborough Rd. DA14: Sidc 2C 12
Ellen Cl. BR1: Brom 7A 10
Ellery Rd. SE19 4C 6
Ellesmere Av. BR3: Beck 6C 8
Elliott Rd. BR2: Brom 1A 18
CR7: Thor H 1A 14
Ellis Cl. BR8: Swan 1J 21
SE9 6H 5
Ellison Rd. DA15: Sidc 5J 5
Elm Bank Dr. BR1: Brom 6A 10
Elmbrook Gdns. SE9 1D 4
Elmcroft Rd. BR6: Orp 4K 19
Elmdene Cl. BR3: Beck 3A 16
Elm Dr. BR8: Swan 6J 13
ELMERS END 1J 15
Elmers End Rd. BR3: Beck 6H 7
SE20 6H 7
Elmers End Station (Rail & CT) 1J 15
Elmerside Rd. BR3: Beck 1K 15
Elmers Lodge BR3: Beck 1J 15
Elmers Rd. SE25 4F 15
Elmfield Pk. BR1: Brom 5C 35 (7H 9)
Elmfield Rd. BR1: Brom 5C 35 (6H 9)
Elm Gro. BR6: Orp 5J 19
Elmgrove Rd. CR0: Croy 4G 15
Elmhurst Rd. SE9 6D 4
Elmlee Cl. BR7: Chst 3C 10
Elm Pde. DA14: Sidc 1K 11
Elm Pk. Rd. SE25 7E 6
Elm Rd. BR3: Beck 6A 8
BR6: Chels 4K 25
CR7: Thor H 1C 14
DA14: Sidc 1K 11
TN16: Westrm 7K 33
Elms, The *CR0: Croy* *5B 14*
(off Tavistock Rd.)
Elmscott Rd. BR1: Brom 2F 9
Elmside CR0: New Ad 3C 22
ELMSTEAD 3C 10
Elmstead Av. BR7: Chst 2C 10
Elmstead Glade BR7: Chst 3C 10
Elmstead La. BR7: Chst 4B 10
Elmstead Woods Station (Rail) 3B 10
Elmstone Ter. BR5: St M Cry 1B 20
Elm Ter. SE9 3F 5
Elm Wlk. BR6: Farnb 7C 18
Elmwood Rd. CR0: Croy 4A 14
Elsa Ct. BR3: Beck 5A 8
Elstan Way CR0: Croy 4K 15
Elstow Cl. SE9 2E 4
(not continuous)
Elstree Hill BR1: Brom 4F 9
ELTHAM 4C 4
Eltham Crematorium
SE9 1J 5
Eltham Grn. SE9 2C 4
Eltham Grn. Rd. SE9 1B 4
Eltham High St. SE9 3E 4
Eltham Hill SE9 2C 4
Eltham Palace 4D 4
Eltham Pal. Rd. SE9 3B 4
ELTHAM PARK 1F 5
Eltham Pk. Gdns. SE9 1F 5
Eltham Pools 3D 4
Eltham Rd. SE9 2A 4
SE12 2A 4
Eltham Station (Rail) 2E 4
Elvington Grn. BR2: Brom 2G 17
Elvino Rd. SE26 2K 7
Elwill Way BR3: Beck 1D 16
Elwyn Gdns. SE12 4A 4
Ely Rd. CR0: Croy 2C 14
Elysian Av. BR5: St M Cry 3J 19
Embassy Ct. DA14: Sidc 1A 12
Embassy Gdns. BR3: Beck 5A 8
Ember Cl. BR5: Pet W 4F 19
Emersons Av. BR8: Swan 2A 34
Empire Sq. *SE20* *4J 7*
(off High St.)
Empress Dr. BR7: Chst 3E 10
Engadine Cl. CR0: Croy 7E 14
Englefield Cl. BR5: St M Cry 2J 19
CR0: Croy 3B 14
Englefield Cres.
BR5: St M Cry 1J 19
Englefield Path BR5: St M Cry 1K 19
Enmore Av. SE25 2F 15
Enmore Rd. SE25 2F 15
Enslin Rd. SE9 3F 5
Enterprise Cen., The *BR3: Beck* *2K 7*
(off Cricket La.)
Epsom Rd. CR0: Wadd 7A 14
Eresby Dr. BR3: Beck 5B 16
Erica Ct. BR8: Swan 1K 21
Erica Gdns. CR0: Croy 7C 16
Eric Liddell Sports Cen. 6C 4
Eridge Grn. Cl. BR5: Orp 5B 20
Erin Cl. BR1: Brom 4F 9
Ermington Rd. SE9 6H 5
Ernest Av. SE27 1A 6
Ernest Cl. BR3: Beck 2B 16
Ernest Gro. BR3: Beck 2A 16
Esam Way SW16 2A 6
Escott Gdns. SE9 1B 10
Eskmont Ridge SE19 4C 6
Esporta Health & Fitness
Chislehurst 2H 11
Essex Gro. SE19 3C 6
Essex Twr. *SE20* *5G 7*
(off Jasmine Gro.)
Estcourt Rd. SE25 3G 15
Etfield Gro. DA14: Sidc 2A 12
Ethelbert Cl. BR1: Brom 6H 9
Ethelbert Ct. BR1: Brom 5B 35
Ethelbert Rd. BR1: Brom 5B 35 (7H 9)
BR5: St P 7C 12
Ethel Ter. BR6: Prat B 5B 26
Eton Rd. BR6: Chels 1A 26
Eugenie M. BR7: Chst 5E 10
Euston Rd. CR0: Croy 5A 14
Evelina Rd. SE20 4H 7
Evelyn Av. RH8: T'sey 6B 32
Evening Hill BR3: Beck 4D 8
Everard Av. BR2: Hayes 5H 17
Everest Pl. BR8: Swan 1J 21
Everest Rd. SE9 2E 4
Everglade TN16: Big H 7F 29
Evergreen Cl. SE20 4H 7
Eversley Rd. SE19 4C 6
Eversley Way CR0: Croy 1B 22
Everton Rd. CR0: Croy 5F 15
Evry Rd. DA14: Sidc 3B 12
Exchange Apartments BR2: Brom 7D 35
Exeter Rd. CR0: Croy 4D 14
Exford Gdns. SE12 5A 4
Exford Rd. SE12 6A 4
Eyebright Cl. CR0: Croy 5J 15
Eylewood Rd. SE27 2B 6
Eynsford Cl. BR5: Pet W 4F 19
Eynsford Rd. BR8: Crock 3J 21
Eynswood Dr. DA14: Sidc 2A 12

F

Factory La. CR0: Croy 6A 14
Faesten Way DA5: Bexl 1K 13
Fair Acres BR2: Brom 2H 17
CR0: Sels 5A 22
Fairbank Av. BR6: Farnb 6E 18
Fairby Rd. SE12 2A 4
Fairchildes Av. CR0: New Ad 7E 22
Fairchildes Rd. CR6: Warl 3A 28
Fairfield Halls 7C 14
Fairfield Path CR0: Croy 7C 14
Fairfield Rd. BR1: Brom 4H 9
BR3: Beck 6B 8
BR5: Pet W 3G 19
CR0: Croy 7C 14
Fairford Av. CR0: Croy 2J 15
Fairford Cl. CR0: Croy 2K 15
Fairgreen Rd. CR7: Thor H 2A 14
Fairhaven Av. CR0: Croy 3J 15
Fairholme Rd. CR0: Croy 4A 14
Fairland Ho. BR2: Brom 7E 35 (1J 17)
Fairlands Ct. SE9 3F 5
Fairlawn Pk. SE26 2K 7
Fairline Ct. BR3: Beck 6D 8
Fairmead BR1: Brom 1C 18
Fairmead Cl. BR1: Brom 1C 18
Fairoak Cl. BR5: Pet W 4E 18
Fairoak Dr. SE9 2J 5
Fairtrough Rd. BR6: Prat B 1F 31
Fairview Cl. SE26 2K 7
Fairview Dr. BR6: Orp 1G 25
Fairway BR5: Pet W 2G 19
Fairway, The BR1: Brom 2C 18
Fairway Cl. CR0: Croy 2K 15
Fairway Gdns. BR3: Beck 3E 16
Fairwyn Rd. SE26 1K 7
Falcon Av. BR1: Brom 1B 18
Falcons Cl. TN16: Big H 6F 29
FALCONWOOD 1K 5
FALCONWOOD 1J 5
Falconwood Pde. DA16: Well 1K 5
Falconwood Rd. CR0: Sels 5A 22
Falconwood Station (Rail) 1J 5
Falkland Ho. SE6 1D 8
Falkland Pk. Av. SE25 7D 6
Fambridge Cl. SE26 1A 8
FANTAIL, THE 7C 18
Faraday Way BR5: St M Cry 1A 20
Faringdon Av. BR2: Brom 4D 18
Farleigh Av. BR2: Hayes 4G 17
Farleigh Dean Cres. CR0: Sels 7C 22
Farley Pl. SE25 1F 15
Farm Av. BR8: Swan 7H 13
Farm Cl. BR4: W W'ck 7G 17
Farmcote Rd. SE12 5A 4
Farm Dr. CR0: Croy 6A 16
Farmfield Rd. BR1: Brom 2F 9
Farmland Wlk. BR7: Chst 2E 10
Farm La. CR0: Croy 6A 16
Farmstead Rd. SE6 1C 8
Farnaby Rd. BR1: Brom 4E 8
BR2: Brom 4E 8
SE9 1B 4
FARNBOROUGH 2F 25
Farnborough Comn. BR6: Farnb 7C 18
Farnborough Cres. BR2: Hayes 5G 17
Farnborough Hill BR6: Chels, Farnb 2G 25
Farnborough Way BR6: Chels, Farnb 2F 25
Farningham Hill Rd. DA4: Farn 7D 34
Farnley Rd. SE25 1C 14
Faro Cl. BR1: Brom 6D 10
Farquhar Rd. SE19 2E 6
Farquharson Rd. CR0: Croy 5B 14
Farrant Cl. BR6: Chels 4K 25
Farrer's Pl. CR0: Croy 7J 15
Farrier Cl. BR1: Brom 7A 10
Farrington Av. BR5: St P 7A 12
Farrington Pl. BR7: Chst 4G 11
Farthing Barn La.
BR6: Downe 5D 24
FARTHING STREET 5C 24
Farthing St. BR6: Downe 4C 24
Farwell Rd. DA14: Sidc 1A 12
Farwig La. BR1: Brom 1A 35 (5G 9)
Fashoda Rd. BR2: Brom 1A 18
Faversham Rd. BR3: Beck 6A 8
Fawcett Rd. CR0: Croy 7B 14

Featherbed La. CR0: Sels 4A 22
CR6: Warl 2A 28
Felhampton Rd. SE9 6G 5
Felix Mnr. BR7: Chst 3H 11
Fellmongers Yd. *CR0: Croy 7B 14*
(off Surrey St.)
Fell Rd. CR0: Croy 7B 14
(not continuous)
Felmingham Rd. SE20 6H 7
Felstead Rd. BR6: Chels 6K 19
Felton Cl. BR5: Pet W 3E 18
Felton Ho. SE3 1A 4
Felton Lea DA14: Sidc 2J 11
Fen Gro. DA15: Sidc 2K 5
Fenn Cl. BR1: Brom 3H 9
Fennel Cl. CR0: Croy 5J 15
Fens Way BR8: Swan 1B 34
Fenton Cl. BR7: Chst 2C 10
Ferby Ct. *DA14: Sidc 1J 11*
(off Main Rd.)
SE9 7J 5
(off Main Rd.)
Ferguson Cl. BR2: Brom 7E 8
Fernbrook Av. DA15: Sidc 2K 5
Ferndale BR1: Brom 6K 9
Ferndale Rd. SE25 2G 15
Ferndale Way BR6: Farnb 2G 25
Ferndell Av. DA5: Bexl 1J 13
Ferndown Av. BR6: Orp 5G 19
Ferndown Rd. SE9 4C 4
Fernham Rd. CR7: Thor H 7B 6
Fernheath Way DA2: Dart 2J 13
Fern Hill Pl. BR6: Farnb 2F 25
Fernhurst Rd. CR0: Croy 4G 15
Fernwood Cl. BR1: Brom 3E 35 (6K 9)
Ferris Av. CR0: Croy 7A 16
FICKLESHOLE 3A 28
Fidgeon Cl. BR1: Brom 7D 10
Field Cl. BR1: Brom 6K 9
Fieldpark Gdns. CR0: Croy 5K 15
Fieldside Cl. BR6: Farnb 1F 25
Fieldside Rd. BR1: Brom 2E 8
Fieldway BR5: Pet W 3G 19
CR0: New Ad 4C 22
Fieldway Stop (CT) 4C 22
Filey Cl. TN16: Big H 1A 32
Film Terrace Fitness Cen. 3F 5
Finch Av. SE27 1C 6
Finglesham Cl. BR5: Orp 5C 20
Finucane Dr. BR5: Orp 4B 20
Fir Dene BR6: Farnb 7C 18
Fire Sta. M. BR3: Beck 5B 8
Firhill Rd. SE6 1B 8
Firmingers Rd. BR6: Orp 2G 27
Firs, The SE26 2G 7
(Border Rd.)
SE26 2H 7
(Waverley Ct.)
Firsby Av. CR0: Croy 5J 15
Fir Tree Cl. BR6: Chels 2J 25
Firtree Gdns. CR0: Croy 1B 22
Fisher Cl. CR0: Croy 5E 14
Fishponds Rd. BR2: Kes 2A 24
Fitness First Health Club
Croydon 5A 14
Fitzjames Av. CR0: Croy 6F 15
Fitzroy Ct. CR0: Croy 4C 14
Fitzroy Gdns. SE19 4D 6
Fiveacre Cl. CR7: Thor H 3A 14
Five Elms Rd. BR2: Hayes 7J 17
FIVEWAYS 6G 5
Five Wents BR8: Swan 4B 34
Flag Cl. CR0: Croy 5J 15
Flagon Ct. *CR0: Croy 7B 14*
(off St Andrew's Rd.)
Flamborough Cl. TN16: Big H 1A 32
Flatford Ho. SE6 1D 8
Fleetwood Cl. CR0: Croy 7E 14
Fletchers Cl. BR2: Brom 7E 35 (1J 17)
Flimwell Cl. BR1: Brom 2F 9
Flint Cl. BR6: Chels 3J 25
Flint Down Cl. BR5: St P 5K 11
Flora Gdns. CR0: New Ad 7D 22
Florence Rd. BR1: Brom 2B 35 (5H 9)
BR3: Beck 6K 7
Florida Ct. BR2: Brom 7A 35
Florida Rd. CR7: Thor H 5A 6
Flyers Way, The TN16: Westrm 7J 33
Foley Rd. TN16: Big H 7F 29
Fonthill Cl. SE20 6F 7
Fontwell Dr. BR2: Brom 2D 18
Footbury Hill Rd. BR6: St M Cry 3K 19
FOOTS CRAY 3B 12
Foots Cray High St. DA14: Sidc 3B 12
Footscray Rd. SE9 3F 5
FORCE GREEN 6J 33
Force Grn. La. TN16: Westrm 6J 33
Ford Cl. CR7: Thor H 2A 14
Fordcroft Rd. BR5: St M Cry 2A 20
Forde Av. BR1: Brom 5E 35 (7K 9)
Fordington Ho. SE26 1F 7
Fordwich Cl. BR6: Orp 4J 19
Forest Cl. BR7: Chst 5D 10
FORESTDALE 5A 22
Forestdale Cen., The CR0: Sels 4A 22
Forest Dr. BR2: Kes 1B 24
Forest Ridge BR2: Kes 1B 24
BR3: Beck 7B 8
Forest Way BR5: St M Cry 2J 19
DA15: Sidc 4J 5
Forge Cl. BR2: Hayes 5H 17
Forge Fld. TN16: Big H 5F 29
Forge M. CR0: Addtn 2B 22
Forrester Path SE26 1H 7
Forstal Cl. BR2: Brom 5B 35 (7H 9)
Forster Ho. BR1: Brom 1E 8
Forster Rd. BR3: Beck 7K 7
Forsyte Cres. SE19 5D 6
Forsythe Shades Ct. BR3: Beck 5D 8
Forty Foot Way SE9 4H 5
Fosters Cl. BR7: Chst 2C 10
Foulsham Rd. CR7: Thor H 7B 6
Founders Gdns. SE19 4B 6
Fountain Dr. SE19 1E 6
Fountain Rd. CR7: Thor H 7B 6
Fowlers Cl. DA14: Sidc 2D 12
Foxbury Av. BR7: Chst 3G 11
Foxbury Cl. BR1: Brom 3J 9
BR6: Chels 2K 25
Foxbury Dr. BR6: Chels 3K 25
Foxbury Rd. BR1: Brom 3H 9
Fox Cl. BR6: Chels 2K 25
Foxcombe CR0: New Ad 3C 22
(not continuous)
Foxearth Cl. TN16: Big H 7G 29
Foxes Dale BR2: Brom 7E 8
Foxfield Rd. BR6: Orp 6G 19
Foxgrove Av. BR3: Beck 4C 8
Foxgrove Rd. BR3: Beck 4C 8
Fox Hill BR2: Kes 2K 23
SE19 4E 6
Fox Hill Gdns. SE19 4E 6
Foxhole Rd. SE9 2D 4
Foxhome Cl. BR7: Chst 3D 10
Fox La. BR2: Kes 2J 23
Foxleas Ct. BR1: Brom 4F 9
Foxley Rd. CR7: Thor H 1A 14
Foxwood Gro. BR6: Prat B 6B 26
Framlingham Cres. SE9 1B 10
Francis Rd. BR5: St P 7C 12
CR0: Croy 4A 14
Frank Godley Ct. DA14: Sidc 2A 12
Franklin Cl. SE27 1A 6
Franklin Ho. BR2: Brom 7F 9
Franklin Ind. Est. *SE20 5H 7*
(off Franklin Rd.)
Franklin Pas. SE9 1D 4
Franklin Rd. SE20 4H 7
Franks Wood Av. BR5: Pet W 2E 18
Fransfield Gro. SE26 1G 7
Frant Cl. SE20 4H 7
Frant Rd. CR7: Thor H 2A 14
Frederick Gdns. CR0: Croy 3A 14
Freeland Ct. DA15: Sidc 1K 11
Freelands Gro. BR1: Brom 1E 35 (5J 9)
Freelands Rd. BR1: Brom 2E 35 (5J 9)
Freemasons Pl. *CR0: Croy 5D 14*
(off Freemasons Rd.)
Freemasons Rd. CR0: Croy 5D 14
Freesia Cl. BR6: Chels 2J 25
Freethorpe Cl. SE19 4C 6
Frensham Dr. CR0: New Ad 4D 22
Frensham Rd. SE9 6J 5
Fresham Ho. BR2: Brom 6A 35
Freshfields CR0: Croy 5A 16
Freshwood Cl. BR3: Beck 5C 8
Frewing Cl. BR7: Chst 3C 10
Friar M. SE27 1A 6
Friar Rd. BR5: St M Cry 2K 19
Friars M. SE9 2F 5
Friarswood CR0: Sels 5A 22
Friends Rd. CR0: Croy 7C 14
Frimley Cl. CR0: New Ad 4D 22
Frimley Ct. DA14: Sidc 2B 12
Frimley Cres. CR0: New Ad 4D 22
Frinsted Gro. BR5: St M Cry 1C 20
Frith Rd. CR0: Croy 6B 14
Frognal Av. DA14: Sidc 2K 11
FROGNAL CORNER 3J 11
Frognal Pl. DA14: Sidc 3K 11
Froissart Rd. SE9 2C 4
Frylands Ct. CR0: New Ad 7D 22
Fryston Av. CR0: Croy 6F 15
Fuller Cl. BR6: Chels 2J 25
Fuller's Wood CR0: Croy 2B 22
Fullerton Rd. CR0: Croy 4E 14
Furneaux Av. SE27 2A 6
Furzefield Cl. BR7: Chst 3E 10
Furzehill Sq. BR5: St M Cry 1A 20
Furze Rd. CR7: Thor H 7B 6
Fyfe Way BR1: Brom 3C 35 (6H 9)
Fyfield Cl. BR2: Brom 1E 16

G

Gable Ct. SE26 1G 7
Gables, The BR1: Brom 4J 9
Gainsborough Cl. BR3: Beck 4B 8
Gainsborough Ct. BR2: Brom 1K 17
Gainsborough M. SE26 1G 7
Gaitskell Rd. SE9 5H 5
Gala Bingo
Crystal Palace 3E 6
Galahad Rd. BR1: Brom 1H 9
Gallus Sq. SE3 1A 4
Garden Cl. SE12 7A 4
Garden Cotts. BR5: St P 6B 12
Garden Ct. CR0: Croy 6E 14
Gardeners Cl. SE9 7D 4
Gardeners Rd. CR0: Croy 5A 14
Gardenia Rd. BR1: Brom 7D 10
Garden La. BR1: Brom 3J 9
Garden Rd. BR1: Brom 4J 9
SE20 5H 7
Gardens, The BR3: Beck 5D 8
Garden Wlk. BR3: Beck 5A 8
Gardiner Cl. BR5: St P 6B 12
Gardner Ind. Est. SE26 2A 8
Gareth Gro. BR1: Brom 1H 9
Garlands Ct. *CR0: Croy 7C 14*
(off Chatsworth Rd.)
Garnet Rd. CR7: Thor H 1B 14
Garnett Cl. SE9 1E 4
Garrard Cl. BR7: Chst 2E 10
Garrick Cres. CR0: Croy 6D 14
Garrolds Cl. BR8: Swan 6J 13
Gascoigne Rd. CR0: New Ad 6D 22
Gatcombe Ct. BR3: Beck 4B 8
Gateacre Ct. DA14: Sidc 1A 12
Gates Grn. Rd. BR2: Kes 7G 17
BR4: W W'ck 7G 17
Gatestone Ct. SE19 3D 6
Gatestone Rd. SE19 3D 6
Gateway Bus. Cen. BR3: Beck 3K 7
Gattons Way DA14: Sidc 1E 12
Gavestone Cres. SE12 4A 4
Gavestone Rd. SE12 4A 4
Geffery's Ct. SE9 7D 4
Geneva Rd. CR7: Thor H 2B 14
Genoa Rd. SE20 5H 7
George Gro. Rd. SE20 5F 7
George La. BR2: Hayes 5J 17
Georges Cl. BR5: St P 7B 12
George's Rd. TN16: Tats 2C 32
George St. CR0: Croy 6B 14
George Street Stop (CT) 6B 14
Georgetown Cl. SE19 2D 6
Georgian Cl. BR2: Hayes 5J 17
Georgian Ct. *CR0: Croy 5C 14*
(off Cross Rd.)
Georgia Rd. CR7: Thor H 5A 6
Geraint Rd. BR1: Brom 1H 9
Gerda Rd. SE9 6H 5
Gibbs Av. SE19 2C 6
Gibbs Cl. SE19 3C 6
Gibbs Ho. BR1: Brom 1A 35
Gibbs Sq. SE19 2C 6
Gibney Ter. BR1: Brom 1G 9
Gibsons Hill SW16 3A 6
(not continuous)
Giggs Hill BR5: St P 6K 11
Gilbert Rd. BR1: Brom 4H 9
Gildenhill Rd. BR8: Swan 2D 34
Giles Coppice SE19 1E 6
Gillan Ct. SE12 7A 4

Gillett Rd. CR7: Thor H . . . 1C **14**
Gillmans Rd. BR5: Orp . . . 5A **20**
Gilroy Way BR5: Orp . . . 4A **20**
Gilsland Rd. CR7: Thor H . . . 1C **14**
Gipsy Hill SE19 . . . 1D **6**
Gipsy Hill Station (Rail) . . . 2D **6**
Gipsy Rd. SE27 . . . 1B **6**
Gipsy Rd. Gdns. SE27 . . . 1B **6**
Girton Gdns. CR0: Croy . . . 7B **16**
Girton Rd. SE26 . . . 2J **7**
Gittens Cl. BR1: Brom . . . 1G **9**
Glade, The BR1: Brom . . . 6A **10**
BR4: W W'ck . . . 7C **16**
CR0: Croy . . . 4K **15**
Glade Gdns. CR0: Croy . . . 4K **15**
Gladeside CR0: Croy . . . 3J **15**
Glades Pl. BR1: Brom . . . 3C **35** (6H **9**)
Glades Shop. Cen., The
BR1: Brom . . . 4C **35** (6H **9**)
Gladstone M. SE20 . . . 4H **7**
Gladstone Rd. BR6: Farnb . . . 2F **25**
CR0: Croy . . . 4C **14**
Gladstone Ter. *SE27 . . . 2B 6*
(off Bentons La.)
Gladwell Rd. BR1: Brom . . . 3H **9**
Glanfield Rd. BR3: Beck . . . 1A **16**
Glanville Rd. BR2: Brom . . . 6E **35** (7J **9**)
Glasbrook Rd. SE9 . . . 4C **4**
Glassmill La. BR2: Brom . . . 4A **35** (6G **9**)
(not continuous)
Glastonbury Cl. BR5: Orp . . . 5B **20**
Glebe, The BR7: Chst . . . 5F **11**
Glebe Ho. Dr. BR2: Hayes . . . 5J **17**
Glebe Hyrst SE19 . . . 1D **6**
Glebe Knoll BR2: Brom . . . 3A **35**
Glebe Rd. BR1: Brom . . . 1B **35** (5H **9**)
Glebe Way BR4: W W'ck . . . 6D **16**
Gleeson Dr. BR6: Chels . . . 2J **25**
Glen, The BR2: Brom . . . 6F **9**
BR6: Farnb . . . 7C **18**
CR0: Croy . . . 7J **15**
Glenavon Lodge BR3: Beck . . . 4B **8**
Glenbarr Cl. SE9 . . . 1G **5**
Glenbow Rd. BR1: Brom . . . 3F **9**
Glencar Ct. SE19 . . . 3A **6**
Glen Ct. DA15: Sidc . . . 1K **11**
Glendale BR8: Swan . . . 6A **34**
Glendale Cl. SE9 . . . 1F **5**
Glendale M. BR3: Beck . . . 5C **8**
Glendower Cres. BR6: St M Cry . . . 3K **19**
Gleneagles Cl. BR6: Orp . . . 5G **19**
Gleneagles Grn. BR6: Orp . . . 5G **19**
Glenesk Rd. SE9 . . . 1F **5**
Glen Gdns. CR0: Wadd . . . 7A **14**
Glenhead Cl. SE9 . . . 1G **5**
Glenhouse Rd. SE9 . . . 2F **5**
Glenhurst BR3: Beck . . . 5D **8**
Glenhurst Ri. SE19 . . . 4B **6**
Glenlea Rd. SE9 . . . 2E **4**
Glenlyon Rd. SE9 . . . 2F **5**
Glenmore Lodge BR3: Beck . . . 5C **8**
Glennie Rd. SE27 . . . 1A **6**
Glenrose Ct. DA14: Sidc . . . 2A **12**
Glenshiel Rd. SE9 . . . 2F **5**
Glenthorne Av. CR0: Croy . . . 5G **15**
Glentrammon Av. BR6: Chels . . . 3J **25**
Glentrammon Cl. BR6: Chels . . . 2J **25**
Glentrammon Gdns. BR6: Chels . . . 3J **25**
Glentrammon Rd. BR6: Chels . . . 3J **25**
Glenure Rd. SE9 . . . 2F **5**
Glenview Rd. BR1: Brom . . . 6A **10**
Glenwood Ct. DA14: Sidc . . . 1K **11**
Glenwood Way CR0: Croy . . . 3J **15**
Gload Cres. BR5: Orp . . . 6C **20**
Gloucester Av. DA15: Sidc . . . 6K **5**
Gloucester Rd. CR0: Croy . . . 5C **14**
Glovers Cl. TN16: Big H . . . 5D **28**
Glyn Cl. SE25 . . . 6D **6**
Glyndebourne Pk. BR6: Farnb . . . 6E **18**
Glyn Dr. DA14: Sidc . . . 1A **12**
Goat Ho. Bri. SE25 . . . 7F **7**
Goatsfield Rd. TN16: Tats . . . 2B **32**
Goddard Rd. BR3: Beck . . . 1J **15**
GODDINGTON . . . **6C 20**
Goddington Chase BR6: Chels . . . 1A **26**
Goddington La. BR6: Chels . . . 7K **19**
Godric Cres. CR0: New Ad . . . 6E **22**
Godwin Rd. BR2: Brom . . . 7K **9**
Goldcrest Way CR0: New Ad . . . 5E **22**
Golden M. SE20 . . . 5H **7**
Goldfinch Cl. BR6: Chels . . . 2K **25**
Goldmark Ho. SE3 . . . 1A **4**
Goldsel Rd. BR8: Crock, Swan . . . 2J **21**
Golf Cl. CR7: Thor H . . . 5A **6**
Golf Rd. BR1: Brom . . . 7D **10**
Goodhart Way BR4: W W'ck . . . 4F **17**
Goodhew Rd. CR0: Croy . . . 3F **15**
Goodmead Rd. BR6: Orp . . . 4K **19**
Goodwood Pde. BR3: Beck . . . 1K **15**
Goose Grn. Cl. BR5: St P . . . 6K **11**
Gordon Cres. CR0: Croy . . . 5D **14**
Gordon Rd. BR3: Beck . . . 7A **8**
DA15: Sidc . . . 2K **5**
Gordon Way BR1: Brom . . . 2B **35** (5H **9**)
Gorse Rd. BR5: St M Cry . . . 6F **21**
CR0: Croy . . . 1B **22**
Goss Hill BR8: Swan . . . 1D **34**
Gosshill Rd. BR7: Chst . . . 6D **10**
Gossington Cl. BR7: Chst . . . 1E **10**
Goudhurst Rd. BR1: Brom . . . 2F **9**
Goulding Gdns. CR7: Thor H . . . 6A **6**
Gourock Rd. SE9 . . . 2F **5**
Gowland Pl. BR3: Beck . . . 6A **8**
Gowlland Cl. CR0: Croy . . . 4F **15**
Grace Cl. SE9 . . . 7C **4**
Grace Ct. *CR0: Croy . . . 7A 14*
(off Waddon Rd.)
Grace M. *SE20 . . . 6H 7*
(off Marlow Rd.)
Grace Path SE26 . . . 1H **7**
Grace Rd. CR0: Croy . . . 3B **14**
Gradient, The SE26 . . . 1F **7**
Grafton Rd. CR0: Croy . . . 5A **14**
Graham Cl. CR0: Croy . . . 6B **16**
Grampian Cl. BR6: St M Cry . . . 3J **19**
Gramsci Way SE6 . . . 1C **8**
Granby Rd. SE9 . . . 1E **4**
Grand Vw. Av. TN16: Big H . . . 6E **28**
Grange, The CR0: Croy . . . 6A **16**
Grange Av. SE25 . . . 6D **6**
Grangecliffe Gdns. SE25 . . . 6D **6**
Grange Dr. BR6: Prat B . . . 5B **26**
BR7: Chst . . . 3B **10**
Grange Gdns. SE25 . . . 6D **6**
Grange Hill SE25 . . . 6D **6**
Grangehill Rd. SE9 . . . 1E **4**
Grange Pk. Rd. CR7: Thor H . . . 1C **14**
Grange Rd. BR6: Orp . . . 6G **19**
CR7: Thor H . . . 1C **14**
SE19 . . . 7C **6**
SE25 . . . 7C **6**
Grangewood La. BR3: Beck . . . 3A **8**
Grangewood Ter. SE25 . . . 6C **6**
Granton Rd. DA14: Sidc . . . 3B **12**
Grant Pl. CR0: Croy . . . 5E **14**
Grant Rd. CR0: Croy . . . 5E **14**
Granville Cl. CR0: Croy . . . 6D **14**
Granville M. DA14: Sidc . . . 1K **11**
Granville Rd. DA14: Sidc . . . 1K **11**
Grasmere Av. BR6: Farnb . . . 7E **18**
Grasmere Ct. SE26 . . . 2F **7**
Grasmere Gdns. BR6: Farnb . . . 7E **18**
Grasmere Rd. BR1: Brom . . . 5G **9**
BR6: Farnb . . . 7E **18**
SE25 . . . 3G **15**
Grassington Rd. DA14: Sidc . . . 1K **11**
Gravel Hill CR0: Addtn . . . 3A **22**
Gravel Hill Stop (CT) . . . **3A 22**
Gravel Pit La. SE9 . . . 2G **5**
Gravel Pit Way BR6: Orp . . . 6K **19**
Gravel Rd. BR2: Brom . . . 7B **18**
Gravelwood Cl. BR7: Chst . . . 7H **5**
Graveney Gro. SE20 . . . 4H **7**
Grayland Cl. BR1: Brom . . . 5A **10**
Grays Farm Production Village BR5: St P . . . 5A **12**
Grays Farm Rd. BR5: St P . . . 5A **12**
Grays Rd. TN14: Westrm . . . 2J **33**
TN16: Westrm . . . 3G **33**
Grazeley Ct. SE19 . . . 2D **6**
Great Brownings SE21 . . . 1E **6**
Gt. Elms Rd. BR2: Brom . . . 1K **17**
Gt. Gatton Cl. CR0: Croy . . . 4K **15**
Gt. Harry Dr. SE9 . . . 7F **5**
Gt. Thrift BR5: Pet W . . . 1F **19**
Greatwood BR7: Chst . . . 4D **10**
Grecian Cres. SE19 . . . 3A **6**
Green, The BR1: Brom . . . 7A **4**
(not continuous)
BR2: Hayes . . . 4H **17**
BR5: St P . . . 4A **12**
BR6: Farnb . . . 1E **24**
CR0: Sels . . . 5A **22**
DA14: Sidc . . . 1K **11**
DA16: Well . . . 1K **5**
Greenacre Cl. BR8: Swan . . . 1K **21**
Green Acres CR0: Croy . . . 7E **14**
Greenacres DA14: Sidc . . . 1K **11**
SE9 . . . 3F **5**
Greenacres Cl. BR6: Farnb . . . 1F **25**
Greenbank Lodge *BR7: Chst . . . 6D 10*
(off Forest Cl.)
Green Cl. BR2: Brom . . . 7F **9**
Greencourt Av. CR0: Croy . . . 6G **15**
Greencourt Gdns. CR0: Croy . . . 5G **15**
Green Ct. Rd. BR8: Crock . . . 2J **21**
Greencourt Rd. BR5: Pet W . . . 2G **19**
Grn. Farm Cl. BR6: Chels . . . 3J **25**
Greenfield Dr. BR1: Brom . . . 6K **9**
Greenfield Gdns. BR5: Pet W . . . 4G **19**
Greenfield Rd. DA2: Dart . . . 2J **13**
Green Gdns. BR6: Farnb . . . 2F **25**
Green Hill BR6: Downe . . . 1H **29**
Greenhithe Cl. DA15: Sidc . . . 4K **5**
Greenholm Rd. SE9 . . . 2G **5**
Greenhurst Rd. SE27 . . . 2A **6**
Green La. BR7: Chst . . . 6G **5**
CR7: Thor H . . . 5A **6**
SE9 . . . 5G **5**
SE20 . . . 4J **7**
SW16 . . . 5A **6**
Green La. Bus. Pk. SE9 . . . 6F **5**
Green La. Gdns. CR7: Thor H . . . 6B **6**
Greenleigh Av. BR5: St P . . . 1A **20**
Greenmead Cl. SE25 . . . 2F **15**
Greenoak Ri. TN16: Big H . . . 7E **28**
Greenside BR8: Swan . . . 6J **13**
Greenside Rd. CR0: Croy . . . 4A **14**
Greenside Wlk. TN16: Big H . . . 7D **28**
GREEN STREET GREEN . . . **3J 25**
Greenvale Rd. SE9 . . . 1E **4**
Greenview Av. BR3: Beck . . . 3K **15**
CR0: Croy . . . 3K **15**
Green Way BR2: Brom . . . 3B **18**
SE9 . . . 2C **4**
Greenway BR7: Chst . . . 2D **10**
TN16: Tats . . . 2B **32**
Greenway, The BR5: St M Cry . . . 3A **20**
Greenway Gdns. CR0: Croy . . . 7A **16**
Greenways BR3: Beck . . . 7B **8**
Greenwood Bus. Cen. CR0: Croy . . . 4E **14**
Greenwood Cl. BR5: Pet W . . . 3H **19**
Greenwood Rd. CR0: Croy . . . 4A **14**
DA5: Bexl . . . 1J **13**
Gregory Cl. BR2: Brom . . . 1F **17**
Gregory Cres. SE9 . . . 4C **4**
Grenaby Av. CR0: Croy . . . 4C **14**
Grenaby Rd. CR0: Croy . . . 4C **14**
Grenville Rd. CR0: New Ad . . . 5D **22**
Gresham Rd. BR3: Beck . . . 6K **7**
SE25 . . . 1F **15**
Greycot Rd. BR3: Beck . . . 2B **8**
Greyfriars *SE26 . . . 1F 7*
(off Wells Pk. Rd.)
Greys Pk. Cl. BR2: Kes . . . 2A **24**
Grice Av. TN16: Big H . . . 2D **28**
Grimwade Av. CR0: Croy . . . 7F **15**
Grindley Gdns. CR0: Croy . . . 3E **14**
Groom Cl. BR2: Brom . . . 7E **35** (1J **17**)
Grosvenor Rd. BR4: W W'ck . . . 5C **16**
BR5: St M Cry . . . 3H **19**
SE25 . . . 1E **14**
Grove, The BR4: W W'ck . . . 7C **16**
BR8: Swan . . . 5A **34**
DA14: Sidc . . . 2D **12**
TN16: Big H . . . 7F **29**
Grove Cl. BR2: Hayes . . . 6H **17**
Grovehill Ct. BR1: Brom . . . 3G **9**
Groveland Rd. BR3: Beck . . . 7A **8**
Grovelands Rd. BR5: St P . . . 4K **11**
Grove Mkt. Pl. SE9 . . . 3E **4**
GROVE PARK . . . **7A 4**
Grove Pk. Rd. SE9 . . . 7B **4**
Grove Park Station (Rail) . . . 7A **4**
Grove Rd. TN16: Tats . . . 2B **32**
Grove Va. BR7: Chst . . . 3D **10**
Guibal Rd. SE12 . . . 4A **4**
Guildford Rd. CR0: Croy . . . 3C **14**
Guinness Ct. CR0: Croy . . . 6E **14**
Gulliver Rd. DA15: Sidc . . . 6J **5**
Gumping Rd. BR5: Farnb . . . 6F **19**
Gundulph Rd. BR2: Brom . . . 7K **9**
Gunnell Cl. CR0: Croy . . . 3E **14**
SE25 . . . 3F 15
(off Backley Gdns.)
SE26 . . . 1F **7**
Gwydor Rd. BR3: Beck . . . 7J **7**

Gwydyr Rd. BR2: Brom 5A 35 (7G 9)
Gwynne Av. CR0: Croy 4J 15

H

Hackington Cres. BR3: Beck 3B 8
Haddington Rd. BR1: Brom 1E 8
Haddon Rd. BR5: St M Cry 2B 20
Hadlow Pl. SE19 4F 7
Hadlow Rd. DA14: Sidc 1K 11
Haig Rd. TN16: Big H 6G 29
Haileybury Rd. BR6: Chels 1K 25
Hailing M. BR2: Brom 6E 35
Haimo Rd. SE9 2C 4
Hainault St. SE9 5G 5
Hainthorpe Rd. SE27 1A 6
Hale Cl. BR6: Farnb 1F 25
Hale Path SE27 1A 6
Halfway St. DA15: Sidc 4J 5
Halifax St. SE26 1G 7
Hallam Cl. BR7: Chst 2C 10
Hallane Ho. SE27 2B 6
Hall Dr. SE26 2H 7
Hall Vw. SE9 6C 4
Halons Rd. SE9 4F 5
HALSTEAD 2K 31
Halstead Cl. CR0: Croy 7B 14
Halstead La. TN14: Knock, Hals 4J 31
Hambledon Gdns. SE25 7E 6
Hambledown Rd. DA15: Sidc 4J 5
Hamblehyrst BR3: Beck 6C 8
Hambro Av. BR2: Hayes 5H 17
Hambrook Rd. SE25 7G 7
Hamilton Ct. CR0: Croy 5F 15
Hamilton Rd. CR7: Thor H 7C 6
DA15: Sidc 1K 11
SE27 1C 6
Hamilton Rd. Ind. Est. *SE27* *1C 6*
(off Hamilton Rd.)
Hamlet Rd. SE19 4E 6
Hamlyn Gdns. SE19 4D 6
Hammelton Ct. BR1: Brom 1A 35
Hammelton Rd. BR1: Brom 1A 35 (5G 9)
Hampden Av. BR3: Beck 6K 7
Hampden Rd. BR3: Beck 6K 7
Hampton Rd. CR0: Croy 3B 14
Hampton Rd. Ind. Pk. CR0: Croy 3B 14
Ham Vw. CR0: Croy 3K 15
Hanbury Dr. TN16: Big H 2D 28
Hancock Rd. SE19 3C 6
Handcroft Rd. CR0: Croy 4A 14
Hangrove Hill BR6: Downe 2K 29
Hanley Pl. BR3: Beck 4B 8
Hannah Cl. BR3: Beck 7D 8
Hannen Rd. SE27 1A 6
Hanover Ct. *SE19* *4F 7*
(off Anerley Rd.)
Hanover Dr. BR7: Chst 1F 11
Hanover St. CR0: Croy 7A 14
Hansom Ter. BR1: Brom 1E 35
Hanson Cl. BR3: Beck 3C 8
Harbledown Pl. BR5: St M Cry 1B 20
Harborough Av. DA15: Sidc 4K 5
Hardcastle Cl. CR0: Croy 3F 15
Hardcourts Cl. BR4: W W'ck 7C 16
Harding Cl. CR0: Croy 7E 14
Hardings La. SE20 3J 7
Hardres Ter. BR5: Orp 5C 20
Hares Bank CR0: New Ad 6E 22
Harfst Way BR8: Swan 5H 13
Harland Av. CR0: Croy 7E 14
DA15: Sidc 7J 5
Harland Rd. SE12 5A 4
Harlands Gro. BR6: Farnb 1E 24
Harleyford BR1: Brom 1E 35 (5J 9)
Harley Gdns. BR6: Orp 1H 25
Harmony Way BR1: Brom 3B 35 (6H 9)
Harnetts Cl. BR8: Crock 4J 21
Harold Rd. SE19 4C 6
Harriet Gdns. CR0: Croy 6F 15
Harrington Ct. CR0: Croy 6C 14
Harrington Rd. SE25 1F 15
Harrington Road Stop (CT) 7H 7
HARRIS HOSPISCARE 1J 25
Harrison Dr. BR1: Brom 1D 18
Harrison's Ri. CR0: Wadd 7A 14
Harrogate Ct. *SE26* *1F 7*
(off Droitwich Cl.)
Harrow Gdns. BR6: Chels 1A 26
Harrow Rd. TN14: Knock 4J 31
Hart Dyke Cres. BR8: Swan 7J 13
Hart Dyke Rd. BR5: Orp 6C 20
BR8: Swan 7J 13
Hartfield Cres. BR4: W W'ck 7H 17
Hartfield Gro. SE20 5H 7
Hartfield Rd. BR4: W W'ck 1H 23
Harting Rd. SE9 7D 4
Hartington Cl. BR6: Farnb 2F 25
Hartland Way CR0: Croy 7K 15
Hartley Cl. BR1: Brom 6C 10
Hartley Rd. CR0: Croy 4B 14
TN16: Westrm 7J 33
Harton Cl. BR1: Brom 5A 10
Harts Cft. CR0: Sels 5A 22
Hartsmead Rd. SE9 6E 4
Harvel Cl. BR5: St P 7K 11
Harvest Bank Rd. BR4: W W'ck 7G 17
Harvest Way BR8: Crock 4J 21
Harvill Rd. DA14: Sidc 2D 12
Harwood Av. BR1: Brom 3D 35 (6J 9)
Haseltine Rd. SE26 1A 8
Haslemere Rd. CR7: Thor H 2A 14
Hassock Wood BR2: Kes 1A 24
Hassop Wlk. SE9 1B 10
Hastings Rd. BR2: Brom 5B 18
CR0: Croy 5E 14
Hathaway Cl. BR2: Brom 5C 18
Hathaway Rd. CR0: Croy 4A 14
Hatherley Rd. DA14: Sidc 1K 11
Hathern Gdns. SE9 1D 10
Hatton Rd. CR0: Croy 5A 14
Havelock Rd. BR2: Brom 1K 17
CR0: Croy 6E 14
Haven Cl. BR8: Swan 4A 34
DA14: Sidc 3B 12
SE9 7E 4
Haven Ct. BR3: Beck 6D 8
Haverstock Ct. *BR5: St P* *6A 12*
(off Cotmandene Cres.)
Haverthwaite Rd. BR6: Orp 6G 19
Havisham Pl. SE19 4A 6
Hawes La. BR4: W W'ck 5D 16
Hawes Rd. BR1: Brom 1D 35 (5J 9)
(not continuous)
Hawfield Bank BR6: Chels 7C 20
(not continuous)
Hawke Rd. SE19 3C 6
Hawkhurst Way BR4: W W'ck 6C 16
Hawkinge Wlk. BR5: St P 7A 12
Hawkins Way SE6 2B 8
Hawksbrook La. BR3: Beck 3C 16
(not continuous)
Hawkshead Cl. BR1: Brom 4F 9
Hawkwood La. BR7: Chst 5F 11
HAWLEY'S CORNER 3G 33
Hawstead La. BR6: Chels 2E 26
Hawthorn Av. CR7: Thor H 5A 6
Hawthorn Cl. BR5: Pet W 3G 19
Hawthorndene Cl. BR2: Hayes 6G 17
Hawthorndene Rd. BR2: Hayes 6G 17
Hawthorn Dr. BR4: W W'ck 1F 23
Hawthorne Av. TN16: Big H 4F 29
Hawthorne Cl. BR1: Brom 7C 10
Hawthorne Rd. BR1: Brom 7B 10
Hawthorn Gro. SE20 4G 7
Haxted Rd. BR1: Brom 1E 35 (5J 9)
Haydens Cl. BR5: Orp 3B 20
HAYES 5H 17
Hayes Chase BR4: W W'ck 3E 16
Hayes Cl. BR2: Hayes 6H 17
Hayesford Pk. Dr. BR2: Brom 2G 17
Hayes Gdn. BR2: Hayes 6H 17
Hayes Hill BR2: Hayes 5F 17
Hayes Hill Rd. BR2: Hayes 5G 17
Hayes La. BR2: Brom, Hayes 7E 35 (2J 17)
BR3: Beck 7D 8
Hayes Mead Rd. BR2: Hayes 5F 17
Hayes Rd. BR2: Brom 7C 35 (1H 17)
Hayes Station (Rail) 5H 17
Hayes St. BR2: Hayes 5J 17
Hayes Way BR3: Beck 1D 16
Hayes Wood Av. BR2: Hayes 5J 17
Hayfield Rd. BR5: St M Cry 2K 19
Hayne Rd. BR3: Beck 6A 8
Haynes La. SE19 3D 6
Haysleigh Gdns. SE20 6F 7
Haywood Ri. BR6: Orp 2H 25
Haywood Rd. BR2: Brom 1A 18
Hazel Bank SE25 6D 6
Hazel Cl. CR0: Croy 4J 15
Hazel End BR8: Swan 2K 21
Hazel Gro. BR6: Farnb 6E 18
SE26 1J 7
Hazelhurst BR3: Beck 5E 8
Hazelhurst Ct. *SE6* *2D 8*
(off Beckenham Hill Rd.)
Hazelmere Rd. BR5: Pet W 1F 19
Hazelmere Way BR2: Hayes 3H 17
Hazel Wlk. BR2: Brom 3D 18
HAZELWOOD 7G 25
Hazelwood Ho's. BR2: Brom 7F 9
Hazelwood Rd. TN14: Cud 1B 30
Hazledean Rd. CR0: Croy 6C 14
Headcorn Rd. BR1: Brom 2G 9
Headley Ct. SE26 2H 7
Headley Dr. CR0: New Ad 4C 22
Healy Dr. BR6: Orp 1J 25
Hearn's Rd. BR5: St P 1B 20
Heath Cl. BR5: Orp 4B 20
BR8: Swan 6K 13
Heatherbank BR7: Chst 6D 10
Heather Ct. DA14: Sidc 3C 12
Heather End BR8: Swan 1J 21
Heather Rd. SE12 6A 4
Heathfield BR7: Chst 3F 11
Heathfield Cl. BR2: Kes 2K 23
Heathfield Ct. SE20 4H 7
Heathfield Gdns. CR0: Croy 7C 14
Heathfield La. BR7: Chst 3E 10
Heathfield Pde. BR8: Swan 6H 13
Heathfield Rd. BR1: Brom 4G 9
BR2: Kes 2K 23
CR0: Croy 7C 14
Heathfield Ter. BR8: Swan 6J 13
Heath Gro. SE20 4H 7
Heath Ho. DA15: Sidc 1J 11
Heathley End BR7: Chst 3F 11
Heath Pk. Dr. BR1: Brom 7B 10
Heath Ri. BR2: Hayes 3G 17
Heath Rd. CR7: Thor H 7B 6
Heathside BR5: Pet W 5F 19
Heathway CR0: Croy 7A 16
Heathwood Gdns. BR8: Swan 6H 13
Heathwood Point SE23 1J 7
Hedge Wlk. SE6 2C 8
Heights, The BR3: Beck 4D 8
(not continuous)
Helegan Cl. BR6: Chels 1J 25
Henderson Rd. CR0: Croy 3C 14
TN16: Big H 1E 28
Heneage Cres. CR0: New Ad 6D 22
Hengist Rd. SE12 4A 4
Hengist Way BR2: Brom 1F 17
Henry Cooper Way SE9 7C 4
Henry St. BR1: Brom 1E 35 (5J 9)
Henry Tudor Ct. SE9 4H 5
Hensford Gdns. SE26 1G 7
Henson Cl. BR6: Farnb 6E 18
Henville Rd. BR1: Brom 2E 35 (5J 9)
Henwick Rd. SE9 1D 4
Hepburn Gdns. BR2: Hayes 5F 17
Herbert Rd. BR2: Brom 2A 18
BR8: Swan 1C 34
Heritage Hill BR2: Kes 2K 23
Hermitage Gdns. SE19 4B 6
Hermitage La. SE25 3F 15
(not continuous)
Hermitage Rd. SE19 4B 6
Heron Ct. BR2: Brom 1K 17
Heron Cres. DA14: Sidc 7K 5
Herongate Rd. BR8: Swan 3K 13
Heron Rd. CR0: Croy 6D 14
Herron Ct. BR2: Brom 1G 17
Hesiers Hill CR6: Warl 6A 28
Hesiers Rd. CR6: Warl 5A 28
Hetley Gdns. SE19 4E 6
Hever Cft. SE9 1D 10
Hever Gdns. BR1: Brom 6D 10
Hewett Pl. BR8: Swan 1J 21
Hewitt Cl. CR0: Croy 7B 16
Hewitts Rd. BR6: Chels 4E 26
HEWITTS RDBT. 5E 26
HEXTABLE 2A 34
Hextable Dance Cen. 5K 13
Hextable Heritage Cen. & Gardens 4K 13
Hibbs Cl. BR8: Swan 6J 13
Highams Hill CR6: Big H 1C 28
Highbarrow Rd. CR0: Croy 5F 15
High Beeches BR6: Chels 3K 25
DA14: Sidc 2D 12
High Broom Cres. BR4: W W'ck 4C 16
Highbury Av. CR7: Thor H 6A 6
Highbury Cl. BR4: W W'ck 6C 16
Highclere St. SE26 1K 7
Highcombe Cl. SE9 5C 4

High Cft. Cotts. BR8: Swan 6B **34**
High Elms Country Pk. 4G 25
High Elms Nature Cen. 4G 25
High Elms Rd. BR6: Downe 7D **24**
Highfield Av. BR6: Chels 2J **25**
Highfield Cotts. DA2: Dart 1C **34**
Highfield Dr. BR2: Brom 1F **17**
BR4: W W'ck 6C **16**
Highfield Hill SE19 . . . . 4C **6**
Highfield Rd. BR1: Brom 1C **18**
BR7: Chst 7J **11**
TN16: Big H 6E **28**
High Firs BR8: Swan 1K **21**
High Gables BR2: Brom 6F **9**
Highgate Ho. SE26 . . . . 1F **7**
High Gro. BR1: Brom 5A **10**
Highgrove Cl. BR7: Chst 5B **10**
Highgrove Ct. BR3: Beck 4B **8**
High Hill Rd. CR6: Warl 3A **28**
(not continuous)
Highland Cft. BR3: Beck 2C **8**
Highland Rd. BR1: Brom 1A **35** (5G **9**)
BR2: Brom 4F **9**
SE19 . . . . 3D **6**
TN14: Hals 6G **27**
Highlands Ct. SE19 . . . . 3D **6**
Highlands Farm Bus. Pk. BR8: Swan 3B **34**
Highlands Hill BR8: Swan 3B **34**
Highlands Rd. BR5: Orp 4A **20**
High Level Dr. SE26 . . . . 1F **7**
High Mead BR4: W W'ck 6E **16**
High Point SE9 . . . . 7G **5**
High St. BR1: Brom 3B **35** (6H **9**)
BR3: Beck 6B **8**
BR4: W W'ck 5C **16**
BR5: St M Cry 3B **20**
(not continuous)
BR6: Chels 4J **25**
BR6: Downe 7D **24**
BR6: Farnb 2E **24**
BR6: Orp 6K **19**
BR7: Chst 3E **10**
BR8: Swan 5A **34**
CR0: Croy 6B **14**
(not continuous)
CR7: Thor H 1B **14**
SE20 . . . . 3H **7**
SE25 . . . . 1E **14**
High Tor Cl. BR1: Brom 1D **35** (4J **9**)
High Trees CR0: Croy 5K **15**
High Vw. Cl. SE19 . . . . 6E **6**
High Vw. Rd. BR6: Downe 6D **24**
DA14: Sidc 1A **12**
Highview Rd. SE19 . . . . 3C **6**
Highway, The BR6: Chels 2A **26**
Highwood BR2: Brom 7E **8**
Highwood Cl. BR6: Farnb 6F **19**
Highwood Dr. BR6: Farnb 6F **19**
Hilborough Way BR6: Farnb 2G **25**
Hilda May Av. BR8: Swan 7K **13**
Hilda Va. Cl. BR6: Farnb 1E **24**
Hilda Va. Rd. BR6: Farnb 1D **24**
Hildenborough Gdns. BR1: Brom 3F **9**
Hildenborough Ho. *BR3: Beck 4A **8***
(off Bethersden Cl.)
Hildenlea Pl. BR2: Brom 6E **8**
Hill Brow BR1: Brom 5A **10**
Hill Brow Cl. DA5: Bexl 1J **13**
Hillbrow Rd. BR1: Brom 4F **9**
Hill Cl. BR7: Chst 2E **10**
Hillcrest Cl. BR3: Beck 3A **16**
SE26 . . . . 1F **7**
Hillcrest Rd. BR1: Brom 2H **9**
BR6: Chels 6K **19**
TN16: Big H 5F **29**
Hillcrest Vw. BR3: Beck 3A **16**
Hilldown Rd. BR2: Hayes 5F **17**
Hilldrop Rd. BR1: Brom 3J **9**
Hill End BR6: Orp 6J **19**
Hill Ho. BR2: Brom 3A **35** (6G **9**)
Hill Ho. M. BR2: Brom 3A **35** (6G **9**)
Hillingdale TN16: Big H 7D **28**
Hillmore Gro. SE26 . . . . 2K **7**
HILL PARK **5G 33**
Hillside, The BR6: Prat B 5A **26**
Hillside Ct. BR8: Swan 6B **34**
Hillside Ho. *CR0: Wadd 7A **14***
(off Violet La.)
Hillside La. BR2: Hayes 6G **17**
(not continuous)
Hillside Rd. BR2: Brom 7G **9**
CR0: Wadd 7A **14**
Hillside Rd. TN16: Tats 1D **32**
Hilltop Gdns. BR6: Orp 6H **19**
Hill Vw. Cres. BR6: Orp 5H **19**
Hill Vw. Rd. BR6: Orp 5J **19**
Hillview Rd. BR7: Chst 2D **10**
Hillworth BR3: Beck 6C **8**
Hinton Cl. SE9 . . . . 5D **4**
Hitherwood Dr. SE19 . . . . 1E **6**
Hobart Gdns. CR7: Thor H 7C **6**
Hobbs Rd. SE27 . . . . 1B **6**
Hoblands End BR7: Chst 3H **11**
HOCKENDEN **7F 13**
Hockenden La. BR8: Swan 7F **13**
Hodsoll Ct. BR5: St M Cry 2C **20**
Hodson Cres. BR5: St M Cry 2C **20**
Hoever Ho. SE6 . . . . 1D **8**
Hogarth Ct. SE19 . . . . 1E **6**
Hogarth Cres. CR0: Croy 4B **14**
Hogs Orchard BR8: Swan 3C **34**
Holbeach Gdns. DA15: Sidc 3K **5**
Holbrook Ho. BR7: Chst 5G **11**
Holbrook La. BR7: Chst 4G **11**
Holbrook Way BR2: Brom 3C **18**
Holderness Way SE27 . . . . 2A **6**
Holland Cl. BR2: Hayes 6G **17**
Holland Dr. SE23 . . . . 1K **7**
Holland Rd. SE25 . . . . 2F **15**
Holland Way BR2: Hayes 6G **17**
Hollies Av. DA15: Sidc 6K **5**
Hollies Cl. SW16 . . . . 3A **6**
Holligrave Rd. BR1: Brom 1C **35** (5H **9**)
Hollington Ct. BR7: Chst 3E **10**
Hollingworth Rd. BR5: Pet W 3E **18**
Hollman Gdns. SW16 . . . . 3A **6**
Hollybrake Cl. BR7: Chst 4G **11**
Holly Bush La. BR6: Chels 3F **27**
Holly Cl. BR3: Beck 1D **16**
Holly Ct. *DA14: Sidc 1A **12***
(off Sidcup Hill)
Holly Cres. BR3: Beck 2A **16**
Hollydale Dr. BR2: Brom 7C **18**
Hollydene BR2: Brom 2A **35**
Holly Rd. BR6: Chels 4K **25**
Hollytree Av. BR8: Swan 6K **13**
Hollytree Pde. *DA14: Sidc 3B **12***
(off Sidcup Hill)
Hollywoods CR0: Sels 5A **22**
Holmbury Gro. CR0: Sels 4A **22**
Holmbury Mnr. DA14: Sidc 1K **11**
Holmbury Pk. BR1: Brom 4B **10**
Holm Ct. SE12 . . . . 7A **4**
Holmcroft Way BR2: Brom 2C **18**
Holmdale Rd. BR7: Chst 2F **11**
Holmdene Cl. BR3: Beck 6D **8**
Holmdene Ct. BR1: Brom 7B **10**
Holmesdale Cl. SE25 . . . . 7E **6**
Holmesdale Rd. CR0: Croy 2C **14**
SE25 . . . . 2C **14**
Holmes Place Health Club
Bromley 1A 18
Croydon 7B 14
Holmewood Rd. SE25 . . . . 7D **6**
Holmlea Ct. *CR0: Croy 7C **14***
(off Chatsworth Rd.)
Holmoaks Ho. BR3: Beck 6D **8**
Holmshaw Cl. SE26 . . . . 1K **7**
Holwood Pk. Av. BR6: Farnb 1C **24**
Holywell Cl. BR6: Chels 1K **25**
Homecroft Rd. SE26 . . . . 2H **7**
Home Farm BR6: Chels 2F **27**
Homefield Cl. BR5: St P 1A **20**
BR8: Swan 5A **34**
Homefield Ho. SE23 . . . . 1J **7**
Homefield M. BR3: Beck 5B **8**
Homefield Ri. BR6: Orp 5K **19**
Homefield Rd. BR1: Brom 2E **35** (5K **9**)
Home Hill BR8: Swan 2A **34**
Homelands Dr. SE19 . . . . 4D **6**
Home Lea BR6: Chels 2J **25**
Homemead Rd. BR2: Brom 2C **18**
Homer Rd. CR0: Croy 3J **15**
Homesdale Rd. BR1: Brom 7K **9**
BR2: Brom 7E **35** (1K **17**)
BR5: Pet W 4H **19**
Homestead Rd. BR6: Chels 4A **26**
Homestead Way CR0: New Ad . . . . 7D **22** & 7E **22**
Homewood Cres. BR7: Chst 3H **11**
Homildon Ho. SE26 . . . . 1F **7**
Honeybourne Way BR5: Pet W 5G **19**
Honeyden Rd. DA14: Sidc 3D **12**
Honeyfield BR8: Swan 1A **34**
Honeysuckle Gdns. CR0: Croy 4J **15**
Hood Av. BR5: St M Cry 2A **20**
Hood Cl. CR0: Croy 5A **14**
Hook Farm Rd. BR2: Brom 2A **18**
Hook La. DA16: Well 2K **5**
Hookwood Cotts. BR6: Prat B 7B **26**
Hookwood Rd. BR6: Prat B 7B **26**
Hope Cl. SE12 . . . . 7A **4**
Hope Ho. *CR0: Croy 7D **14***
(off Steep Hill)
Hope Pk. BR1: Brom 1A **35** (4G **9**)
Hopton Ct. BR2: Hayes 5J **17**
Horizon Ho. BR8: Swan 1K **21**
Horley Rd. SE9 . . . . 1B **10**
Hornbeam Way BR2: Brom 3D **18**
Horncastle Rd. SE12 . . . . 4A **4**
Horning Cl. SE9 . . . . 1B **10**
HORN PARK **2A 4**
Horn Pk. Cl. SE12 . . . . 2A **4**
Hornpark La. SE12 . . . . 2A **4**
HORNS GREEN **6C 30**
Horsa Rd. SE12 . . . . 4B **4**
Horsecroft Cl. BR6: Orp 5A **20**
Horsell Rd. BR5: St P 5A **12**
Horsfeld Gdns. SE9 . . . . 2D **4**
Horsfeld Rd. SE9 . . . . 2C **4**
Horsley Dr. CR0: New Ad 4D **22**
Horsley Rd. BR1: Brom 1D **35** (5J **9**)
Horsmonden Cl. BR6: Orp 4J **19**
Horton Pl. TN16: Westrm 7J **33**
Hortons Way TN16: Westrm 7J **33**
Horton Twr. *BR5: St M Cry 1B **20***
(off Harbledown Pl.)
Horton Way CR0: Croy 2J **15**
Hotham Cl. BR8: Swan 3C **34**
Howard Rd. BR1: Brom 1B **35** (4H **9**)
SE20 . . . . 5H **7**
SE25 . . . . 2F **15**
Howards Crest Cl. BR3: Beck 6D **8**
Howberry Rd. CR7: Thor H 5C **6**
Howden Rd. SE25 . . . . 6E **6**
Howley Rd. CR0: Croy 7A **14**
Hubbard Rd. SE27 . . . . 1B **6**
Hudson Gdns. BR6: Chels 3J **25**
Hughes Wlk. CR0: Croy 4B **14**
Hunter Rd. CR7: Thor H 7C **6**
Hunters Cl. DA5: Bexl 1K **13**
Hunters Gro. BR6: Farnb 1F **25**
Hunters Mdw. SE19 . . . . 1D **6**
Hunters Wlk. TN14: Knock 3J **31**
Hunter's Way CR0: Croy 7D **14**
Huntingfield CR0: Sels 4A **22**
Huntly Rd. SE25 . . . . 1D **14**
Huntsmead Cl. BR7: Chst 4C **10**
Hurlstone Rd. SE25 . . . . 2D **14**
Huron Cl. BR6: Chels 3H **25**
Hurst Cl. BR2: Hayes 5G **17**
Hurstdene Av. BR2: Hayes 5G **17**
Hurstfield BR2: Brom 2H **17**
Hurstwood Dr. BR1: Brom 7C **10**
Husseywell Cres. BR2: Hayes 5H **17**
Hutchingsons Rd.
CR0: New Ad 7D **22**
Hutchinson's Bank Nature Reserve 7D 22
Hyde Dr. BR5: St P 7A **12**
Hythe Cl. BR5: St M Cry 1B **20**
Hythe Rd. CR7: Thor H 6C **6**

I

Ickleton Rd. SE9 . . . . 1B **10**
Iden Cl. BR2: Brom 7F **9**
Ightham Ho. *BR3: Beck 4A **8***
(off Bethersden Cl.)
Ilfracombe Rd. BR1: Brom 1G **9**
Ilkley Cl. SE19 . . . . 3C **6**
Impact Ct. SE20 . . . . 6G **7**
Imperial Pl. BR7: Chst 5D **10**
Imperial Way BR7: Chst 7H **5**
Inca Dr. SE9 . . . . 4G **5**
Inchwood CR0: Addtn 1C **22**
Ingatestone Rd. SE25 . . . . 1G **15**
Ingleby Way BR7: Chst 2D **10**
Inglenorth Ct. BR8: Crock 3H **21**
Ingleside Cl. BR3: Beck 4B **8**
Inglewood BR8: Swan 6K **13**
Inglewood Copse
BR1: Brom 6B **10**
Inglis Rd. CR0: Croy 5E **14**
Ingram Rd. CR7: Thor H 5B **6**
Ingrebourne Ho. *BR1: Brom 2E **8***
(off Brangbourne Rd.)

Innes Yd. CR0: Croy 7B **14**
Innova Ct. CR0: Croy 5D **14**
Inspirations Way BR6: Orp 4K **19**
Invicta Cl. BR7: Chst 2D **10**
Invicta Pde. DA14: Sidc 1A **12**
Inwood Cl. CR0: Croy 6K **15**
Irene Rd. BR6: Orp 4J **19**
Iris Cl. CR0: Croy 5J **15**
Irvine Way BR6: Orp 4J **19**
Irving Way BR8: Swan 6J **13**
Isabella Dr. BR6: Farnb 1F **25**
Isard Ho. BR2: Hayes 5J **17**
Islehurst Cl. BR7: Chst 5D **10**
Iveagh Ct. BR3: Beck 7D **8**
Ivers Way CR0: New Ad 4C **22**
Ivor Gro. SE9 5G **5**
Ivorydown BR1: Brom 1H **9**
Ivybridge Ct. *BR7: Chst* *5D* ***10***
(off Old Hill)
Ivychurch Cl. SE20 4H **7**
Ivy La. TN14: Knock 5J **31**

J

Jackass La. BR2: Kes 2J **23**
Jackson Rd. BR2: Brom 6C **18**
Jacksons Pl. CR0: Croy 5C **14**
Jackson's Way CR0: Croy 7B **16**
Jaffray Pl. SE27 1A **6**
Jaffray Rd. BR2: Brom 1A **18**
Jail La. TN16: Big H 4F **29**
Jamaica Rd. CR7: Thor H 3A **14**
James Newman Ct. SE9 7F **5**
Jane Seymour Ct. SE9 4J **5**
Jasmine Cl. BR6: Farnb 6E **18**
Jasmine Gdns. CR0: Croy 7C **16**
Jasmine Gro. SE20 5G **7**
Jason Wlk. SE9 1D **10**
Jasper Pas. SE19 3E **6**
Jasper Rd. SE19 2E **6**
Jay Gdns. BR7: Chst 1C **10**
Jeffrey Row SE12 2A **4**
Jeken Rd. SE9 1B **4**
Jenner Cl. DA14: Sidc 1K **11**
Jenson Way SE19 4E **6**
Jersey Dr. BR5: Pet W 3G **19**
Jerviston Gdns. SW16 3A **6**
Jesmond Rd. CR0: Croy 4E **14**
Jevington Way SE12 5A **4**
Jewels Hill TN16: Big H 1C **28**
Jews' Wlk. SE26 1G **7**
Joan Cres. SE9 4C **4**
Joe Hunte Ct. SE27 2A **6**
John Baird Ct. SE26 1H **7**
Johnson Rd.
BR2: Brom 2A **18**
CR0: Croy 4C **14**
Johnson's Av. TN14: Hals 6G **27**
John's Rd. TN16: Tats 2C **32**
John's Ter. CR0: Croy 5D **14**
John St. SE25 1F **15**
JOYDENS WOOD **1J 13**
Joydens Wood (Nature Reserve) 1G 13
Joydens Wood Rd. DA5: Bexl 1J **13**
Jubilee Country Pk. 1E 18
Jubilee Ct. BR4: W W'ck 5D **16**
Jubilee Rd. BR6: Chels 3F **27**
Jug Hill TN16: Big H 5F **29**
Juglans Rd. BR6: Orp 5K **19**
Julian Ho. SE21 1D **6**
Julian Rd. BR6: Chels 3K **25**
Juniper Cl. TN16: Big H 6G **29**
Juniper Wlk. BR8: Swan 6J **13**

K

Kangley Bri. Rd. SE26 3A **8**
Kangley Bus. Cen. SE26 2A **8**
Karen Ct. BR1: Brom 1A **35** (5G **9**)
Katharine Ho. *CR0: Croy* *7B* ***14***
(off Katharine St.)
Katharine St. CR0: Croy 7B **14**
Katherine Gdns. SE9 1C **4**
Keats Way CR0: Croy 3H **15**
Kechill Gdns. BR2: Hayes 4H **17**
Kedleston Dr. BR5: St M Cry 3J **19**
Keedonwood Rd. BR1: Brom 2F **9**
Keeley Rd. CR0: Croy 6B **14**
Keeling Rd. SE9 2C **4**
Keens Rd. CR0: Croy 7B **14**
Keightley Dr. SE9 5H **5**
Keith Pk. Cres. TN16: Big H 1D **28**
Kelby Path SE9 7G **5**
Kelling Gdns. CR0: Croy 4A **14**
Kelsey Ga. BR3: Beck 6C **8**
Kelsey La. BR3: Beck 6B **8**
Kelsey Pk. Av. BR3: Beck 6C **8**
(not continuous)
Kelsey Pk. Rd. BR3: Beck 6B **8**
Kelsey Rd. BR5: St P 6A **12**
Kelsey Sq. BR3: Beck 6B **8**
Kelsey Way BR3: Beck 7B **8**
Kelvin Ct. SE20 5G **7**
Kelvin Gro. SE26 1G **7**
Kelvington Cl. CR0: Croy 4K **15**
Kelvin Pde. BR6: Orp 5H **19**
Kemble Dr. BR2: Brom 7B **18**
Kemble Rd. CR0: Wadd 7A **14**
Kembleside Rd. TN16: Big H 7E **28**
Kemerton Rd. BR3: Beck 6C **8**
CR0: Croy 4E **14**
Kemnal Rd. BR7: Chst 1G **11**
(not continuous)
Kemp Gdns. CR0: Croy 3B **14**
Kempton Wlk. CR0: Croy 3K **15**
Kemsing Cl. BR2: Hayes 6G **17**
CR7: Thor H 1B **14**
Kemsley Rd. TN16: Tats 1C **32**
Kendale Rd. BR1: Brom 2F **9**
Kendal Ho. *SE20* *6F* ***7***
(off Derwent Rd.)
Kendall Av. BR3: Beck 6K **7**
Kendall Lodge BR1: Brom 2D **35**
Kendall Rd. BR3: Beck 6K **7**
Kenilworth Rd. BR5: Pet W 3F **19**
SE20 5J **7**
Kenley Cl. BR7: Chst 7H **11**
Kenley Gdns. CR7: Thor H 1A **14**
Kennedy Cl. BR5: Pet W 5G **19**
Kennel Wood Cres. CR0: New Ad 7E **22**
Kennett Ct. *BR8: Swan* *7K* ***13***
(off Oakleigh Cl.)
Kensington Av. CR7: Thor H 5A **6**
Kent Cl. BR6: Chels 3H **25**
Kent Ga. Way CR0: Addtn 3A **22**
Kent Ho. App. Rd. BR3: Beck 5K **7**
Kent Ho. Rd. BR3: Beck 5J **7**
SE26 2K **7**
Kent House Station (Rail) **5K 7**
Kentish Way BR1: Brom 3D **35** (6J **9**)
BR2: Brom 6J **9**
Kenton Ct. *SE26* *1K* ***7***
(off Adamsrill Rd.)
Kentone Ct. SE25 1G **15**
Kent Rd. BR4: W W'ck 5C **16**
BR5: St M Cry 3A **20**
Kenward Rd. SE9 2B **4**
Kenwood Dr. BR3: Beck 7D **8**
Kersey Gdns. SE9 1B **10**
KESTON **2K 23**
Keston Av. BR2: Kes 2K **23**
Keston Gdns. BR2: Kes 1K **23**
KESTON MARK **1B 24**
KESTON MARK **7B 18**
Keston Pk. Cl. BR2: Kes 7C **18**
Kestrel Way CR0: New Ad 5E **22**
Keswick Ct. BR2: Brom 1G **17**
Keswick Rd. BR4: W W'ck 6F **17**
BR6: Orp 5J **19**
Kettering Ct. CR7: Thor H 1B **14**
Kettlewell Ct. BR8: Swan 4A **34**
KEVINGTON **3D 20**
Kevington Cl. BR5: St P 1J **19**
Kevington Dr. BR5: St P 1J **19**
BR7: Chst 1J **19**
Keymer Cl. TN16: Big H 5E **28**
Keynsham Gdns. SE9 2D **4**
Keynsham Rd. SE9 2C **4**
Keys Ct. *CR0: Croy* *7C* ***14***
(off Beech Ho. Rd.)
Kidbrooke Est. SE3 1B **4**
Kidbrooke La. SE9 1D **4**
Kidbrooke Pk. Rd. SE3 1A **4**
Kidbrooke Station Station (Rail) **1A 4**
Kidderminster Pl. CR0: Croy 5A **14**
Kidderminster Rd. CR0: Croy 5A **14**
Killewarren Way BR5: Orp 3B **20**
Killigarth Ct. DA14: Sidc 1K **11**
Kilmartin Av. SW16 7A **6**
Kilnfields BR6: Chels 3F **27**
Kilnwood TN14: Hals 2K **31**
Kimbell Pl. SE3 1B **4**
Kimberley Ga. BR1: Brom 4F **9**
Kimberley Rd. BR3: Beck 6J **7**
CR0: Croy 3A **14**
Kimmeridge Gdns. SE9 1B **10**
Kimmeridge Rd. SE9 1B **10**
King Alfred Av. SE6 1B **8**
(not continuous)
King & Queen Cl. SE9 1B **10**
Kingcup Cl. CR0: Croy 4J **15**
Kingfisher Cl. BR5: St P 1C **20**
Kingfisher Way BR3: Beck 2J **15**
King George VI Av. TN16: Big H 5F **29**
King Henry M. BR6: Chels 2J **25**
King Henry's Dr. CR0: New Ad 5C **22**
King Henry's Drive Stop (CT) **5C 22**
King John's Wlk. SE9 4D **4**
(not continuous)
Kingsand Rd. SE12 6A **4**
Kings Av. BR1: Brom 3G **9**
Kingscote Rd. CR0: Croy 4G **15**
Kingsdale Rd. SE20 4J **7**
Kingsdown Way BR2: Hayes 4H **17**
Kingsfield Ho. SE9 7C **4**
Kingsgate Cl. BR5: St P 6B **12**
Kingsground SE9 4C **4**
Kings Hall Rd. BR3: Beck 4K **7**
Kingsholm Gdns. SE9 1C **4**
Kingshurst Rd. SE12 4A **4**
Kings Keep BR2: Brom 6F **9**
Kingsleigh Wlk. BR2: Brom 7A **35**
Kingsley M. BR7: Chst 3E **10**
Kingsley Rd. BR6: Chels 4J **25**
Kingsley Wood Dr. SE9 7E **4**
Kingslyn Cres. SE19 5D **6**
Kingsmead TN16: Big H 5F **29**
Kingsmead Cotts. BR2: Brom 5B **18**
King's Orchard SE9 3D **4**
Kings Rd. BR6: Orp 1J **25**
SE25 7F **7**
TN16: Big H 5E **28**
Kingsthorpe Rd. SE26 1J **7**
Kingston Cres. BR3: Beck 5A **8**
Kingston Sq. SE19 2C **6**
Kingsway BR4: W W'ck 7F **17**
BR5: Pet W 2G **19**
Kingswood Av. BR2: Brom 7F **9**
BR8: Swan 6A **34**
CR7: Thor H 2A **14**
Kingswood Cl. BR6: Orp 4H **19**
Kingswood Dr. SE19 1D **6**
Kingswood Est. SE21 1D **6**
Kingswood Rd. BR2: Brom 1E **16**
SE20 3H **7**
Kingsworth Cl. BR3: Beck 2K **15**
King William IV Gdns. SE20 3H **7**
Kinnaird Av. BR1: Brom 3G **9**
Kinnaird Cl. BR1: Brom 3G **9**
Kinross Ct. *BR1: Brom* *5G* ***9***
(off Highland Rd.)
Kinver Rd. SE26 1H **7**
Kippington Dr. SE9 5C **4**
Kirkdale Cnr. SE26 1H **7**
Kirkland Cl. DA15: Sidc 3K **5**
Kirkland Ter. BR3: Beck 3B **8**
Kirkstone Way BR1: Brom 4F **9**
Kirtley Rd. SE26 1K **7**
Kitchener Rd. CR7: Thor H 7C **6**
Kitley Gdns. SE19 5E **6**
Knighton Pk. Rd. SE26 2J **7**
Knights Hill SE27 2A **6**
Knight's Hill Sq. SE27 1A **6**
Knights Ridge BR6: Chels 2A **26**
KNOCKHOLT **6F 31**
Knockholt Main Rd. TN14: Knock 7D **30**
KNOCKHOLT POUND **4J 31**
Knockholt Rd. SE9 2C **4**
TN14: Hals 3K **31**
Knockholt Station (Rail) **5D 26**
Knole, The SE9 1D **10**
Knole Cl. CR0: Croy 3H **15**
Knole Ga. DA15: Sidc 7K **5**
Knoll, The BR2: Hayes 6H **17**
BR3: Beck 5C **8**
Knoll Ri. BR6: Orp 5J **19**
Knoll Rd. DA14: Sidc 2A **12**
Knowle Rd. BR2: Brom 6C **18**
Knowlton Grn. BR2: Brom 2G **17**
Koonowla Cl. TN16: Big H 4F **29**
Kydbrook Cl. BR5: Pet W 4F **19**
Kynaston Av. CR7: Thor H 2B **14**
Kynaston Cres.
CR7: Thor H 2B **14**

Kynaston Rd. BR1: Brom 2H 9
BR5: Orp 4A 20
CR7: Thor H 2B 14

L

Laburnum Av. BR8: Swan 7H 13
Laburnum Gdns. CR0: Croy 4J 15
Laburnum Ho. BR2: Brom 5E 8
Laburnum Pl. SE9 2F 5
Laburnum Way BR2: Brom 4D 18
Ladas Rd. SE27 1B 6
Ladbrooke Cres. DA14: Sidc 1C 12
Ladbrook Rd. SE25 1C 14
Ladds Way BR8: Swan 1J 21
Ladycroft Gdns. BR6: Farnb 2F 25
Ladycroft Way BR6: Farnb 2F 25
Ladysmith Rd. SE9 3F 5
Ladywood Av. BR5: Pet W 2H 19
LA Fitness
Bromley 3C 35
Sydenham 1H 7
Lagoon Rd. BR5: St M Cry 2B 20
Lait Ho. BR3: Beck 5C 8
Lake Av. BR1: Brom 3H 9
Lakefield Cl. SE20 4G 7
Lakehall Gdns. CR7: Thor H 2A 14
Lakehall Rd. CR7: Thor H 2A 14
Laker Ind. Est. *BR3* *2K 7*
(off Kent Ho. La.)
Lake Rd. CR0: Croy 6A 16
Lakeside BR3: Beck 7C 8
Lakeside Cl. SE25 6F 7
Lakeside Dr. BR2: Brom 7B 18
Lakes Rd. BR2: Kes 2K 23
Lakeswood Rd. BR5: Pet W 3E 18
Lakeview Rd. SE27 2A 6
Lambarde Av. SE9 1D 10
Lambardes Cl. BR6: Prat B 7B 26
Lamberhurst Cl. BR5: Orp 5C 20
Lamberhurst Rd. SE27 1A 6
Lambert Cl. TN16: Big H 5F 29
Lambert's Pl. CR0: Croy 5C 14
Lambeth Rd. CR0: Croy 4A 14
Lambscroft Av. SE9 7B 4
Lamerock Rd. BR1: Brom 1G 9
Lamorbey Cl. DA15: Sidc 5K 5
Lamorna Cl. BR6: Orp 4K 19
Lancaster Cl. BR2: Brom 1G 17
Lancaster Gdns. BR1: Brom 2B 18
Lancaster Rd. SE25 6E 6
Lancelot Ct. BR6: Orp 6A 20
Lancing Ho. *CR0: Croy* *7C 14*
(off Coombe Rd.)
Lancing Rd. BR6: Orp 6K 19
Landway, The BR5: St P 7B 12
Laneside BR7: Chst 2E 10
Langdale Cl. BR6: Farnb 7E 18
Langdale Rd. CR7: Thor H 1A 14
Langdon Rd. BR2: Brom 6D 35 (7J 9)
Langdon Shaw DA14: Sidc 2J 11
Langford Pl. DA14: Sidc 1K 11
Langham Pk. Pl. BR2: Brom 1G 17
Langland Gdns. CR0: Croy 6A 16
Langley Gdns. BR2: Brom 1K 17
BR5: Pet W 3E 18
Langley Pk. Girls School Sports Cen. 3D 16
Langley Rd. BR3: Beck 1K 15
Langley Way BR4: W W'ck 5E 16
Langmead St. SE27 1A 6
Langthorne Ct. BR1: Brom 1D 8
Langton Way CR0: Croy 7D 14
Lankton Cl. BR3: Beck 5D 8
Lannoy Rd. SE9 5H 5
Lansdowne Av. BR6: Farnb 5E 18
Lansdowne Pl. SE19 4E 6
Lansdowne Rd. BR1: Brom 4H 9
CR0: Croy 6C 14
Lapworth Cl. BR6: Chels 6B 20
Larch Dene BR6: Farnb 6D 18
Larch Ho. BR2: Brom 5F 9
Larch Tree Way CR0: Croy 7B 16
Larch Wlk. BR8: Swan 6J 13
Larch Way BR2: Brom 4D 18
Larchwood Rd. SE9 6G 5
Larkbere Rd. SE26 1K 7
Larkfield Cl. BR2: Hayes 6G 17
Larkfield Rd. DA14: Sidc 7K 5
Larkspur Cl. BR6: Chels 6B 20
Larkspur Lodge DA14: Sidc 1A 12
Lassa Rd. SE9 2D 4

Latham Cl. TN16: Big H 5E 28
Lathkill Ct. BR3: Beck 5A 8
Latimer Ct. BR2: Brom 7A 35
Latimer Rd. CR0: Croy 7A 14
La Tourne Gdns. BR6: Farnb 7F 19
Laud St. CR0: Croy 7B 14
Launcelot Rd. BR1: Brom 1H 9
Laura Dr. BR8: Swan 2B 34
Laurel Cres. CR0: Croy 7B 16
Laurel Gdns. BR1: Brom 1B 18
Laurel Gro. SE20 4G 7
SE26 1J 7
Laurel Ho. BR2: Brom 5F 9
Laurels, The BR1: Brom 2E 35 (5J 9)
BR2: Brom 7B 35 (1H 17)
Laurier Rd. CR0: Croy 4E 14
Lavender Cl. BR2: Brom 3B 18
Lavender Hill BR8: Swan 7J 13
Lavender Way CR0: Croy 3J 15
Lavidge Rd. SE9 6D 4
Lavisham Ho. BR1: Brom 2H 9
Lawn Cl. BR1: Brom 3J 9
BR8: Swan 6H 13
Lawn Rd. BR3: Beck 4A 8
Lawns, The DA14: Sidc 1A 12
SE19 5C 6
Lawrence Rd. BR4: W W'ck 1H 23
SE25 1E 14
Lawrie Pk. Av. SE26 2G 7
Lawrie Pk. Cres. SE26 2G 7
Lawrie Pk. Gdns. SE26 1G 7
Lawrie Pk. Rd. SE26 3G 7
Laws Cl. SE25 1C 14
Laxey Rd. BR6: Chels 3J 25
Laxton Ct. CR7: Thor H 1B 14
Layard Rd. CR7: Thor H 6C 6
Layhams Rd. BR2: Kes 7E 16
BR4: W W'ck 7E 16
CR6: Big H 1B 28
Layzell Wlk. SE9 5C 4
Leafield Cl. SW16 3A 6
Leafield La. DA14: Sidc 1E 12
Leafy Gro. BR2: Kes 2K 23
Leafy Oak Rd. SE12 1K 9
Leafy Way CR0: Croy 6E 14
Leamington Av. BR1: Brom 2K 9
BR6: Orp 1H 25
Leamington Cl. BR1: Brom 1K 9
Lea Rd. BR3: Beck 6B 8
Leas Dale SE9 7F 5
Leas Grn. BR7: Chst 3J 11
Leaveland Cl. BR3: Beck 1B 16
LEAVES GREEN 7A 24
Leaves Grn. Cres. BR2: Kes 7K 23
Leaves Grn. Rd. BR2: Kes 7A 24
Lebanon Gdns. TN16: Big H 6F 29
Lebanon Rd. CR0: Croy 5D 14
Lebanon Road Stop (CT) 6D 14
Lebrun Sq. SE3 1A 4
Le Chateau *CR0: Croy* *7C 14*
(off Chatsworth Rd.)
Leclair Ho. SE3 1A 4
Ledrington Rd. SE19 3F 7
Leechcroft Av. BR8: Swan 5A 34
Leeds Cl. BR6: Chels 6C 20
Lee Grn. BR5: St M Cry 2K 19
Lee M. BR3: Beck 7K 7
Lees, The CR0: Croy 6A 16
Leesons Hill BR5: St P 7H 11
BR7: Chst 7H 11
Leeson's Way BR5: St P 6J 11
Leewood Pl. BR8: Swan 1J 21
Lefa Bus. & Ind. Est. DA14: Sidc 3C 12
Legatt Rd. SE9 2C 4
Leicester Rd. CR0: Croy 4D 14
Leigh Cres. CR0: New Ad 4C 22
Leigh Ter. BR5: St P 7A 12
Leighton Gdns. CR0: Croy 5A 14
Leighton St. CR0: Croy 5A 14
Leith Hill BR5: St P 5K 11
Leith Hill Grn. BR5: St P 5K 11
Le May Av. SE12 7A 4
Lemonwell Dr. SE9 2H 5
Lenham Rd. CR7: Thor H 6C 6
Lennard Av. BR4: W W'ck 6F 17
Lennard Cl. BR4: W W'ck 6F 17
Lennard Rd. BR2: Brom 5C 18
BR3: Beck 3J 7
CR0: Croy 5B 14
SE20 3J 7
Lentmead Rd. BR1: Brom 1G 9
Leof Cres. SE6 2C 8

Lesley Cl. BR8: Swan 7J 13
Leslie Gro. CR0: Croy 5D 14
Leslie Gro. Pl. CR0: Croy 5D 14
Leslie Pk. Rd. CR0: Croy 5D 14
Lestock Cl. *SE25* *7F 7*
(off Manor Rd.)
Letchworth Cl. BR2: Brom 2H 17
Letchworth Dr. BR2: Brom 2H 17
LETT'S GREEN 5D 30
Levehurst Ho. SE27 2B 6
Leveret Cl. CR0: New Ad 7E 22
Leverholme Gdns. SE9 7F 5
Lewes Rd. BR1: Brom 6A 10
Lewing Cl. BR6: Orp 5H 19
Lewis Sports and Leisure Cen. 5E 6
Leybourne Cl. BR2: Brom 3H 17
Leyburn Gdns. CR0: Croy 6D 14
Leydenhatch La. BR8: Dart, Swan 5H 13
Leyhill Cl. BR8: Swan 2K 21
Leysdown Rd. SE9 6D 4
Lezayre Rd. BR6: Chels 3J 25
Library and Lifetime Mus. *7B 14*
(off High St.)
Lichlade Cl. BR6: Orp 1J 25
Liddon Rd. BR1: Brom 7K 9
Lilac Gdns. BR8: Swan 7J 13
CR0: Croy 7B 16
Lilah M. BR2: Brom 6G 9
Lila Pl. BR8: Swan 1K 21
Lilburne Gdns. SE9 2D 4
Lilburne Rd. SE9 2D 4
Lilian Barker Cl. SE12 2A 4
Lillie Rd. TN16: Big H 7F 29
Lilliput Ct. SE12 2A 4
Lime Cl. BR1: Brom 1B 18
Lime Ct. SE9 6G 5
Lime Gro. BR6: Farnb 6E 18
Limekiln Pl. SE19 4E 6
Lime Rd. BR8: Swan 7J 13
Limes, The BR2: Brom 6B 18
Limes Av. SE20 4G 7
Limes Pl. CR0: Croy 4C 14
Limes Rd. BR3: Beck 6C 8
CR0: Croy 4C 14
Limes Row BR6: Farnb 2E 24
Lime Tree Gro. CR0: Croy 7A 16
Lime Tree Wlk. BR4: W W'ck 1G 23
Limewood Cl. BR3: Beck 2D 16
Lincoln Cl. SE25 3F 15
Lincoln Ct. SE12 7B 4
Lincoln Grn. Rd. BR5: St M Cry 2J 19
Lincoln Rd. DA14: Sidc 2A 12
SE25 7G 7
Linden Av. CR7: Thor H 1A 14
Linden Cl. BR6: Chels 2K 25
Linden Ct. DA14: Sidc 1H 11
Lindenfield BR7: Chst 6E 10
Linden Leas BR4: W W'ck 6E 16
Lindens, The CR0: New Ad 3D 22
Lindfield Rd. CR0: Croy 3E 14
Lindsay Ct. *CR0: Croy* *7C 14*
(off Eden Rd.)
Lindsey Cl. BR1: Brom 7A 10
Lindway SE27 2A 6
Lingfield Cres. SE9 1J 5
Link, The *SE9* *7F 5*
(off William Barefoot Dr.)
Linkfield BR2: Hayes 3H 17
Links Rd. BR4: W W'ck 5D 16
Links Vw. Rd. CR0: Croy 7B 16
Links Way BR3: Beck 3B 16
Link Way BR2: Brom 4B 18
Linslade Rd. BR6: Chels 3K 25
Linsted Ct. SE9 3K 5
Linton Glade CR0: Sels 6A 22
(not continuous)
Linton Gro. SE27 2A 6
Lionel Gdns. SE9 2C 4
Lionel Rd. SE9 2C 4
Lion Rd. CR0: Croy 2B 14
Lions Cl. SE9 7C 4
Liskeard Cl. BR7: Chst 3F 11
Little Acre BR3: Beck 7B 8
Little Birches DA15: Sidc 6K 5
Little Bornes SE21 1D 6
Littlebrook Cl. CR0: Croy 3J 15
Little Ct. BR4: W W'ck 6F 17
Littlejohn Rd.
BR5: St M Cry 3K 19
Littlemede SE9 7E 4
Little Redlands BR1: Brom 6B 10
Littlestone Cl. BR3: Beck 3B 8

Little Theatre, The 2B 35 (5H 9)
Little Thrift BR5: Pet W 1F 19
Lit. Wood Cl. BR5: St P 5K 11
Liverpool Rd. CR7: Thor H 7B 6
Livingstone Rd. CR7: Thor H 6B 6
Llewellyn Ct. SE20 5H 7
Lloyd Ho. BR3: Beck 3C 8
Lloyds Way BR3: Beck 2K 15
Lockesley Dr. BR5: St M Cry 3J 19
Lockie Pl. SE25 7F 7
LOCKSBOTTOM 7D 18
Lockwood Cl. SE26 1J 7
Lodge Cl. BR6: Orp 5A 20
Lodge Cres. BR6: Orp 5A 20
Lodge Gdns. BR3: Beck 2A 16
Lodge La. CR0: New Ad 3B 22
Lodge Rd. BR1: Brom 4K 9
CR0: Croy 3A 14
Logs Hill BR1: Brom 4B 10
BR7: Chst 4B 10
Logs Hill Cl. BR7: Chst 5B 10
Lomas Cl. CR0: New Ad 4D 22
LONDON - BIGGIN HILL AIRPORT 1E 28
London La. BR1: Brom 4G 9
London Rd. BR1: Brom 1A 35 (4G 9)
BR8: Swan 5H 13
(Birchwood Rd.)
BR8: Swan 6A 34
(High St.)
CR0: Croy 2A 14
TN14: Hals 5E 26
(not continuous)
TN16: Westrm 5H 33
London Towers Basketball
(Crystal Palace National Sports Cen.) 3F 7
Long Acre BR6: Orp 6C 20
Longbury Cl. BR5: St P 7A 12
Longbury Dr. BR5: St P 7A 12
Longcroft SE9 7E 4
Longdon Wood BR2: Kes 7B 18
Longdown Rd. SE6 1B 8
Longfield BR1: Brom 1A 35 (5G 9)
Longford Ho. *BR1: Brom* *2E 8*
(off Brangbourne Rd.)
Longheath Gdns. CR0: Croy 2H 15
Longhedge Ho. *SE26* *1F 7*
(off High Level Dr.)
Longhill Rd. SE6 1E 8
Longhurst Rd. CR0: Croy 3G 15
LONGLANDS 7H 5
Longlands Pk. Cres.
DA15: Sidc 7K 5
Longlands Rd. DA15: Sidc 7K 5
Long La. CR0: Croy 3G 15
Longleat M. BR5: St M Cry 1B 20
Longley Rd. CR0: Croy 4A 14
Longmead BR7: Chst 6D 10
Longmead Ho. SE27 2B 6
Long Mdw. Cl. BR4: W W'ck 4D 16
Longmeadow Rd. DA15: Sidc 5K 5
Longton Av. SE26 1F 7
Longton Gro. SE26 1G 7
Lonsdale Cl. SE9 7C 4
Lonsdale Rd. SE25 1G 15
Loop Rd. BR7: Chst 3F 11
Loraine Ct. BR7: Chst 2E 10
Lorne Av. CR0: Croy 4J 15
Lorne Gdns. CR0: Croy 4J 15
Lotus Rd. TN16: Big H 7H 29
Louis Gdns. BR7: Chst 1C 10
Lovelace Av. BR2: Brom 3D 18
Lovelace Grn. SE9 1E 4
Love La. BR1: Brom 6D 35
(Elmfield Rd.)
BR1: Brom 4D 35 (7J 9)
(Rafford Way)
SE25 7G 7
(not continuous)
Lovibonds Av. BR6: Farnb 1E 24
Low Cross Wood La. SE21 1E 6
Lwr. Addiscombe Rd. CR0: Croy 5D 14
Lower Camden BR7: Chst 4C 10
Lwr. Church St. CR0: Croy 6A 14
Lwr. Coombe St. CR0: Croy 7B 14
Lower Cft. BR8: Swan 6A 34
Lwr. Drayton Pl. CR0: Croy 6A 14
Lwr. Gravel Rd. BR2: Brom 5B 18
Lower Rd. BR5: St M Cry 3A 20
BR8: Swan 2A 34
LOWER SYDENHAM 1J 7
Lwr. Sydenham Ind. Est. SE26 2A 8
Lower Sydenham Station (Rail) 2A 8
Lower Ter. *SE27* *2A 6*
(off Woodcote Pl.)
Lownds Ct. BR1: Brom 3C 35 (6H 9)
Loxley Cl. SE26 2J 7
Loxwood Cl. BR5: Orp 6C 20
Lubbock Rd. BR7: Chst 4C 10
Lucas Ct. SE26 2K 7
Lucas Rd. SE20 3H 7
Lucerne Rd. BR6: Orp 5J 19
CR7: Thor H 2A 14
Ludford Cl. CR0: Wadd 7A 14
Ludlow Cl. BR2: Brom 6B 35 (7H 9)
Luffman Rd. SE12 7A 4
Lullarook Cl. TN16: Big H 5E 28
Lullingstone Av. BR8: Swan 5A 34
Lullingstone Cl. BR5: St P 4A 12
Lullingstone Cres. BR5: St P 4K 11
Lullington Gth. BR1: Brom 4F 9
Lullington Rd. SE20 4F 7
Lulworth Rd. SE9 6D 4
Lunar Cl. TN16: Big H 5F 29
Luna Rd. CR7: Thor H 7B 6
Lunham Rd. SE19 3D 6
Lupin Cl. CR0: Croy 5J 15
Lupton Cl. SE12 7A 4
Luscombe Ct. BR2: Brom 6F 9
Lushington Rd. SE6 1C 8
Lusted Hall La. TN16: Big H, Tats 2B 32
Luxfield Rd. SE9 5D 4
LUXTED 3J 29
Luxted Rd. BR6: Downe 1J 29
Lyall Av. SE21 1D 6
Lych Ga. Rd. BR6: Orp 5K 19
Lyconby Gdns. CR0: Croy 4K 15
Lydd Cl. DA14: Sidc 7K 5
Lydden Ct. SE9 3K 5
Lydstep Rd. BR7: Chst 1D 10
Lyme Farm Rd. SE12 1A 4
Lymer Av. SE19 2E 6
Lyminge Cl. DA14: Sidc 1J 11
Lynden Hyrst CR0: Croy 6E 14
Lynden Way BR8: Swan 7H 13
Lyndhurst Cl. BR6: Farnb 1E 24
CR0: Croy 7E 14
Lyndhurst Rd. CR7: Thor H 1A 14
Lynmouth Ri. BR5: St M Cry 1A 20
Lynne Cl. BR6: Chels 3J 25
Lynstead Ct. BR3: Beck 6K 7
Lynsted Cl. BR1: Brom 6K 9
Lynsted Gdns. SE9 1C 4
Lynton Av. BR5: St M Cry 1A 20
Lynwood Gro. BR6: Orp 4H 19
Lyoth Rd. BR5: Farnb 6F 19
Lyric M. SE26 1H 7
Lysander Way BR6: Farnb 7F 19
Lytchet Rd. BR1: Brom 4H 9

M

Mabel Rd. BR8: Swan 1B 34
Maberley Cres. SE19 4F 7
Maberley Rd. BR3: Beck 7J 7
SE19 5E 6
McAuley Cl. SE9 2G 5
Macclesfield Rd. SE25 2H 15
Mace La. TN14: Cud 2B 30
Mackenzie Rd. BR3: Beck 6H 7
McKillop Way DA14: Sidc 4B 12
Madan Cl. TN16: Westrm 7K 33
Madan Rd. TN16: Westrm 7J 33
Mada Rd. BR6: Farnb 7E 18
Maddocks Cl. DA14: Sidc 2D 12
Madeira Av. BR1: Brom 4F 9
Madeline Rd. SE20 4F 7
Madison Gdns. BR2: Brom 6A 35 (7G 9)
Maesmaur Rd. TN16: Tats 3C 32
Magdalen Gro. BR6: Chels 1A 26
Magnolia Dr. TN16: Big H 5F 29
Magpie Hall Cl. BR2: Brom 3B 18
Magpie Hall La. BR2: Brom 2C 18
Maidstone Rd. DA14: Sidc, Swan 3C 12
Mainridge Rd. BR7: Chst 1D 10
Main Rd. BR2: Kes 2E 28
BR5: St P 5B 12
BR8: Crock 3J 21
BR8: Swan 2A 34
DA14: Sidc 7J 5
TN16: Big H, Westrm 2E 28
Main Rd. Cotts. BR6: Prat B 5B 26
Maitland Rd. SE26 3J 7
Malan Cl. TN16: Big H 6G 29
Malcolm Rd. SE20 4H 7
SE25 3F 15
Malden Av. SE25 1G 15
Malibu Ct. SE26 1G 7
Mall, The BR1: Brom 5C 35 (7H 9)
BR8: Swan 7K 13
CR0: Croy 6B 14
Mallard Wlk. BR3: Beck 2J 15
DA14: Sidc 3B 12
Malling Cl. CR0: Croy 3H 15
Malling Way BR2: Hayes 4G 17
Mallow Cl. CR0: Croy 5J 15
Malmains Cl. BR3: Beck 1E 16
Malmains Way BR3: Beck 1D 16
Malory Cl. BR3: Beck 6K 7
Maltby Cl. BR6: Orp 5K 19
Maltings, The BR6: Orp 5J 19
Malvern Cl. SE20 6F 7
Malvern Rd. BR6: Chels 1A 26
CR7: Thor H 1A 14
Malyons Rd. BR8: Swan 2A 34
Manchester Rd. CR7: Thor H 7B 6
Manitoba Gdns. BR6: Chels 3J 25
Mann Cl. CR0: Croy 7B 14
Manning Rd. BR5: St M Cry 2C 20
Manor Brook SE3 1A 4
Manor Ct. BR4: W W'ck 5C 16
Manorfields Cl. BR7: Chst 7J 11
Manor Gro. BR3: Beck 6C 8
Manor Pk. BR7: Chst 6G 11
Manor Pk. Cl. BR4: W W'ck 5C 16
Manor Pk. Rd. BR4: W W'ck 5C 16
BR7: Chst 5F 11
Manor Pl. BR7: Chst 6G 11
Manor Rd. BR3: Beck 6C 8
BR4: W W'ck 6C 16
SE25 1F 15
TN16: Tats 2D 32
Manor Way BR2: Brom 3B 18
BR3: Beck 6B 8
BR5: Pet W 1F 19
SE3 1A 4
Manse Pde. BR8: Swan 6B 34
Manse Way BR8: Swan 6B 34
Mansfield Cl. BR5: St M Cry 4C 20
Mansfield Rd. BR8: Swan 3K 13
Manston Cl. SE20 5H 7
Maple Cl. BR5: Pet W 2G 19
BR8: Swan 6K 13
Maple Ct. *CR0: Croy* *7B 14*
(off Lwr. Coombe St.)
Mapledale Av. CR0: Croy 6F 15
Mapledene BR7: Chst 2F 11
Maplehurst BR2: Brom 6F 9
Mapleleaf Cl. TN16: Big H 5F 29
Maple Leaf Dr. DA15: Sidc 5K 5
Maple Rd. SE20 5G 7
Maplethorpe Rd. CR7: Thor H 1A 14
Mapleton Cl. BR2: Brom 3H 17
Marbrook Ct. SE12 7B 4
Marcellina Way BR6: Orp 7H 19
Mardell Rd. CR0: Croy 2J 15
Marden Av. BR2: Hayes 3H 17
Marechal Niel Av. DA15: Sidc 7J 5
Marechal Niel Pde. *DA14: Sidc* *7J 5*
(off Main Rd.)
Mares Fld. CR0: Croy 7D 14
Margaret Gardner Dr. SE9 6E 4
Marigold Way CR0: Croy 5J 15
Marina Cl. BR2: Brom 5B 35 (7H 9)
Marion Cres. BR5: St M Cry 2K 19
Marion Rd. CR7: Thor H 2B 14
Marke Cl. BR2: Kes 1B 24
Market Mdw. BR5: St M Cry 1B 20
Market Pde. BR1: Brom 2C 35
DA14: Sidc 1A 12
Market Sq. BR1: Brom 3B 35 (6H 9)
(not continuous)
Market Way TN16: Westrm 7J 33
Markfield CR0: Sels 6A 22
(not continuous)
Mark Way BR8: Swan 7B 34
Markwell Cl. SE26 1G 7
Marlborough Cl. BR6: Orp 3J 19
Marlborough Rd. BR2: Brom 1K 17
Marlings Cl. BR7: Chst 1H 19
Marlings Pk. Av. BR7: Chst 1H 19
Marlow Cl. SE20 7G 7
Marlowe Cl. BR7: Chst 3G 11
Marlowe Gdns. SE9 3F 5
Marlow Rd. SE20 7G 7

Marlwood Cl. DA15: Sidc 6K **5**
Maroons Way SE6 2B **8**
Marriett Ho. SE6 1D **8**
Marsden Way BR6: Orp 1J **25**
Marsham Cl. BR7: Chst 2E **10**
Marston Way SE19 4A **6**
Martell Rd. SE21 1C **6**
Martindale Av. BR6: Chels 2K **25**
Martins Cl. BR4: W W'ck 5E **16**
BR5: St P 7C **12**
Martin's Rd. BR2: Brom 6F **9**
Marton Cl. SE6 1B **8**
Marvels Cl. SE12 6A **4**
Marvels La. SE12 6A **4**
(not continuous)
Marwell Cl. BR4: W W'ck 6G **17**
Maryfield Cl. DA5: Bexl 1K **13**
Maryland Rd. CR7: Thor H 5A **6**
Masefield Vw. BR6: Farnb 7F **19**
Mason's Av. CR0: Croy 7B **14**
Masons Hill BR2: Brom 6C **35** (7H **9**)
Matfield Cl. BR2: Brom 2H **17**
Matilda Cl. SE19 4C **6**
Matthews Gdns. CR0: New Ad 7E **22**
Matthews Yd. *CR0: Croy 7B 14*
(off Surrey St.)
Maude Rd. BR8: Swan 1B **34**
Maureen Ct. BR3: Beck 6H **7**
Mavelstone Cl. BR1: Brom 5B **10**
Mavelstone Rd. BR1: Brom 5A **10**
Maxim Apartments BR2: Brom 7D **35**
Maxwell Gdns. BR6: Orp 7J **19**
May Av. BR5: St M Cry 2A **20**
Mayberry Ct. *BR3: Beck 4A 8*
(off Copers Cope Rd.)
Maybourne Cl. SE26 3G **7**
Maybury Cl. BR5: Pet W 2E **18**
Mayday Rd. CR7: Thor H 3A **14**
MAYDAY UNIVERSITY HOSPITAL 3A 14
Mayerne Rd. SE9 2C **4**
Mayes Cl. BR8: Swan 6B **34**
Mayeswood Rd. SE12 1K **9**
Mayfair Cl. BR3: Beck 5C **8**
Mayfield Av. BR6: Orp 5J **19**
Mayfield Cl. SE20 5G **7**
Mayfield Rd. BR1: Brom 2B **18**
Mayfield Vs. DA14: Sidc 3B **12**
Mayfly Cl. BR5: St P 1C **20**
Mayford Cl. BR3: Beck 7J **7**
Maylands Dr. DA14: Sidc 1C **12**
Mayne Ct. SE26 2G **7**
Mayo Rd. CR0: Croy 2C **14**
Mayow Rd. SE23 1J **7**
SE26 1J **7**
MAYPOLE 3F **27**
Maypole Rd. BR6: Chels 2E **26**
Mays Hill Rd. BR2: Brom 6F **9**
Maywood Cl. BR3: Beck 4C **8**
Mead, The BR3: Beck 5D **8**
BR4: W W'ck 5E **16**
Mead Cl. BR8: Swan 7B **34**
Meadow, The BR7: Chst 3F **11**
Meadow Av. CR0: Croy 3J **15**
Meadow Cl. BR7: Chst 2E **10**
SE6 2B **8**
Meadowcroft BR1: Brom 7C **10**
Meadow La. SE12 7A **4**
Meadow Rd. BR2: Brom 6F **9**
Meadows, The BR6: Chels 3B **26**
TN14: Hals 2K **31**
Meadows Ct. DA14: Sidc 3A **12**
Meadowside SE9 1B **4**
Meadowside Leisure Cen. 1B 4
Meadow Stile CR0: Croy 7B **14**
Meadow Vw. BR5: St P 7B **12**
Meadow Vw. Rd. CR7: Thor H 2A **14**
Meadowview Rd. SE6 2A **8**
Meadow Way BR6: Farnb 7D **18**
Mead Pl. CR0: Croy 5B **14**
Mead Rd. BR7: Chst 3F **11**
Meadside Cl. BR3: Beck 5K **7**
Meadvale Rd. CR0: Croy 4E **14**
Mead Way BR2: Hayes 3G **17**
CR0: Croy 6K **15**
Meadway BR3: Beck 5D **8**
TN14: Hals 2K **31**
Meadway, The BR6: Chels 3A **26**
Meaford Way SE20 4G **7**
Meath Cl. BR5: St M Cry 2A **20**
Mecca Bingo
Croydon 6B 14
(off Tamworth Rd.)
Mede Ho. *BR1: Brom 2J 9*
(off Pike Cl.)
Medway Cl. CR0: Croy 3H **15**
Meerbrook Rd. SE3 1B **4**
Melanda Cl. BR7: Chst 2C **10**
Melbourne Cl. BR6: Orp 4H **19**
SE20 4F **7**
Melbury Cl. BR7: Chst 3B **10**
Meldrum Cl. BR5: Orp 3B **20**
Melfield Gdns. SE6 1D **8**
Melfort Av. CR7: Thor H 7A **6**
Melfort Rd. CR7: Thor H 7A **6**
Mells Cres. SE9 1C **10**
Melody Rd. TN16: Big H 7E **28**
Melrose Av. SW16 6A **6**
Melrose Cl. SE12 5A **4**
Melrose Cres. BR6: Orp 1G **25**
Melrose Rd. TN16: Big H 5E **28**
Melvin Rd. SE20 5H **7**
Mendip Cl. SE26 1H **7**
Menlo Gdns. SE19 4C **6**
Merchants Cl. SE25 1F **15**
Merchland Rd. SE9 5H **5**
Mere Cl. BR6: Farnb 6D **18**
Mere End CR0: Croy 4J **15**
Mere Side BR6: Farnb 6D **18**
Merewood Cl. BR1: Brom 6D **10**
Merewood Gdns. CR0: Croy 4J **15**
Mereworth Cl. BR2: Brom 2G **17**
Meriden Cl. BR1: Brom 4A **10**
Meridian Cen. CR0: New Ad 6F **23**
Merifield Rd. SE9 1B **4**
Merlewood Dr. BR7: Chst 5C **10**
Merlin Cl. CR0: Croy 7D **14**
Merlin Ct. BR2: Brom 7G **9**
Merlin Gdns. BR1: Brom 1H **9**
Merlin Gro. BR3: Beck 1A **16**
Merrilees Rd. DA15: Sidc 4K **5**
Merrow Way CR0: New Ad 3D **22**
Merrydown Way BR7: Chst 5B **10**
Merryfield Ho. *SE9 7B 4*
(off Grove Pk. Rd.)
Merryhills Cl. TN16: Big H 5F **29**
Mersham Pl. *CR7: Thor H 6C 6*
(off Livingstone Rd.)
SE20 5G **7**
Mersham Rd. CR7: Thor H 7C **6**
Merton Gdns. BR5: Pet W 2E **18**
Merton Rd. SE25 2E **14**
Mervyn Av. SE9 7H **5**
Messent Rd. SE9 2B **4**
Messeter Pl. SE9 3F **5**
Metro Bus. Cen., The SE26 3A **8**
Metro Cen. BR5: St M Cry 3A **20**
Metropolitan Police Norwood Cadet Training Cen. 5D 6
Mews, The DA14: Sidc 1K **11**
Mews End TN16: Big H 7F **29**
Miall Wlk. SE26 1K **7**
Michael Rd. SE25 7D **6**
Michelle Ct. BR1: Brom 2A **35**
Mickleham Cl. BR5: St P 6J **11**
Mickleham Rd. BR5: St P 5J **11**
Mickleham Way CR0: New Ad 4E **22**
Middle Pk. Av. SE9 3C **4**
Middle St. CR0: Croy 6B **14**
(not continuous)
Middleton Av. DA14: Sidc 3A **12**
Midfield Av. BR8: Swan 1B **34**
Midfield Way BR5: St P 5K **11**
Midholm Rd. CR0: Croy 6K **15**
Midhurst SE26 3H **7**
Midhurst Av. CR0: Croy 4A **14**
Miles Ct. *CR0: Croy 6A 14*
(off Cuthbert Rd.)
Milestone Rd. SE19 3E **6**
Milford Gdns. CR0: Croy 2H **15**
Milking La. BR2: Kes 7A **24**
BR6: Downe 1G **29**
Milk St. BR1: Brom 3J **9**
Millbro BR8: Swan 3B **34**
Millbrook Av. DA16: Well 1J **5**
Mill Brook Rd. BR5: St M Cry 1B **20**
Millcroft Ho. *SE6: 1D 8*
(off Melfield Gdns.)
Miller Cl. BR1: Brom 2J **9**
Millfield Cotts. BR5: St P 7A **12**
Millfields Cl. BR5: St P 1A **20**
Mill Gdns. SE26 1G **7**
Millhouse Pl. SE27 1A **6**
Mill La. BR6: Downe 6D **24**
Mill Pl. BR7: Chst 5E **10**
Mill Va. BR2: Brom 4A **35** (6G **9**)
Mill Vw. Gdns. CR0: Croy 7J **15**
Millwood Rd. BR5: St P 7B **12**
Milne Gdns. SE9 2D **4**
Milne Pk. E. CR0: New Ad 7E **22**
Milne Pk. W. CR0: New Ad 7E **22**
Milner Rd. CR7: Thor H 7C **6**
Milner Wlk. SE9 6J **5**
Milton Av. CR0: Croy 4C **14**
TN14: Hals 6G **27**
Milton Lodge DA14: Sidc 1K **11**
Milton Rd. CR0: Croy 4C **14**
Milverton Ho. SE6 1K **7**
Milverton Way SE9 1D **10**
Mimosa Cl. BR6: Chels 6B **20**
Minden Rd. SE20 5G **7**
Minerva Cl. DA14: Sidc 7K **5**
Ministry Way SE9 6E **4**
Minshaw Ct. DA14: Sidc 1J **11**
Minshull Pl. BR3: Beck 4B **8**
Minster Dr. CR0: Croy 7D **14**
Minster Rd. BR1: Brom 4J **9**
Mint Wlk. CR0: Croy 7B **14**
Mirror Path SE9 7B **4**
Mistletoe Cl. CR0: Croy 5J **15**
Mitcham Rd. CR0: Croy 5A **14**
Mitchell Rd. BR6: Orp 1J **25**
Mitchell Way BR1: Brom 2C **35** (5H **9**)
Mitre Cl. BR2: Brom 3A **35** (6G **9**)
Moat Cl. BR6: Chels 3J **25**
Moat Ct. SE9 3E **4**
Model Farm Cl. SE9 7D **4**
Moffat Rd. CR7: Thor H 6B **6**
Moira Rd. SE9 1E **4**
Molash Rd. BR5: St M Cry 1C **20**
Molescroft SE9 7H **5**
Moliner Ct. BR3: Beck 4B **8**
Monarch Cl. BR4: W W'ck 1G **23**
Monarch M. SW16 2A **6**
Monivea Rd. BR3: Beck 4A **8**
MONKS ORCHARD 4K **15**
Monks Orchard Rd. BR3: Beck 5B **16**
Monks Way BR3: Beck 3B **16**
BR5: Farnb 5F **19**
Mons Way BR2: Brom 3B **18**
Montacute Rd. CR0: New Ad 5D **22**
Montague Ct. DA15: Sidc 1K **11**
Montague Pl. BR8: Swan 6A **34**
Montague Rd. CR0: Croy 5A **14**
Montague Ter. BR2: Brom 7A **35** (1G **17**)
Montana Gdns. SE26 2A **8**
Montbelle Rd. SE9 7G **5**
Montbretia Cl. BR5: St M Cry 1B **20**
Montcalm Cl. BR2: Hayes 3H **17**
Montgomery Cl. DA15: Sidc 3K **5**
Montpelier Ct. BR2: Brom 7A **35**
Montrave Rd. SE20 3H **7**
Montrose Av. DA16: Well 1J **5**
Montserrat Cl. SE19 2C **6**
Moon Ct. SE12 1A **4**
Moorcroft Gdns. BR2: Brom 2B **18**
Moorehead Way SE3 1A **4**
Mooreland Rd. BR1: Brom 1A **35** (4G **9**)
Moore Rd. SE19 3B **6**
Moorfield Rd. BR6: Orp 4K **19**
Moorside Rd. BR1: Brom 1F **9**
Morello Cl. BR8: Swan 1J **21**
Moremead Rd. SE6 1A **8**
Moreton Cl. BR8: Swan 6K **13**
Moreton Ind. Est. BR8: Swan 6C **34**
Morgan Rd. BR1: Brom 1B **35** (4H **9**)
Morgan Wlk. BR3: Beck 1C **16**
Moriaty Cl. BR1: Brom 1D **18**
Morland Av. CR0: Croy 5D **14**
Morland Rd. CR0: Croy 5D **14**
SE20 3J **7**
Morley Cl. BR6: Farnb 6E **18**
Morley Ct. BR2: Brom 7A **35** (1G **17**)
Morley Rd. BR7: Chst 5F **11**
Mornington Av. BR1: Brom 7K **9**
Mornington Cl.
TN16: Big H 6F **29**
Morris Cl. BR6: Orp 7H **19**
CR0: Croy 2K **15**
Morston Gdns. SE9 1C **10**
Mortimer Rd. BR6: Orp 5K **19**
TN16: Big H 1E **28**
Moselle Rd. TN16: Big H 7G **29**
Mosslea Rd. BR2: Brom 2A **18**
BR6: Farnb 7F **19**
SE20 3H **7**
(not continuous)

Mosul Way BR2: Brom 3B 18
Mosyer Dr. BR5: Orp 6C 20
MOTTINGHAM 6D 4
Mottingham Gdns. SE9 5C 4
Mottingham La. SE9 5B 4
SE12 5B 4
Mottingham Rd. SE9 6D 4
Mottingham Station (Rail) 5E 4
Mouchotte Cl. TN16: Big H 1D 28
Moultain Hill BR8: Swan 6B 34
Mound, The SE9 7F 5
Mountacre Cl. SE26 1E 6
Mt. Arlington *BR2: Brom* *6F 9*
(off Pk. Hill Rd.)
Mountbatten Cl. SE19 2D 6
Mountbatten Gdns. BR3: Beck 1K 15
Mount Cl. BR1: Brom 5B 10
Mount Ct. BR4: W W'ck 6F 17
Mt. Culver Av. DA14: Sidc 3C 12
Mountfield Way BR5: St M Cry 1B 20
Mount Hill TN14: Knock 6E 30
Mounthurst Rd. BR2: Hayes 4G 17
Mt. Pleasant SE27 1B 6
TN16: Big H 6F 29
Mount Rd. SE19 3C 6
Mountview Rd. BR6: St M Cry 4K 19
(not continuous)
Mowbray Ct. SE19 4E 6
Mowbray Rd. SE19 5E 6
Mulberry Ho. BR2: Brom 5F 9
Mulberry La. CR0: Croy 5E 14
Mulberry Pl. SE9 1C 4
Mulgrave Rd. CR0: Croy 7C 14
Mungo Pk. Way BR5: Orp 4B 20
Munnery Way BR6: Farnb 7D 18
Murray Av. BR1: Brom 5E 35 (7J 9)
Murray Bus. Cen. BR5: St P 7A 12
Murray Rd. BR5: St P 7A 12
Mylis Cl. SE26 1G 7
Myrtle Rd. CR0: Croy 7B 16

N

Napier Ct. SE12 7A 4
Napier Rd. BR2: Brom 7E 35 (1J 17)
SE25 1G 15
Narrow Way BR2: Brom 3B 18
Naseby Ct. DA14: Sidc 1J 11
Naseby Rd. SE19 3C 6
NASH 3H 23
Nash Grn. BR1: Brom 3H 9
Nash La. BR2: Kes 4H 23
Natal Rd. CR7: Thor H 7C 6
NHS WALK-IN CENTRE (CROYDON) 7B 14
Naval Wlk. BR1: Brom 3B 35
Nayland Ho. SE6 1D 8
Nello James Gdns. SE27 1C 6
Nelson Cl. CR0: Croy 5A 14
TN16: Big H 6G 29
Nelson Pl. DA14: Sidc 1K 11
Nelson Rd. BR2: Brom 1K 17
DA14: Sidc 1K 11
Nesbit Rd. SE9 1C 4
Nesbitt Sq. SE19 4D 6
Netley Cl. CR0: New Ad 4D 22
Nettlefold Pl. SE27 1A 6
Nettlestead Cl. BR3: Beck 4A 8
Neville Cl. DA15: Sidc 1J 11
Neville Rd. CR0: Croy 4C 14
NEW ADDINGTON 6D 22
New Addington Pools & Fitness Cen. 6D 22
New Addington Stop (CT) 6D 22
New Barn La. TN14: Cud 7A 30
TN16: Cud, Westrm 7A 30
New Barn Rd. BR8: Swan 5K 13
NEW BECKENHAM 3A 8
New Beckenham Station (Rail) 4A 8
Newbury Ct. DA14: Sidc 1J 11
Newbury Rd. BR2: Brom 6B 35 (7H 9)
NEW ELTHAM 6H 5
New Eltham Station (Rail) 5G 5
New Farm Av. BR2: Brom 7B 35 (1H 17)
Newgate CR0: Croy 5B 14
New Grn. Pl. SE19 3D 6
Newhaven Gdns. SE9 1C 4
Newhaven Rd. SE25 2C 14
Newing Grn. BR1: Brom 4A 10
Newlands Ct. SE9 3F 5
Newlands Pk. SE26 3H 7
Newlands Wood CR0: Sels 5A 22
Newlyn Cl. BR6: Chels 1K 25
Newman Ct. BR1: Brom 2C 35
Newman Rd. BR1: Brom 2C 35 (5H 9)
Newmarket Grn. SE9 4C 4
New Mill Rd. BR5: St P 5B 12
Newnham Cl. CR7: Thor H 6B 6
Newnhams Cl. BR1: Brom 7C 10
New Pl. CR0: Addtn 3B 22
Newports BR8: Crock 4J 21
New Rd. BR6: Orp 4K 19
BR8: Swan 2A 34
(Egerton Av.)
BR8: Swan 5A 34
(Swanley La.)
New Rd. Hill BR2: Kes 5B 24
BR6: Downe 5B 24
Newstead Av. BR6: Orp 7G 19
New St. Hill BR1: Brom 2J 9
Newton Ho. SE20 4J 7
Newton Ter. BR2: Brom 3A 18
New Years La. BR6: Knock 5D 30
TN14: Knock 5D 30
Nichol La. BR1: Brom 4H 9
Nicholson Rd. CR0: Croy 5E 14
Nicolson Rd. BR5: Orp 4C 20
Niederwald Rd. SE26 1K 7
Nightingale Cl. TN16: Big H 4E 28
Nightingale Cnr. BR5: St M Cry 1C 20
Nightingale Ct. BR2: Brom 6F 9
Nightingale La. BR1: Brom 6K 9
Nightingale Rd. BR5: Pet W 3F 19
Nightingale Way BR8: Swan 7K 13
Ninehams Rd. TN16: Tats 3B 32
Ninhams Wood BR6: Farnb 1D 24
Nita Ct. SE12 5A 4
Noel Ter. DA14: Sidc 1A 12
Norbury Av. CR7: Thor H 6A 6
Norbury Cl. SW16 5A 6
Norbury Cres. SW16 6A 6
Norbury Hill SW16 4A 6
Norbury Rd. CR7: Thor H 6B 6
Norfield Rd. DA2: Dart 1H 13
Norfolk Cres. DA15: Sidc 4K 5
Norfolk Ho. *BR2: Brom* *1G 17*
(off Westmoreland Rd.)
SE20 5H 7
Norfolk Rd. CR7: Thor H 7B 6
Norheads La. TN16: Big H 7C 28
Norhyrst Av. SE25 7E 6
Norlands Cres. BR7: Chst 5E 10
Norman Cl. BR6: Farnb 7F 19
Normandy Cl. SE26 1K 7
Normanhurst Rd. BR5: St P 6A 12
Norman Pk. Athletics Track 3J 17
Norman Rd. CR7: Thor H 2A 14
Norsted La. BR6: Prat B 1E 30
Northampton Rd. CR0: Croy 6F 15
Northbourne BR2: Hayes 4H 17
Northbrook Rd. CR0: Croy 2C 14
Northcote Rd. CR0: Croy 3C 14
DA14: Sidc 1H 11
North Ct. BR1: Brom 2C 35
NORTH CRAY 2D 12
Nth. Cray Rd. DA14: Sidc 3D 12
Northdale Ct. SE25 7E 6
Nth. Downs Cres. CR0: New Ad 5C 22
(not continuous)
Nth. Downs Rd. CR0: New Ad 6C 22
North Dr. BR3: Beck 1C 16
BR6: Orp 1H 25
North End CR0: Croy 6B 14
North End La. BR6: Downe 7D 24
Northfield Av. BR5: Orp 3B 20
Northfield Cl. BR1: Brom 5B 10
Northlands Av. BR6: Orp 1H 25
Northolme Ri. BR6: Orp 6H 19
Northover BR1: Brom 1G 9
North Pk. SE9 3E 4
Nth. Pole La. BR2: Kes 3G 23
North Rd. BR1: Brom 1D 35 (5J 9)
BR4: W W'ck 5C 16
Northside Rd. BR1: Brom 2C 35 (5H 9)
North St. BR1: Brom 2B 35 (5H 9)
Northumberland Av. DA16: Well 1J 5
Northumberland Gdns. BR1: Brom 1D 18
Northview BR8: Swan 6K 13
North Wlk. CR0: New Ad 3C 22
(not continuous)
Northway Rd. CR0: Croy 3E 14
Nth. Wood Ct. SE25 7F 7
Northwood Ho. SE27 1C 6
Northwood Rd. CR7: Thor H 6A 6
Northwood Way SE19 3C 6
Norton Ct. BR3: Beck 5A 8
Norwich Rd. CR7: Thor H 7B 6
NORWOOD 3D 6
Norwood High St. SE27 1A 6
Norwood Junction Station (Rail) 1F 15
NORWOOD NEW TOWN 3B 6
Norwood Pk. Rd. SE27 2B 6
Notson Rd. SE25 1G 15
Novar Cl. BR6: Orp 4J 19
Nova Rd. CR0: Croy 5A 14
Novar Rd. SE9 5H 5
Nower, The TN14: Knock 1K 33
Nubia Way BR1: Brom 1F 9
Nuffield Rd. BR8: Swan 1B 34
Nugent Ind. Pk. BR5: St M Cry 1B 20
Nugent Rd. SE25 7E 6
Nunnington Cl. SE9 7D 4
Nursery Av. CR0: Croy 6J 15
Nursery Cl. BR6: Orp 4J 19
BR8: Swan 6H 13
CR0: Croy 6J 15
Nursery Gdns. BR7: Chst 3E 10
Nursery Rd. CR7: Thor H 1C 14
Nutfield Ct. BR1: Brom 5C 35 (7H 9)
Nutfield Pas. *CR7: Thor H* *1A 14*
(off Nutfield Rd.)
Nutfield Rd. CR7: Thor H 1A 14
Nutfield Way BR6: Farnb 6E 18
Nutley Cl. BR8: Swan 3A 34
Nut Tree Cl. BR6: Chels 7C 20

O

Oak Av. CR0: Croy 5B 16
Oak Bank CR0: New Ad 3D 22
Oakbrook Cl. BR1: Brom 1J 9
Oakdene Av. BR7: Chst 2D 10
Oakdene Rd. BR5: St M Cry 2J 19
Oakfield Cen. SE20 4G 7
Oakfield Gdns. BR3: Beck 2C 16
SE19 2D 6
(not continuous)
Oakfield La. BR2: Kes 1K 23
Oakfield Rd. BR6: Orp 4K 19
CR0: Croy 5B 14
SE20 4G 7
Oakfield Rd. Ind. Est. SE20 4G 7
Oak Gdns. CR0: Croy 6B 16
Oak Gro. BR4: W W'ck 5D 16
Oak Gro. Rd. SE20 5H 7
Oakham Dr. BR2: Brom 7B 35 (1G 17)
Oakhill Rd. BR3: Beck 6D 8
BR6: Orp 5J 19
Oakhurst Cl. BR7: Chst 5C 10
Oaklands BR3: Beck 5C 8
Oaklands Av. BR4: W W'ck 7C 16
DA15: Sidc 4K 5
Oaklands Cl. BR5: Pet W 3H 19
Oaklands Ct. *SE20* *4H 7*
(off Chestnut Gro.)
Oaklands La. TN16: Big H 2D 28
Oaklands Rd. BR1: Brom 4F 9
Oakleigh Cl. BR8: Swan 7K 13
Oakleigh Gdns. BR6: Orp 1H 25
Oakleigh Pk. Av. BR7: Chst 5D 10
Oakley Dr. BR2: Brom 7B 18
SE9 5J 5
Oakley Rd. BR2: Brom 7B 18
SE25 2G 15
Oak Lodge Dr. BR4: W W'ck 4C 16
Oak Lodge La. TN16: Westrm 7J 33
Oakmead Av. BR2: Hayes 3H 17
Oakmont Pl. BR6: Orp 5G 19
Oakridge La. BR1: Brom 2E 8
Oakridge Rd. BR1: Brom 1E 8
Oak Rd. BR6: Chels 4K 25
TN16: Westrm 7J 33
Oaks, The BR2: Brom 3D 18
BR8: Swan 6K 13
Oaks Av. SE19 2D 6
Oaksford Av. SE26 1G 7
Oakshade Rd. BR1: Brom 1E 8
Oaks La. CR0: Croy 7G 15
Oaks Rd. CR0: Croy 7H 15
Oak Tree Gdns.
BR1: Brom 2J 9
Oakview Gro. CR0: Croy 5K 15
Oakview Rd. SE6 2C 8
Oak Way CR0: Croy 3J 15
Oakway BR2: Brom 6E 8
Oakways SE9 3G 5

Oakwood Av. BR2: Brom .6D **35** (7J **9**)
BR3: Beck .6D **8**
Oakwood Cl. BR7: Chst .3C **10**
Oakwood Ct. *BR8: Swan .6H 13*
(off Lawn Cl.)
Oakwood Dr. SE19 .3C **6**
Oakwood Gdns. BR6: Farnb .6F **19**
Oakwood Rd. BR6: Farnb .6F **19**
Oasis, The BR1: Brom .3E **35** (6K **9**)
Oasthouse Way BR5: St M Cry .1A **20**
Oates Cl. BR2: Brom .7E **8**
Oatfield Rd. BR6: Orp .5J **19**
Oban Rd. SE25 .1C **14**
Ockham Dr. BR5: St P .4K **11**
Ockley Ct. DA14: Sidc .7K **5**
Odeon Cinema
Beckenham .6A **8**
Bromley .3B **35**
Eltham Park .1D 4
(off Well Hall Rd.)
Odeon Pde. *SE9 .1D 4*
(off Well Hall Rd.)
Offenham Rd. SE9 .1C **10**
Okemore Gdns. BR5: St M Cry .1B **20**
Old Bromley Rd. BR1: Brom .2E **8**
Oldbury Cl. BR5: St M Cry .1C **20**
Old Chapel Rd. BR8: Crock .4H **21**
Old Courtyard, The BR1: Brom .2E **35** (5J **9**)
Old Farm Av. DA15: Sidc .5J **5**
Old Farm Gdns. BR8: Swan .5A **34**
Oldfield Cl. BR1: Brom .1C **18**
Oldfield Rd. BR1: Brom .1C **18**
Old Forge Way DA14: Sidc .1A **12**
Old Harrow La. TN16: Westrm .1H **33**
Old Hill BR6: Downe .3G **25**
BR7: Chst .5D **10**
Old Homesdale Rd. BR2: Brom .1K **17**
Old La. TN16: Tats .2C **32**
Old Laundry, The BR7: Chst .5F **11**
Old London Rd. DA14: Sidc, Swan .4F **13**
TN14: Hals .5E **26**
TN14: Knock .4J **31**
Old Maidstone Rd. DA14: Sidc .4E **12**
Old Mnr. Way BR7: Chst .2C **10**
Old Mill Equestrian Cen. .1E **34**
Old Pal. Rd. CR0: Croy .7A **14**
Old Perry St. BR7: Chst .3H **11**
Old School Cl. BR3: Beck .6J **7**
Old School Ct. *BR8: Swan .6K 13*
(off Bonney Way)
Oldstead Rd. BR1: Brom .1D **8**
Old Town CR0: Croy .7A **14**
Old Tye Av. TN16: Big H .5G **29**
Oleander Cl. BR6: Farnb .2G **25**
Oliver Av. SE25 .7E **6**
Oliver Gro. SE25 .1E **14**
Oliver Rd. BR8: Swan .7J **13**
Olyffe Dr. BR3: Beck .5D **8**
Olympic Golf & Leisure Cen., The .6C **34**
Onslow Cres. BR7: Chst .5E **10**
Onslow Rd. CR0: Croy .5A **14**
Orange Ct. La. BR6: Downe .5D **24**
Orangery La. SE9 .2E **4**
Orchard, The BR8: Swan .6J **13**
Orchard Av. CR0: Croy .6K **15**
Orchard Bus. Cen. SE26 .2A **8**
Orchard Grn. BR6: Orp .6H **19**
Orchard Gro. BR6: Orp .6J **19**
CR0: Croy .4K **15**
SE20 .4F **7**
Orchard Pl. BR2: Kes .5K **23**
BR5: St P .7B **12**
Orchard Ri. CR0: Croy .5K **15**
Orchard Ri. E. DA15: Sidc .2K **5**
Orchard Ri. W. DA15: Sidc .2K **5**
Orchard Rd. BR1: Brom .5K **9**
BR6: Farnb .2E **24**
BR6: Prat B .6B **26**
DA14: Sidc .1H **11**
Orchard Vs. DA14: Sidc .3B **12**
Orchard Way BR3: Beck .5K **15**
CR0: Croy .5K **15**
Oregon Sq. BR6: Orp .5G **19**
Oriel Ct. CR0: Croy .5C **14**
Orleans Rd. SE19 .3C **6**
Orlestone Gdns. BR6: Chels .2D **26**
Ormanton Rd. SE26 .1F **7**
Ormonde Av. BR6: Farnb .6F **19**
ORPINGTON .5K **19**
Orpington By-Pass BR6: Chels, Orp .6A **20**
Orpington By-Pass Rd. BR6: Hals .5E **26**
TN14: Hals .5E **26**
ORPINGTON HOSPITAL .1J **25**
Orpington Retail Pk. BR5: St M Cry .1B **20**
Orpington Rd. BR7: Chst .7H **11**
Orpington Station (Rail) .6H **19**
Orpington Superbowl .5K **19**
Orpington Trade Cen. BR5: St P .7A **12**
Osborne Cl. BR3: Beck .1K **15**
Osborne Gdns. CR7: Thor H .6B **6**
Osborne Rd. CR7: Thor H .6B **6**
Osgood Av. BR6: Chels .2J **25**
Osgood Gdns. BR6: Chels .2J **25**
Oslac Rd. SE6 .2C **8**
Osprey Cl. BR2: Brom .5B **18**
Osprey Ct. BR3: Beck .4B **8**
Ospringe Cl. SE20 .4H **7**
Ospringe Ct. SE9 .3J **5**
Osterley Cl. BR5: St P .5K **11**
Osterley Gdns. CR7: Thor H .6B **6**
Osward CR0: Sels .5A **22**
(not continuous)
Otford Cl. BR1: Brom .7D **10**
SE20 .5H **7**
Otford La. TN14: Hals .1K **31**
Otlinge Rd. BR5: St M Cry .1C **20**
Otterbourne Rd. CR0: Croy .6B **14**
Otterden Cl. BR6: Orp .7H **19**
Otterden St. SE6 .1B **8**
Otters Cl. BR5: St P .1C **20**
Outram Rd. CR0: Croy .6E **14**
Oval Ho. *CR0: Croy .5D 14*
(off Oval Rd.)
Oval Rd. CR0: Croy .6C **14**
Overbrae BR3: Beck .3B **8**
Overbury Av. BR3: Beck .7C **8**
Overbury Cres. CR0: New Ad .6D **22**
Overdown Rd. SE6 .1B **8**
Overhill Way BR3: Beck .2E **16**
Overmead BR8: Swan .2K **21**
DA15: Sidc .4J **5**
Overstand Cl. BR3: Beck .2B **16**
Overstone Gdns. CR0: Croy .4A **16**
Overton's Yd. CR0: Croy .7B **14**
Ovett Cl. SE19 .3D **6**
Owen Cl. CR0: Croy .3C **14**
Owen Wlk. SE20 .5F **7**
Ownsted Hill CR0: New Ad .6D **22**
Oxenden Wood Rd. BR6: Chels .3A **26**
Oxford Rd. DA14: Sidc .2A **12**
SE19 .3C **6**
Oxhawth Cres. BR2: Brom .2D **18**
Oxlip Cl. CR0: Croy .5J **15**

P

Packham Cl. BR6: Chels .6B **20**
Packmores Rd. SE9 .2J **5**
Paddock, The TN16: Westrm .7H **33**
Paddock Cl. BR6: Farnb .1E **24**
SE26 .1J **7**
Paddock Gdns. SE19 .3D **6**
Paddock Mobile Home Pk. BR2: Kes .5B **24**
Paddock Pas. *SE19 .3D 6*
(off Paddock Gdns.)
Paddocks, The CR0: Addtn .3B **22**
Paddocks Cl. BR5: Orp .6C **20**
Paddock Way BR7: Chst .4G **11**
Padstow Cl. BR6: Chels .1J **25**
Padua Rd. SE20 .5H **7**
Pageant Wlk. CR0: Croy .7D **14**
Page Heath La. BR1: Brom .7A **10**
Page Heath Vs. BR1: Brom .7A **10**
Pagehurst Rd. CR0: Croy .4G **15**
Paget Gdns. BR7: Chst .5E **10**
Palace Ct. BR1: Brom .2D **35**
Palace Grn. CR0: Sels .4A **22**
Palace Gro. BR1: Brom .2D **35** (5J **9**)
SE19 .4E **6**
Palace Rd. BR1: Brom .2D **35** (5J **9**)
SE19 .4E **6**
TN16: Westrm .3F **33**
Palace Sq. SE19 .4E **6**
Palace Vw. BR1: Brom .5D **35** (7J **9**)
(not continuous)
CR0: Croy .1A **22**
SE12 .6A **4**
Palewell Cl. BR5: St P .6A **12**
Pallant Way BR6: Farnb .7D **18**
Palmarsh Rd. BR5: St M Cry .1C **20**
Palm Av. DA14: Sidc .3C **12**
Palmer Cl. BR4: W W'ck .7E **16**
Palmer Dr. BR1: Brom .1E **18**
Palmerston Rd. BR6: Farnb .1F **25**
CR0: Croy .2C **14**
Panmure Rd. SE26 .1G **7**
Panter's BR8: Swan .2A **34**
Pantiles, The BR1: Brom .7B **10**
Parade, The *SE26 .1G 7*
(off Wells Pk. Rd.)
Parchmore Rd. CR7: Thor H .6A **6**
Parchmore Way CR7: Thor H .6A **6**
Parish Ga. Dr. DA15: Sidc .3K **5**
Parish La. SE20 .3J **7**
Parish M. SE20 .4J **7**
Park, The DA14: Sidc .2K **11**
Park & Ride
Bromley .3J **17**
Park Av. BR1: Brom .3G **9**
BR4: W W'ck .6D **16**
BR6: Chels .6K **19**
BR6: Farnb .7C **18**
Park Ct. SE26 .3G **7**
Park End BR1: Brom .1A **35** (5G **9**)
Park Farm Rd. BR1: Brom .5A **10**
Parkfields CR0: Croy .5A **16**
Parkfield Way BR2: Brom .3C **18**
Parkgate Rd. BR6: Orp .1G **27**
Park Gro. BR1: Brom .2E **35** (5J **9**)
Park Hall Trad. Est. SE21 .1B **6**
Parkham Ct. BR2: Brom .6F **9**
Park Hill BR1: Brom .1B **18**
Park Hill Ri. CR0: Croy .6D **14**
Park Hill Rd. BR2: Brom .6F **9**
CR0: Croy .6D **14**
DA15: Sidc .7K **5**
Parkland Mead BR1: Brom .7E **10**
Park La. BR8: Swan .4D **34**
CR0: Croy .7C **14**
Park La. Mans. *CR0: Croy .7C 14*
(off Edridge Rd.)
PARK LANGLEY .1D **16**
Park M. BR7: Chst .3E **10**
Park Pl. BR1: Brom .2D **35**
Park Rd. BR1: Brom .3D **35** (5J **9**)
BR3: Beck .4A **8**
BR5: St M Cry .2B **20**
BR7: Chst .3E **10**
BR8: Swan .6A **34**
CR6: Warl .3A **28**
SE25 .1D **14**
Park Rd. Ind. Est. BR8: Swan .5A **34**
Parkside TN14: Hals .2K **31**
Parkside Av. BR1: Brom .1B **18**
Parkside Cl. SE20 .4H **7**
Parkside Ter. *BR6: Farnb .7E 18*
(off Willow Wlk.)
Park St. CR0: Croy .6B **14**
Park Vw. *BR6: Orp .4A 20*
(off High St.)
Park Vw. Ct. SE20 .5G **7**
Park Vw. Rd. CR0: Croy .5F **15**
Parkview Rd. SE9 .5G **5**
Park Way DA5: Bexl .1K **13**
Parkway CR0: New Ad .5C **22**
Parkwood BR3: Beck .4B **8**
Parkwood Rd. TN16: Tats .3D **32**
Parnham Cl. BR1: Brom .7E **10**
Parry Rd. SE25 .7D **6**
Parsley Gdns. CR0: Croy .5J **15**
Parsonage La. DA14: Sidc .1E **12**
Parson's Mead CR0: Croy .5A **14**
Partridge Dr. BR6: Farnb .7F **19**
Partridge Grn. SE9 .7F **5**
Partridge Rd. DA14: Sidc .7K **5**
Passey Pl. SE9 .3E **4**
Paston Cres. SE12 .4A **4**
Patricia Ct. BR7: Chst .5G **11**
Patterdale Cl. BR1: Brom .3G **9**
Patterson Ct. SE19 .4E **6**
Patterson Rd. SE19 .3E **6**
Paul Gdns. CR0: Croy .6E **14**
Paulinus Cl. BR5: St P .6B **12**
Pavement Sq. CR0: Croy .5F **15**
Pavilion La. BR3: Beck .3A **8**
Pavilion Leisure Cen., The .4C **35** (6H **9**)
Pawleyne Cl. SE20 .4H **7**
Pawsons Rd. CR0: Croy .3B **14**
Paxton Ct. SE12 .7B **4**
SE26 .1K 7
(off Adamsrill Rd.)
Paxton Pl. SE27 .1D **6**
Paxton Rd. BR1: Brom .4H **9**
Paynesfield Rd. TN16: Tats .3B **32**
(not continuous)

Peabody Cl. CR0: Croy 5H **15**
Peace Cl. SE25 1D **14**
Peak, The SE26 1H **7**
Peak Hill SE26 1H **7**
Peak Hill Av. SE26 1H **7**
Peak Hill Gdns. SE26 1H **7**
Peartree SE26 2K **7**
Pear Tree Cl. BR2: Brom 2A **18**
BR8: Swan 6J **13**
Peatfield Cl. DA15: Sidc 7K **5**
Pedham Pl. Ind. Est. BR8: Swan 7B **34**
Peel Rd. BR6: Farnb 2F **25**
Pegley Gdns. SE12 6A **4**
Pelham Ct. DA14: Sidc 1K **11**
Pelham Rd. BR3: Beck 6H **7**
Pemberton Gdns. BR8: Swan 7K **13**
Pemberton Ho. *SE26* *1F 7*
(off High Level Dr.)
Pembroke Rd. BR1: Brom 6K **9**
SE25 1D **14**
Pembury Cl. BR2: Hayes 4G **17**
Pembury Rd. SE25 1F **15**
Pemdevon Rd. CR0: Croy 4A **14**
Pendennis Rd. BR6: Chels 6B **20**
Pendle Ho. SE26 1F **7**
Penfold Cl. CR0: Wadd 7A **14**
Penford Gdns. SE9 1C **4**
PENGE 4H **7**
Penge East Station (Rail) 3H **7**
Penge La. SE20 4H **7**
Penge Rd. SE20 7F **7**
SE25 7F **7**
Penge West Station (Rail) 3G **7**
Penhale Cl. BR6: Chels 1K **25**
Penn Gdns. BR7: Chst 6E **10**
Pennington Cl. SE27 1C **6**
Pennington Way SE12 6A **4**
Penrith Cl. BR3: Beck 5C **8**
Penrith Rd. CR7: Thor H 6B **6**
Penshurst Grn. BR2: Brom 2G **17**
Penshurst Rd. CR7: Thor H 2A **14**
Penshurst Wlk. BR2: Brom 2G **17**
Penshurst Way BR5: St M Cry 1B **20**
Peppercorn Cl. CR7: Thor H 6C **6**
Pepys Ri. BR6: Orp 5J **19**
Percival Rd. BR6: Farnb 6E **18**
Percy Rd. SE20 5J **7**
SE25 2F **15**
Percy Ter. BR1: Brom 7E **10**
Peregrine Gdns. CR0: Croy 6K **15**
Periton Rd. SE9 1C **4**
Perpins Rd. SE9 3K **5**
Perry Hall Cl. BR6: St M Cry 4K **19**
Perry Hall Rd. BR6: St M Cry 3J **19**
Perry Hill SE6 1A **8**
Perry Ri. SE23 1K **7**
Perrys La. BR6: Prat B 2F **31**
Perry St. BR7: Chst 3G **11**
Perry St. Gdns. BR7: Chst 3H **11**
Perry St. Shaw BR7: Chst 4H **11**
Perth Rd. BR3: Beck 6D **8**
Peter Kennedy Ct. BR3: Beck 3A **16**
Petersham Dr. BR5: St P 6J **11**
Petersham Gdns. BR5: St P 6J **11**
Peter's Path SE26 1G **7**
Petten Cl. BR5: Orp 5C **20**
Petten Gro. BR5: Orp 5B **20**
PETTS WOOD 2F **19**
Petts Wood Rd. BR5: Pet W 2F **19**
Petts Wood Station (Rail) 2F **19**
Philip Av. BR8: Swan 1J **21**
Philip Gdns. CR0: Croy 6A **16**
Philipot Path SE9 3E **4**
Philippa Gdns. SE9 2C **4**
Phoenix Cl. BR4: W W'ck 6E **16**
Phoenix Dr. BR2: Kes 1A **24**
Phoenix Rd. SE20 3H **7**
Pickering Gdns. CR0: Croy 3E **14**
Pickhurst Grn. BR2: Hayes 4G **17**
Pickhurst La. BR2: Hayes 2F **17**
BR4: W W'ck 2F **17**
Pickhurst Mead BR2: Hayes 4G **17**
Pickhurst Pk. BR2: Brom 2F **17**
Pickhurst Ri. BR4: W W'ck 4D **16**
Pickwick Ct. SE9 5D **4**
Pickwick Way BR7: Chst 3F **11**
Piermont Pl. BR1: Brom 6B **10**
Pike Cl. BR1: Brom 2J **9**
Pilgrim Hill SE27 1B **6**
Pilgrims La. RH8: T'sey 7A **32**
TN16: Tats 5D **32**
Pilgrims Way TN16: Westrm, Bras 5E **32**
Pilkington Rd. BR6: Farnb 7F **19**
Pilton Est., The CR0: Croy 6A **14**
Pinchbeck Rd. BR6: Chels 3J **25**
Pine Av. BR4: W W'ck 5C **16**
Pine Cl. BR8: Swan 6A **34**
SE20 5H **7**
Pine Coombe CR0: Croy 7J **15**
Pinecrest Gdns. BR6: Farnb 1E **24**
Pine Glade BR6: Farnb 1C **24**
Pinehurst Wlk. BR6: Orp 5G **19**
Pines Rd. BR1: Brom 6B **10**
Pine Tree Lodge BR2: Brom 7A **35** (1G **17**)
Pinewood Av. DA15: Sidc 5K **5**
Pinewood Cl. BR6: Orp 5G **19**
CR0: Croy 7K **15**
Pinewood Dr. BR6: Orp 2H **25**
Pinewood Rd. BR2: Brom 7C **35** (1H **17**)
Pink's Hill BR8: Swan 2K **21**
Pinnell Rd. SE9 1C **4**
Pinto Way SE3 1A **4**
Pioneer Pl. CR0: Sels 5B **22**
Pioneer Way BR8: Swan 7K **13**
Piper's Gdns. CR0: Croy 4K **15**
Pippenhall SE9 3G **5**
Pippin Cl. CR0: Croy 5A **16**
Piquet Rd. SE20 6H **7**
Pirbright Cres. CR0: New Ad 3D **22**
Pitfold Cl. SE12 3A **4**
Pitfold Rd. SE12 3A **4**
Pitlake CR0: Croy 6A **14**
Pitt Rd. BR6: Farnb 1F **25**
CR0: Croy 2B **14**
CR7: Thor H 2B **14**
Pittsmead Av. BR2: Hayes 4H **17**
Pittville Gdns. SE25 7F **7**
Pixfield Ct. *BR2: Brom* *6G 9*
(off Beckenham La.)
Pixton Way CR0: Sels 5A **22**
Place Farm Av. BR6: Orp 5G **19**
PLAISTOW 4H **9**
Plaistow Gro. BR1: Brom 4J **9**
Plaistow La. BR1: Brom 1E **35** (4H **9**)
(not continuous)
Plane Ho. BR2: Brom 6F **9**
Plane St. SE26 1G **7**
Plane Tree Wlk. SE19 3D **6**
Plantation Dr. BR5: Orp 5C **20**
Plantation Rd. BR8: Swan 2B **34**
Plawsfield Rd. BR3: Beck 5J **7**
Plaxtol Cl. BR1: Brom 5K **9**
Playgreen Way SE6 1B **8**
Playground Cl. BR3: Beck 6J **7**
Pleasance Rd. BR5: St P 6A **12**
Pleasant Gro. CR0: Croy 7A **16**
Pleasant Vw. Pl. BR6: Farnb 2E **24**
Pleydell Av. SE19 4E **6**
Pleydell Gdns. *SE19* *3E 6*
(off Anerley Hill)
Plymouth Rd. BR1: Brom 1E **35** (5J **9**)
Pole Cat All. BR2: Hayes 6G **17**
Polesteeple Hill TN16: Big H 6F **29**
Pollard Wlk. DA14: Sidc 3B **12**
Polperro Cl. BR6: St M Cry 3J **19**
Pond Cott. La. BR4: Beck 5B **16**
Pondfield Ho. SE27 2B **6**
Pondfield Rd. BR2: Hayes 5F **17**
BR6: Farnb 7E **18**
Pond Path BR7: Chst 3E **10**
Pondwood Ri. BR6: Orp 4H **19**
Pontefract Rd. BR1: Brom 2G **9**
Pool Cl. BR3: Beck 2B **8**
Pope Rd. BR2: Brom 2A **18**
Popes Gro. CR0: Croy 7A **16**
Poplar Av. BR6: Farnb 6E **18**
Poplar Wlk. CR0: Croy 6B **14**
Poppy La. CR0: Croy 4H **15**
Porchester Mead BR3: Beck 3C **8**
Porcupine Cl. SE9 6D **4**
Porlock Ho. SE26 1F **7**
Porrington Cl. BR7: Chst 5C **10**
Porthallow Cl. BR6: Chels 1J **25**
Porthcawe Rd. SE26 1K **7**
Port Hill BR6: Prat B 1F **31**
Portland Cres. SE9 6D **4**
Portland Pl. *SE25* *1F 15*
(off Sth. Norwood Hill)
Portland Rd. BR1: Brom 1K **9**
SE9 6D **4**
SE25 1F **15**
Postmill Cl. CR0: Croy 7H **15**
Potters Cl. CR0: Croy 5K **15**
Poulters Wood BR2: Kes 2A **24**
Pound Cl. BR6: Orp 6G **19**
Pound Ct. Dr. BR6: Orp 6G **19**
Pound La. TN14: Knock 4H **31**
Pound Pl. SE9 3F **5**
Pound Way BR7: Chst 4F **11**
POVEREST 1K **19**
Poverest Rd. BR5: St M Cry 2J **19**
Powerscroft Rd.
DA14: Sidc 3B **12**
(not continuous)
Powster Rd. BR1: Brom 2H **9**
Poynings Cl. BR6: Chels 6B **20**
Poyntell Cres. BR7: Chst 5G **11**
Pragnell Rd. SE12 6A **4**
PRATT'S BOTTOM 6B **26**
PRATT'S BOTTOM 5B **26**
Precista Ct. BR6: Orp 4A **20**
Prescott Av. BR5: Pet W 3E **18**
Prestbury Sq. SE9 1C **10**
Preston Ct. *DA14: Sidc* *1J 11*
(off The Crescent)
Preston Rd. SE19 3A **6**
Prestons Rd. BR2: Hayes 7H **17**
Prestwood Gdns. CR0: Croy 4B **14**
Prickley Wood BR2: Hayes 5G **17**
Priddy's Yd. CR0: Croy 6B **14**
Pridham Rd. CR7: Thor H 1C **14**
Priestlands Pk. Rd. DA15: Sidc 1J **11**
Primrose Cl. SE6 2D **8**
Primrose La. CR0: Croy 5H **15**
Prince Consort Dr. BR7: Chst 5G **11**
Prince Imperial Rd. BR7: Chst 5E **10**
Prince John Rd. SE9 2D **4**
Prince Rd. SE25 2D **14**
Prince Rupert Rd. SE9 1E **4**
Princes Av. BR5: Pet W 2H **19**
Princes Cl. DA14: Sidc 1C **12**
Prince's Plain BR2: Brom 4B **18**
Princes Rd. BR8: Swan 1B **34**
SE20 3J **7**
Princess Pde. BR6: Farnb 7D **18**
Princess Rd. CR0: Croy 3B **14**
PRINCESS ROYAL UNIVERSITY HOSPITAL
7D 18
Princes Way BR4: W W'ck 1G **23**
Princethorpe Rd. SE26 1J **7**
Prioress Rd. SE27 1A **6**
Priorsford Av. BR5: St M Cry 1K **19**
Priory, The CR0: Wadd 7A **14**
Priory Av. BR5: Pet W 3G **19**
Priory Cl. BR3: Beck 7K **7**
BR7: Chst 5C **10**
Priory Cres. SE19 4B **6**
Priory Gardens 4A 20
Priory Gdns. SE25 1E **14**
PRIORY HOSPITAL, HAYES GROVE, THE
6H 17
Priory Leas SE9 5D **4**
Priory Leisure Cen., The 5B 20
Prospect Cl. SE26 1G **7**
Prospect Pl. BR2: Brom 6D **35** (7J **9**)
Pucknells Cl. BR8: Swan 5H **13**
PUDDLEDOCK 1A **34**
Puddledock La.
DA2: Dart, Swan 2K **13**
Puffin Cl. BR3: Beck 2J **15**
Pullman M. SE12 7A **4**
Pullman Pl. SE9 2D **4**
Pump Ho. Cl. BR2: Brom 6F **9**
Pump La. BR6: Orp 2G **27**
Pump Pail Nth. CR0: Croy 7B **14**
Pump Pail Sth. CR0: Croy 7B **14**
Purneys Rd. SE9 1C **4**
Pyrmont Gro. SE27 1A **6**
Pytchley Cres. SE19 3B **6**

Q

Quadrant Rd. CR7: Thor H 1A **14**
Queen Adelaide Ct. SE20 3H **7**
Queen Adelaide Rd. SE20 3H **7**
Queen Anne Av. BR2: Brom 5A **35** (7G **9**)
Queenborough Gdns. BR7: Chst 3G **11**
Queen Elizabeth's Dr. CR0: New Ad 5E **22**
Queen Elizabeth's Gdns. CR0: New Ad 6E **22**
Queen Mary Rd. SE19 3A **6**
QUEEN MARY'S HOSPITAL 2K 11
Queenscroft Rd. SE9 2C **4**
Queens Ga. Gdns. BR7: Chst 5G **11**
Queen's Mead Rd. BR2: Brom 4A **35** (6G **9**)
Queens Pas. BR7: Chst 3E **10**

Queens Rd. BR1: Brom 3C **35** (6H **9**)
BR3: Beck 6K **7**
BR7: Chst 3E **10**
CR0: Croy 3A **14**
Queensthorpe Rd. SE26 1J **7**
Queen St. CR0: Croy 7B **14**
Queensway BR4: W W'ck 7F **17**
BR5: Pet W 2F **19**
Queenswood Av. CR7: Thor H 2A **14**
Queenswood Ct. SE27 1C **6**
Queenswood Rd. DA15: Sidc 2K **5**
SE23 1J **7**
Quentins Dr. TN16: Big H 5K **29**
Quentins Wlk. *TN16: Big H 5K 29*
(off St Anns Way)
Quernmore Cl. BR1: Brom 3H **9**
Quernmore Rd. BR1: Brom 3H **9**
Quiet Nook BR2: Kes 7A **18**
Quilter Gdns. BR5: Orp 5B **20**
Quilter Rd. BR5: Orp 5B **20**
Quinton Cl. BR3: Beck 7D **8**

R

Radcliffe Rd. CR0: Croy 6E **14**
Radfield Way DA15: Sidc 4J **5**
(not continuous)
Radnor Cl. BR7: Chst 3H **11**
Radnor Wlk. CR0: Croy 3K **15**
Raeburn Rd. DA15: Sidc 3K **5**
Rafford Way BR1: Brom 4D **35** (6J **9**)
Raggleswood BR7: Chst 5D **10**
Rag Hill Cl. TN16: Tats 3D **32**
Rag Hill Rd. TN16: Tats 3C **32**
Raglan Ct. SE12 2A **4**
Raglan Rd. BR2: Brom 1K **17**
Railpit La. CR6: Warl 4A **28**
Railway Children Wlk. SE12 6A **4**
Railway Ter. TN16: Westrm 7J **33**
Rainham Cl. SE9 3K **5**
Raleigh Ct. BR3: Beck 5C **8**
Raleigh Ho. BR1: Brom 1B **35**
Raleigh M. BR6: Chels 2J **25**
Raleigh Rd. SE20 4J **7**
Ralph Perring Ct. BR3: Beck 1B **16**
Rama La. SE19 4E **6**
RAMSDEN 5B **20**
Ramsden Cl. BR5: Orp 5B **20**
Ramsden Rd. BR5: Orp 5A **20**
BR6: Orp 4A **20**
Ramsey Ct. *CR0: Croy 6A 14*
(off Church St.)
Ramuswood Av. BR6: Chels 2H **25**
Rancliffe Gdns. SE9 1D **4**
Randlesdown Rd. SE6 1B **8**
(not continuous)
Randles La. TN14: Knock 4H **31**
Randolph Rd. BR2: Brom 5C **18**
Rangefield Rd. BR1: Brom 2F **9**
Ranmore Av. CR0: Croy 7E **14**
Ranmore Path BR5: St M Cry 1K **19**
Rathbone Sq. CR0: Croy 7B **14**
Ravensbourne Av. BR2: Brom 4E **8**
Ravensbourne Ho. BR1: Brom 2E **8**
Ravensbourne Rd. BR1: Brom 5B **35** (7H **9**)
Ravensbourne Station (Rail) 4E **8**
Ravensbury Rd. BR5: St P 7J **11**
Ravenscar Rd. BR1: Brom 1F **9**
Ravens Cl. BR2: Brom 4A **35** (6G **9**)
Ravenscourt Rd. BR5: St P 7K **11**
Ravenscroft Cres. SE9 7E **4**
Ravenscroft Rd. BR3: Beck 6H **7**
Ravensdale Gdns. SE19 4C **6**
Ravenshill BR7: Chst 5E **10**
Ravensleigh Gdns. BR1: Brom 2J **9**
Ravensmead Rd. BR2: Brom 4E **8**
Ravensquay Bus. Cen.
BR5: St M Cry 2A **20**
Ravens Way SE12 2A **4**
Ravenswood Av. BR4: W W'ck 5D **16**
Ravenswood Cres. BR4: W W'ck 5D **16**
Ravenswood Rd. CR0: Wadd 7A **14**
Ravensworth Rd. SE9 7E **4**
Rawlings Cl. BR3: Beck 2D **16**
BR6: Chels 2J **25**
Rawlins Cl. CR2: Sels 4A **22**
Rayfield Cl. BR2: Brom 3B **18**
Raymead Av. CR7: Thor H 2A **14**
Raymead Pas. *CR7: Thor H 2A 14*
(off Raymead Av.)
Raymond Cl. SE26 2H **7**
Raymond Rd. BR3: Beck 1K **15**
Rays Rd. BR4: W W'ck 4D **16**
Rebecca Ct. DA14: Sidc 1A **12**
Recreation Rd. BR2: Brom 6G **9**
DA15: Sidc 7K **5**
SE26 1J **7**
Rectory Bus. Cen. DA14: Sidc 1A **12**
Rectory Cl. DA14: Sidc 1A **12**
Rectory Gdns. *BR3: Beck 5B 8*
(off Rectory Rd.)
Rectory Grn. BR3: Beck 5A **8**
Rectory Gro. CR0: Croy 6A **14**
Rectory La. DA14: Sidc 1A **12**
TN16: Tats 5D **32**
Rectory Rd. BR2: Kes 4A **24**
BR3: Beck 5B **8**
Red Cedars Rd. BR6: Orp 4H **19**
Redcourt CR0: Croy 7D **14**
Reddons Rd. BR3: Beck 4K **7**
Redgate Dr. BR2: Hayes 6J **17**
Redgrave Cl. CR0: Croy 3E **14**
Red Hill BR7: Chst 2E **10**
Redhouse Rd. TN16: Tats 2B **32**
Redlands, The BR3: Beck 6C **8**
Redlands Ct. BR1: Brom 4G **9**
Red Lion Cl. BR5: St M Cry 3B **20**
Red Lodge BR4: W W'ck 5D **16**
Red Lodge Cres. DA5: Bexl 1J **13**
Red Lodge Rd. BR4: W W'ck 5D **16**
DA5: Bexl 1J **13**
Redmans La. TN14: S'ham 3H **27**
Red Oak Cl. BR6: Farnb 7E **18**
Redroofs Cl. BR3: Beck 5C **8**
Redstart Cl. CR0: New Ad 6E **22**
Redwing Ct. *BR6: Orp 4K 19*
(off High St.)
Reed Av. BR6: Orp 7H **19**
Reed Cl. SE12 2A **4**
Rees Gdns. CR0: Croy 3E **14**
Reeves Cnr. CR0: Croy 6A **14**
Reeves Corner Stop (CT) 6A **14**
Reeves Cres. BR8: Swan 7J **13**
Reflex Apartments BR2: Brom 6D **35**
Regency M. BR3: Beck 4D **8**
Regency Wlk. CR0: Croy 3A **16**
Regent Pl. CR0: Croy 5E **14**
Regents Ct. BR1: Brom 4G **9**
Regents Dr. BR2: Kes 2A **24**
Regina Ho. SE20 5J **7**
Regina Rd. SE25 7F **7**
Reigate Rd. BR1: Brom 7A **4**
Reinickendorf Av. SE9 3H **5**
Rendle Cl. CR0: Croy 2E **14**
Rennets Cl. SE9 2K **5**
Rennets Wood Rd. SE9 2J **5**
Renown Cl. CR0: Croy 5A **14**
Renton Dr. BR5: Orp, St M Cry 4C **20**
Repton Ct. BR3: Beck 5C **8**
Repton Rd. BR6: Chels 7K **19**
Reservoir Cl. CR7: Thor H 7C **6**
Restavon Cvn. Site TN16: Big H 5K **29**
Restons Cres. SE9 3J **5**
Retreat, The BR6: Chels 3A **26**
CR7: Thor H 1C **14**
Reventlow Rd. SE9 5H **5**
Reynard Cl. BR1: Brom 7D **10**
Reynard Dr. SE19 4E **6**
Reynolds Way CR0: Croy 7D **14**
Ribston Cl. BR2: Brom 5C **18**
Rice Pde. BR5: Pet W 2G **19**
Richborough Cl. BR5: St M Cry 1C **20**
Richmond Cl. TN16: Big H 1A **32**
Richmond Rd. CR7: Thor H 7A **6**
Ricketts Hill Rd. TN16: Tats 7F **29**
Rickyard Path SE9 1D **4**
Riddons Rd. SE12 7B **4**
Rider Cl. DA15: Sidc 3K **5**
Ridge, The BR6: Orp 6G **19**
Ridgebrook Rd. SE3 1C **4**
Ridgemount Av. CR0: Croy 5J **15**
Ridgemount Cl. SE20 4G **7**
Ridges Yd. CR0: Croy 7A **14**
Ridge Way SE19 3D **6**
Ridgeway BR2: Hayes 6H **17**
Ridgeway Cres. BR6: Orp 7H **19**
Ridgeway Cres. Gdns. BR6: Orp 6H **19**
Ridgeway Dr. BR1: Brom 1J **9**
Ridgeway E. DA15: Sidc 2K **5**
Ridgeway W. DA15: Sidc 2K **5**
Ridgewell Cl. SE26 1A **8**
Ridings, The TN16: Big H 6G **29**
Ridley Rd. BR2: Brom 5A **35** (7G **9**)
Ridsdale Rd. SE20 5G **7**
Riefield Rd. SE9 1H **5**
Ring Cl. BR1: Brom 4J **9**
Ringers Ct. BR1: Brom 5B **35**
Ringers Rd. BR1: Brom 5B **35** (7H **9**)
Ringmer Way BR1: Brom 2B **18**
Ringshall Rd. BR5: St P 7K **11**
Ringwold Cl. BR3: Beck 4K **7**
Ringwood Av. BR6: Prat B 6B **26**
Ripley Cl. BR1: Brom 2C **18**
CR0: New Ad 3D **22**
Ritchie Rd. CR0: Croy 3G **15**
Riverbank Rd. BR1: Brom 1H **9**
River Gro. Pk. BR3: Beck 5A **8**
River Ho. SE26 1G **7**
River Pk. Gdns. BR2: Brom 4E **8**
River Pk. Vw. BR6: Orp 4A **20**
Riverside Cl. BR5: St P 6B **12**
Riverside Wlk. BR4: W W'ck 5C **16**
Riverwood La. BR7: Chst 5G **11**
Roberton Dr. BR1: Brom 5K **9**
Roberts Cl. BR5: St M Cry 2B **20**
CR7: Thor H 7C **6**
SE9 5J **5**
Roberts Ct. *SE20 5H 7*
(off Maple Rd.)
Roberts M. BR6: Orp 5K **19**
Robert St. CR0: Croy 7B **14**
Robina Cl. *SE20 5F 7*
(off Sycamore Gro.)
Robina Ct. BR8: Swan 6B **34**
Robin Hill Dr. BR7: Chst 3B **10**
Robin Hood Grn. BR5: St M Cry 2K **19**
Robins Ct. BR3: Beck 6E **8**
SE12 7B **4**
Robins Gro. BR4: W W'ck 7H **17**
Robin Way BR5: St P 7A **12**
Rochester Av. BR1: Brom 3D **35** (6J **9**)
Rochester Gdns. CR0: Croy 7D **14**
Rochester Way SE9 1C **4**
Rochester Way Relief Rd.
SE9 1B **4**
Rock Hill BR6: Chels 3G **27**
SE26 1E **6**
(not continuous)
Rockmount Rd. SE19 3C **6**
Rockwell Gdns. SE19 2D **6**
Roden Gdns. CR0: Croy 3D **14**
Rodney Cl. CR0: Croy 5A **14**
Rodney Gdns. BR4: W W'ck 1H **23**
Rodway Rd. BR1: Brom 1D **35** (5J **9**)
Roedean Cl. BR6: Chels 1A **26**
Roehampton Dr. BR7: Chst 3F **11**
Rogers Ct. BR8: Swan 6B **34**
Rokell Ho. *BR3: Beck 2C 8*
(off Beckenham Hill Rd.)
Rolinsden Way BR2: Kes 2A **24**
Rolleston Av. BR5: Pet W 3E **18**
Rolleston Cl. BR5: Pet W 4E **18**
Rollo Rd. BR8: Swan 2A **34**
Rolvenden Gdns. BR1: Brom 4A **10**
Romanhurst Av. BR2: Brom 1F **17**
Romanhurst Gdns. BR2: Brom 1F **17**
Roman Ind. Est. CR0: Croy 4D **14**
Roman Ri. SE19 3C **6**
Roman Way CR0: Croy 6A **14**
Romany Ri. BR5: Farnb 5F **19**
Romero Sq. SE3 1B **4**
Rommany Rd. SE27 1C **6**
(not continuous)
Romney Dr. BR1: Brom 4A **10**
Romsey Cl. BR6: Farnb 1E **24**
Ronald Cl. BR3: Beck 1A **16**
Ronald Ho. SE3 1B **4**
Ronalds Rd. BR1: Brom 1C **35** (5H **9**)
Ronaldstone Rd. DA15: Sidc 3K **5**
Ronfearn Av. BR5: St M Cry 2C **20**
Rookery Dr. BR7: Chst 5D **10**
Rookery Gdns. BR5: St M Cry 2B **20**
Rookery La. BR2: Brom 3A **18**
Rookery Rd. BR6: Downe 6C **24**
Rookesley Rd. BR5: St M Cry 4C **20**
Roper St. SE9 2E **4**
Rosamond St. SE26 1G **7**
Rosebank SE20 4G **7**
Roseberry Av. CR7: Thor H 6B **6**
Roseberry Gdns. BR6: Orp 7H **19**
Rosebery Av. DA15: Sidc 4K **5**
Rose Cotts. BR2: Kes 7K **23**
Rosecroft Cl. BR5: St M Cry 3B **20**
TN16: Big H 7H **29**
Rose Dale BR6: Farnb 6E **18**

Rosedale Pl. CR0: Croy 4J **15**
Rosehill Rd. TN16: Big H 6E **28**
Rosemount Dr. BR1: Brom 1C **18**
Rosemount Point SE23 1J **7**
Rosendale Rd. SE21 1C **6**
Roseneath Cl. BR6: Chels 4B **26**
Rosery, The CR0: Croy 3J **15**
Roseveare Rd. SE12 1K **9**
Rose Wlk. BR4: W W'ck 6D **16**
Rosewell Cl. SE20 4G **7**
Rosewood DA2: Dart 1K **13**
Rosewood Ct. BR1: Brom 5K **9**
Roslin Way BR1: Brom 2H **9**
Rosslare Cl. TN16: Westrm 7J **33**
Rosslyn Cl. BR4: W W'ck 7G **17**
Ross Rd. SE25 7C **6**
Rothesay Ct. SE12 7A **4**
Rothesay Rd. SE25 1C **14**
Rothschild St. SE27 1A **6**
Round Gro. CR0: Croy 4J **15**
Roundlyn Gdns.
BR5: St M Cry 1A **20**
Roundtable Rd. BR1: Brom 1G **9**
Roundway TN16: Big H 5E **28**
Roundwood BR7: Chst 6E **10**
Rouse Gdns. SE21 1D **6**
Rowan Gdns. CR0: Croy 7E **14**
Rowan Ho. BR2: Brom 6F **9**
DA14: Sidc 7K **5**
Rowan Rd. BR8: Swan 7J **13**
Rowan Wlk. BR2: Brom 7C **18**
Rowden Rd. BR3: Beck 5K **7**
Rowdown Cres.
CR0: New Ad 5E **22**
Rowhill Rd. BR8: Swan 1A **34**
DA2: Dart 1A **34**
Rowzill Rd. BR8: Swan 1A **34**
Roxburgh Rd. SE27 2A **6**
Roxton Gdns. CR0: Addtn 2B **22**
Royal Cl. BR6: Farnb 1E **24**
Royal Ct. SE9 5E **4**
Royal Oak Hill TN14: Knock 7D **30**
Royal Pde. BR7: Chst 4F **11**
Royal Pde. M. *BR7: Chst* *4F* ***11***
(off Royal Pde.)
Royston Rd. SE20 5J **7**
Rozel Ter. *CR0: Croy* *6B* ***14***
(off Church Rd.)
Runciman Cl. BR6: Prat B 6B **26**
Rushbrook Rd. SE9 6H **5**
Rushden Cl. SE19 4C **6**
Rushdene Wlk. TN16: Big H 6F **29**
Rushet Rd. BR5: St P 6K **11**
Rushley Cl. BR2: Kes 1A **24**
Rushmead Cl. CR0: Croy 7E **14**
Rushmore Cl. BR1: Brom 7B **10**
Rushmore Hill BR6: Prat B 5B **26**
TN14: Prat B 5B **26**
Rusholme Gro. SE19 2D **6**
Ruskin Dr. BR6: Orp 7H **19**
Ruskin Rd. CR0: Croy 6A **14**
Ruskin Wlk. BR2: Brom 3C **18**
Rusland Av. BR6: Orp 7G **19**
Russell Cl. BR3: Beck 7C **8**
Russet Dr. CR0: Croy 5K **15**
Russett Cl. BR6: Chels 2A **26**
Russett Way BR8: Swan 6J **13**
Rusthall Cl. CR0: Croy 3H **15**
Rutland Ct. BR7: Chst 5D **10**
SE9 6H **5**
Rutland Ga. BR2: Brom 7A **35** (1G **17**)
Rutland Way
BR5: St M Cry 3B **20**
RUXLEY 4D **12**
Ruxley Cl. DA14: Sidc 3C **12**
Ruxley Cnr. Ind. Est.
DA14: Sidc 3C **12**
Ruxton Cl. BR8: Swan 7K **13**
Ruxton Ct. BR8: Swan 7K **13**
Ryan Cl. SE3 1A **4**
Ryarsh Cres. BR6: Orp 1H **25**
Rydal Dr. BR4: W W'ck 6F **17**
Rydal Mt. BR2: Brom 1G **17**
Rydens Ho. SE9 7B **4**
Ryder Cl. BR1: Brom 2J **9**
Rye Cres. BR5: Orp 5B **20**
Ryecroft Rd. BR5: Pet W 3G **19**
SW16 3A **6**
Rye Fld. BR5: Orp 5C **20**
Ryefield Rd. SE19 3B **6**
Ryelands Cres. SE12 3B **4**
Rymer Rd. CR0: Croy 4D **14**

S

Sackville Av. BR2: Hayes 5H **17**
Sainsbury Rd. SE19 2D **6**
St Amunds Cl. SE6 1B **8**
St Andrews Ct. BR8: Swan 7K **13**
St Andrew's Dr. BR5: St M Cry 3A **20**
St Andrew's Rd. CR0: Croy 7B **14**
DA14: Sidc 1C **12**
St Anne's Ct. BR4: W W'ck 1F **23**
St Anns Way TN16: Big H 5K **29**
St Anthony's Ct. BR6: Farnb 6E **18**
St Arvan's Cl. CR0: Croy 7D **14**
St Aubyn's Cl. BR6: Orp 7J **19**
St Aubyn's Gdns. BR6: Orp 6J **19**
St Aubyn's Rd. SE19 3E **6**
St Augustine's Av. BR2: Brom 2B **18**
St Barnabas Cl. BR3: Beck 6D **8**
St Bartholomew's Cl.
SE26 1G **7**
St Benjamins Dr. BR6: Prat B 5B **26**
St Bernards CR0: Croy 7D **14**
St Bernard's Cl. SE27 1C **6**
St Blaise Av. BR1: Brom 3D **35** (6J **9**)
ST CHRISTOPHER'S HOSPICE 2H **7**
St Clair's Rd. CR0: Croy 6D **14**
St Clement's Hgts. SE26 1F **7**
St Cloud Rd. SE27 1B **6**
St Daniel Ct. *BR3: Beck* *4B* ***8***
(off Brackley Rd.)
St David's Cl. BR4: W W'ck 4C **16**
St David's Ct. BR1: Brom 7E **10**
St Davids Rd. BR8: Swan 1A **34**
St Denis Rd. SE27 1C **6**
St Dunstan's La. BR3: Beck 3D **16**
St Dunstan's Rd. SE25 1E **14**
St Edward's Cl. CR0: New Ad 7E **22**
St Francis Cl. BR5: Pet W 3H **19**
St Georges Rd. BR1: Brom 6C **10**
BR3: Beck 5C **8**
BR5: Pet W 3G **19**
BR8: Swan 6A **34**
(not continuous)
DA14: Sidc 3C **12**
St George's Rd. W. BR1: Brom 5B **10**
St George's Wlk. CR0: Croy 7B **14**
St Giles Cl. BR6: Farnb 2G **25**
St Gothard Rd. SE27 1C **6**
(not continuous)
St Hilary's Ct. BR1: Brom 7E **10**
St Hugh's Rd. SE20 5G **7**
St James's Av. BR3: Beck 7K **7**
St James's Pk. CR0: Croy 4B **14**
St James's Rd. CR0: Croy 4A **14**
St James Ter. *BR6: Prat B* *5B* ***26***
(off St Benjamins Dr.)
St James Way DA14: Sidc 2D **12**
St Johns Cl. TN16: Big H 5K **29**
St John's Cotts. SE20 4H **7**
St Johns Pde. *DA14: Sidc* *1K* ***11***
(off Sidcup High St.)
St Johns Ri. TN16: Big H 5K **29**
St John's Rd. BR5: Pet W 3G **19**
CR0: Croy 7A **14**
DA14: Sidc 1A **12**
SE20 3H **7**
St Joseph's Cl. BR6: Orp 1J **25**
St Joseph's College Sports Cen. 3A **6**
St Justin Cl. BR5: St P 7C **12**
St Keverne Rd. SE9 1B **10**
St Kilda Rd. BR6: Orp 5J **19**
St Kitts Ter. SE19 2D **6**
St Laurence Cl. BR5: St P 7C **12**
St Leonard's Ri. BR6: Orp 1H **25**
St Leonard's Rd. CR0: Wadd 7A **14**
St Louis Rd. SE27 1C **6**
St Luke's Cl. BR8: Swan 6J **13**
SE25 3G **15**
St Margarets Av. DA15: Sidc 7J **5**
TN16: Big H 5K **29**
St Margaret's Cl. BR6: Chels 1A **26**
St Mark's Rd. BR2: Brom 6D **35** (7H **9**)
SE25 1F **15**
St Martin's La. BR3: Beck 2C **16**
ST MARY CRAY 1B **20**
St Mary Cray Station (Rail) 1A **20**
St Mary's Av. BR2: Brom 7F **9**
St Mary's Cl. BR5: St P 6A **12**
St Mary's Grn. TN16: Big H 7E **28**
St Mary's Gro. TN16: Big H 7E **28**
St Mary's Pl. SE9 3E **4**
St Mary's Rd. BR8: Swan 1J **21**
SE25 7D **6**
St Matthew's Dr. BR1: Brom 7C **10**
St Merryn Ct. BR3: Beck 4B **8**
St Michael's Cl. BR1: Brom 7B **10**
St Michael's Rd. CR0: Croy 5B **14**
St Nicolas La. BR7: Chst 5B **10**
St Oswald's Rd. SW16 5A **6**
ST PAUL'S CRAY 6A **12**
St Paul's Cray Rd. BR7: Chst 5G **11**
St Paul's Rd. CR7: Thor H 7B **6**
St Paul's Sq. BR2: Brom 3B **35** (6G **9**)
St Paul's Wood Hill BR5: St P 6H **11**
St Peter Claver Ct. *BR3: Beck* *5C* ***8***
(off Albemarle Rd.)
St Peters Av. TN16: Big H 5K **29**
St Peter's Cl. BR7: Chst 4G **11**
St Peter's La. BR5: St P 6K **11**
St Peter's Rd. CR0: Croy 7C **14**
St Saviour's Coll. SE27 1C **6**
St Saviour's Rd. CR0: Croy 3A **14**
Saints Cl. SE27 1A **6**
St Thomas Dr. BR5: Farnb 5F **19**
St Timothys M. BR1: Brom 2D **35** (5J **9**)
St Vincent Cl. SE27 2A **6**
St Winifred's Rd. TN16: Big H 7H **29**
Sala Ho. SE3 1A **4**
Salcot Cres. CR0: New Ad 6D **22**
Salem Pl. CR0: Croy 7B **14**
Salisbury Av. BR8: Swan 6B **34**
Salisbury Rd. BR2: Brom 2B **18**
SE25 3F **15**
Saltbox Hill TN16: Big H 2D **28**
Salter's Hill SE19 2C **6**
Saltwood Cl. BR6: Chels 1B **26**
Samos Rd. SE20 6G **7**
Samuel Palmer Ct. *BR6: Orp* *4K* ***19***
(off Chislehurst Rd.)
Sandby Grn. SE9 1D **4**
Sandersons Av. TN14: Hals 6F **27**
Sanderson Sq. BR1: Brom 7D **10**
Sanderstead Rd. BR5: St M Cry 3A **20**
Sandfield Gdns. CR7: Thor H 7A **6**
Sandfield Pas. CR7: Thor H 7B **6**
Sandfield Pl. CR7: Thor H 7B **6**
Sandfield Rd. CR7: Thor H 7A **6**
Sandford Rd. BR2: Brom 6C **35** (7H **9**)
Sandhurst Rd. BR6: Chels 7K **19**
DA15: Sidc 1J **11**
Sandiland Cres. BR2: Hayes 6G **17**
Sandilands CR0: Croy 6F **15**
Sandilands Stop (CT) 6E **14**
Sandling Ri. SE9 7F **5**
Sandown Ct. SE26 1G **7**
Sandown Rd. SE25 2G **15**
Sandpiper Way BR5: St P 1C **20**
Sandpit Rd. BR1: Brom 2F **9**
Sandpits Rd. CR0: Croy 7J **15**
Sandringham Rd. BR1: Brom 2H **9**
CR7: Thor H 2B **14**
Sandrock Pl. CR0: Croy 7J **15**
Sandstone Rd. SE12 6A **4**
Sandway Path *BR5: St M Cry* *1B* ***20***
(off Okemore Gdns.)
Sandway Rd. BR5: St M Cry 1B **20**
Sandy Bury BR6: Orp 7G **19**
Sandy La. BR5: St P 6C **12**
BR6: Orp 4K **19**
DA14: Sidc 6C **12**
TN16: Westrm 7J **33**
Sandy Ridge BR7: Chst 3D **10**
Sandy Way CR0: Croy 7A **16**
Sangley Rd. SE25 1D **14**
Saphora Cl. BR6: Farnb 2G **25**
Saracen Cl. CR0: Croy 3C **14**
Sarjeant Ct. *BR4: W W'ck* *6E* ***16***
(off Bencurtis Pk.)
Sarre Rd. BR5: St M Cry 2B **20**
Savile Gdns. CR0: Croy 6E **14**
Saville Row BR2: Hayes 5G **17**
Saxon Lodge *CR0: Croy* *5B* ***14***
(off Tavistock Rd.)
Saxon Rd. BR1: Brom 4G **9**
SE25 2C **14**
Saxon Wlk. DA14: Sidc 3B **12**
Saxville Rd. BR5: St P 7A **12**
Sayes Ct. Rd. BR5: St P 1K **19**
Scadbury Gdns. BR5: St P 6K **11**
Scadbury Pk. Nature Reserve 4J **11**
Scads Hill Cl. BR6: Pet W 3J **19**
Scarborough Cl. TN16: Big H 7E **28**
Scarbrook Rd. CR0: Croy 7B **14**

Scarlet Cl. BR5: St P . . . 1A **20**
School La. BR8: Swan . . . 3C **34**
School Rd. BR7: Chst . . . 5F **11**
Scotney Cl. BR6: Farnb . . . 1D **24**
Scotsdale Cl. BR5: Pet W . . . 1H **19**
Scotsdale Rd. SE12 . . . 2A **4**
Scotts Av. BR2: Brom . . . 6E **8**
Scott's La. BR2: Brom . . . 7E **8**
Scotts Rd. BR1: Brom . . . 1B **35** (4H **9**)
Scotts Ter. SE9 . . . 6D **4**
Seabrook Dr. BR4: W W'ck . . . 6F **17**
Sedcombe Cl. DA14: Sidc . . . 1A **12**
Sedgehill Rd. SE6 . . . 1B **8**
Sedgewood Cl. BR2: Hayes . . . 4G **17**
Seeley Dr. SE21 . . . 1D **6**
Sefton Cl. BR5: St M Cry . . . 1J **19**
Sefton Rd. BR5: St M Cry . . . 1J **19**
CR0: Croy . . . 5F **15**
Selah Dr. BR8: Swan . . . 5H **13**
Selborne Rd. CR0: Croy . . . 7D **14**
DA14: Sidc . . . 1A **12**
Selby Cl. BR7: Chst . . . 3D **10**
Selby Rd. SE20 . . . 6F **7**
SELHURST . . . **3D 14**
Selhurst New Rd. SE25 . . . 3D **14**
Selhurst Pk. . . . **1D 14**
Selhurst Pl. SE25 . . . 3D **14**
Selhurst Rd. SE25 . . . 3D **14**
Selhurst Station (Rail) . . . **2D 14**
Sellindge Cl. BR3: Beck . . . 4A **8**
Selsdon Pk. Rd. CR0: Sels . . . 5A **22**
CR2: Sels . . . 5A **22**
Selsdon Rd. SE27 . . . 1A **6**
Selsdon Wood Nature Reserve . . . **7A 22**
Selwood Rd. CR0: Croy . . . 6G **15**
Selwyn Pl. BR5: St P . . . 7A **12**
Seneca Rd. CR7: Thor H . . . 1B **14**
Senlac Rd. SE12 . . . 5A **4**
Sennen Wlk. SE9 . . . 7D **4**
Sequoia Gdns. BR6: Orp . . . 4J **19**
Sermon Dr. BR8: Swan . . . 7H **13**
Serviden Dr. BR1: Brom . . . 5A **10**
Servite Ho. BR3: Beck . . . 5A **8**
Seven Acres BR8: Crock . . . 3J **21**
Sevenoaks Rd. BR6: Chels, Orp . . . 2J **25**
BR6: Prat B . . . 4J **25**
TN14: Hals . . . 5D **26**
Sevenoaks Way BR5: St P . . . 4B **12**
DA14: Sidc . . . 4B **12**
Seward Rd. BR3: Beck . . . 6J **7**
Seymour Dr. BR2: Brom . . . 5C **18**
Seymour Pl. SE25 . . . 1G **15**
Seymour Ter. SE20 . . . 5G **7**
Seymour Vs. SE20 . . . 5G **7**
Shacklands Rd. TN14: Hals, S'ham . . . 7G **27**
Shaftesbury Rd. BR3: Beck . . . 6A **8**
Shalford Cl. BR6: Farnb . . . 1F **25**
Shallons Rd. SE9 . . . 1E **10**
Shannon Ct. *CR0: Croy* . . . *5B* ***14***
(off Tavistock Rd.)
Shannon Way BR3: Beck . . . 3C **8**
Sharman Ct. *DA14: Sidc* . . . *1K* ***11***
(off Carlton Rd.)
Shawbrooke Rd. SE9 . . . 2B **4**
Shawfield Pk. BR1: Brom . . . 6A **10**
Shaw Path BR1: Brom . . . 1G **9**
Shaw Rd. BR1: Brom . . . 1G **9**
TN16: Tats . . . 2B **32**
Shaxton Cres. CR0: New Ad . . . 5D **22**
Sheenewood SE26 . . . 1G **7**
Sheen Rd. BR5: St M Cry . . . 1J **19**
Sheepbarn La. CR6: Big H . . . 1B **28**
Sheepcote La. BR5: St M Cry . . . 2E **20**
BR8: Swan . . . 2E **20**
Shelbourne Pl. BR3: Beck . . . 4A **8**
Shelbury Cl. DA14: Sidc . . . 1K **11**
Sheldon Cl. SE12 . . . 2A **4**
SE20 . . . 5G **7**
Sheldon St. CR0: Croy . . . 7B **14**
Sheldwich Ter. BR2: Brom . . . 3B **18**
Shelford Ri. SE19 . . . 4E **6**
Shell Cl. BR2: Brom . . . 3B **18**
Shelley Cl. BR6: Orp . . . 7H **19**
Shelleys La. TN14: Knock . . . 5D **30**
Shepherd's Cl. BR6: Orp . . . 7J **19**
Shepherds Grn. BR7: Chst . . . 4G **11**
Shepherds Leas SE9 . . . 1H **5**
Sheppards Coll. BR1: Brom . . . 2B **35**
Shepperton Rd. BR5: Pet W . . . 3F **19**
Sherard Rd. SE9 . . . 2D **4**
Sherborne Rd. BR5: St M Cry . . . 1J **19**
Sheridan Cl. BR8: Swan . . . 6A **34**
Sheridan Cres. BR7: Chst . . . 6E **10**
Sheridan Lodge *BR2: Brom* . . . *1K* ***17***
(off Homesdale Rd.)
Sheridan Way BR3: Beck . . . 5A **8**
Sheringham Rd. SE20 . . . 7H **7**
Sherlies Av. BR6: Orp . . . 6H **19**
Sherman Rd. BR1: Brom . . . 2C **35** (5H **9**)
Sherwood Rd. CR0: Croy . . . 4G **15**
Sherwood Way BR4: W W'ck . . . 6D **16**
Shinners Cl. SE25 . . . 2F **15**
Shipfield Cl. TN16: Tats . . . 3B **32**
Ship Hill TN16: Tats . . . 3B **32**
Ship La. BR8: Swan . . . 3E **34**
DA4: Sutt H, Swan . . . 3E **34**
Shire La. BR2: Kes . . . 5B **24**
BR6: Chels, Downe . . . 4E **24**
(not continuous)
SHIRLEY . . . **6H 15**
Shirley Av. CR0: Croy . . . 5H **15**
Shirley Chu. Rd. CR0: Croy . . . 7J **15**
Shirley Cres. BR3: Beck . . . 1K **15**
SHIRLEY OAKS . . . **5J 15**
SHIRLEY OAKS BMI HOSPITAL . . . **4H 15**
Shirley Oaks Rd. CR0: Croy . . . 5J **15**
Shirley Pk. CR0: Croy . . . 6H **15**
Shirley Pk. Rd. CR0: Croy . . . 5G **15**
Shirley Rd. CR0: Croy . . . 4G **15**
DA15: Sidc . . . 7K **5**
Shirley Way CR0: Croy . . . 7K **15**
Shirley Windmill . . . **7H 15**
Sholden Gdns. BR5: St M Cry . . . 2B **20**
SHOREHAM . . . **7K 27**
Shoreham Cl. CR0: Croy . . . 3H **15**
Shoreham La. BR6: Chels . . . 3F **27**
TN14: Hals . . . 7F **27**
Shoreham Rd. BR5: St P . . . 5A **12**
Shoreham Way BR2: Hayes . . . 3H **17**
Shorne Cl. BR5: St M Cry . . . 1C **20**
Shornefield Cl. BR1: Brom . . . 7D **10**
SHORTLANDS . . . **6F 9**
Shortlands Gdns. BR2: Brom . . . 6F **9**
Shortlands Gro. BR2: Brom . . . 7E **8**
Shortlands Rd. BR2: Brom . . . 7E **8**
Shortlands Station (Rail) . . . **6F 9**
Short Way SE9 . . . 1D **4**
Shottery Cl. SE9 . . . 7D **4**
Shrapnel Rd. SE9 . . . 1E **4**
Shrewsbury Rd. BR3: Beck . . . 7K **7**
Shroffold Rd. BR1: Brom . . . 7A **4**
Shrublands Av. CR0: Croy . . . 7B **16**
Shrublands Cl. SE26 . . . 1H **7**
Shrubsall Cl. SE9 . . . 5D **4**
Shurlock Av. BR8: Swan . . . 6J **13**
Shurlock Dr. BR6: Farnb . . . 1F **25**
Shuttle Cl. DA15: Sidc . . . 4K **5**
Sibley Cl. BR1: Brom . . . 2B **18**
Sibley Ct. BR2: Brom . . . 6E **8**
Sibthorpe Rd. SE12 . . . 3A **4**
SIDCUP . . . **1K 11**
Sidcup By-Pass BR5: Sidc, Swan, St P . . . 1H **11**
BR7: Chst, Sidc . . . 7J **5**
DA14: Sidc . . . 1H **11**
Sidcup High St. DA14: Sidc . . . 1K **11**
Sidcup Hill DA14: Sidc . . . 1A **12**
Sidcup Hill Gdns. DA14: Sidc . . . 2B **12**
Sidcup Place . . . **2K 11**
Sidcup Pl. DA14: Sidc . . . 2K **11**
Sidcup Rd. SE9 . . . 5E **4**
SE12 . . . 3B **4**
Sidcup Technical Cen. DA14: Sidc . . . 2C **12**
Siddons Rd. CR0: Wadd . . . 7A **14**
Sidewood Rd. SE9 . . . 5J **5**
Sidmouth Rd. BR5: St M Cry . . . 2A **20**
(not continuous)
Sidney Rd. BR3: Beck . . . 6K **7**
SE25 . . . 2F **15**
Silbury Ho. SE26 . . . 1F **7**
Silver Birch Cl. DA2: Dart . . . 1K **13**
SE6 . . . 1A **8**
Silverdale SE26 . . . 1H **7**
Silverdale Dr. SE9 . . . 6D **4**
Silverdale Rd. BR5: Pet W . . . 1F **19**
BR5: St P . . . 7K **11**
Silver La. BR4: W W'ck . . . 6E **16**
Silverstead La. TN16: Westrm . . . 3J **33**
Silverwood Cl. BR3: Beck . . . 4B **8**
CR0: Sels . . . 5A **22**
Simnel Rd. SE12 . . . 4A **4**
Simone Cl. BR1: Brom . . . 5A **10**
Simpsons Rd. BR2: Brom . . . 6C **35** (7H **9**)
Sinclair Ct. CR0: Croy . . . 6D **14**
Singles Cross La. TN14: Knock . . . 3G **31**
SINGLE STREET . . . **4K 29**
Single St. TN16: Big H . . . 4K **29**
Singleton Cl. CR0: Croy . . . 4B **14**
Sissinghurst Cl. BR1: Brom . . . 2F **9**
Sissinghurst Rd. CR0: Croy . . . 4F **15**
Siward Rd. BR2: Brom . . . 6E **35** (7J **9**)
Skeet Hill La. BR5: Orp . . . 7F **21**
BR6: Orp . . . 5D **20**
Skibbs La. BR5: Orp, St M Cry . . . 6E **20**
BR6: Chels, Orp . . . 2D **26**
Skid Hill La. CR6: Warl . . . 1B **28**
Skyline Ct. *CR0: Croy* . . . *7C* ***14***
(off Park La.)
Skyview Apartments *CR0: Croy* . . . *6B* ***14***
(off Park St.)
Slades Dr. BR7: Chst . . . 7H **5**
Slip, The TN16: Westrm . . . 7H **33**
SLOANE BMI HOSPITAL, THE . . . **5E 8**
Sloane Gdns. BR6: Farnb . . . 7F **19**
Sloane Wlk. CR0: Croy . . . 3A **16**
Smarden Gro. SE9 . . . 1C **10**
Smiths Yd. *CR0: Croy* . . . *7B* ***14***
(off St George's Wlk.)
Smock Wlk. CR0: Croy . . . 3B **14**
Snag La. BR6: Cud, Prat B . . . 7H **25**
TN14: Cud . . . 1B **30**
Snodland Cl. BR6: Downe . . . 6D **24**
Snowdown Cl. SE20 . . . 5H **7**
Socket La. BR2: Hayes . . . 3J **17**
Somerden Rd. BR5: St M Cry . . . 4C **20**
Somerset Rd. BR6: Orp . . . 4K **19**
Somertrees Av. SE12 . . . 6A **4**
Somerville Rd. SE20 . . . 4J **7**
Sonnet Wlk. TN16: Big H . . . 7D **28**
Sonning Rd. SE25 . . . 3F **15**
Sopwith Cl. TN16: Big H . . . 5F **29**
Sounds Lodge BR8: Crock . . . 3H **21**
South Bank TN16: Westrm . . . 7J **33**
Southbank BR8: Swan . . . 2A **34**
SOUTHBOROUGH . . . **2C 18**
Southborough La. BR2: Brom . . . 2B **18**
Southborough Rd. BR1: Brom . . . 7B **10**
Southbourne BR2: Hayes . . . 4H **17**
Southbourne Gdns. SE12 . . . 2A **4**
Southbridge Pl. CR0: Croy . . . 7B **14**
Southbridge Rd. CR0: Croy . . . 7B **14**
Southcote Rd. SE25 . . . 2G **15**
Southcroft Av. BR4: W W'ck . . . 6D **16**
Southcroft Rd. BR6: Orp . . . 7H **19**
Sth. Croxted Rd. SE21 . . . 1C **6**
Southdene TN14: Hals . . . 2K **31**
(not continuous)
South Dr. BR6: Orp . . . 2H **25**
Sth. Eden Pk. Rd. BR3: Beck . . . 3C **16**
SOUTHEND . . . **1E 8**
South End CR0: Croy . . . 7B **14**
Southend Cl. SE9 . . . 3G **5**
Southend Cres. SE9 . . . 3G **5**
Southend La. SE6 . . . 1A **8**
SE26 . . . 1A **8**
Southend Rd. BR3: Beck . . . 5B **8**
Southern Av. SE25 . . . 7E **6**
Southern Pl. BR8: Swan . . . 1J **21**
Southey St. SE20 . . . 4J **7**
Southfield Rd. BR7: Chst . . . 7K **11**
Southfields BR8: Swan . . . 4K **13**
Southfleet Rd. BR6: Orp . . . 7H **19**
South Hill BR7: Chst . . . 3C **10**
Sth. Hill Rd. BR2: Brom . . . 7F **9**
Southholme Cl. SE19 . . . 5D **6**
Southill Ct. BR2: Brom . . . 2G **17**
Southill Rd. BR7: Chst . . . 4B **10**
Southlands Av. BR6: Orp . . . 1G **25**
Southlands Gro. BR1: Brom . . . 7B **10**
Southlands Rd. BR1: Brom . . . 2K **17**
BR2: Brom . . . 2K **17**
South London Theatre . . . ***1A 6***
(off Norwood High St.)
SOUTH NORWOOD . . . **1E 14**
South Norwood Country Pk. . . . **1H 15**
South Norwood Country Pk. Vis. Cen. . . . **1G 15**
Sth. Norwood Hill SE25 . . . 5D **6**
South Norwood Pools & Fitness Cen. . . . **2G 15**
Southold Ri. SE9 . . . 7E **4**
Southover BR1: Brom . . . 2H **9**
South Pk. Ct. BR3: Beck . . . 4B **8**
Southspring DA15: Sidc . . . 4J **5**
SOUTH STREET . . . **1F 33**
South St. BR1: Brom . . . 3C **35** (6H **9**)
Southvale SE19 . . . 3D **6**
South Vw. BR1: Brom . . . 6K **9**
Southview Cl. BR8: Swan . . . 6B **34**

South Vw. Ct. SE19 4B **6**
Southview Rd. BR1: Brom 1E **8**
South Wlk. BR4: W W'ck 7F **17**
Southwark Pl. BR1: Brom 7C **10**
Southwater Cl. BR3: Beck 4C **8**
South Way BR2: Hayes 4H **17**
CR0: Croy 7K **15**
Southwood Cl. BR1: Brom 1C **18**
Southwood Rd. SE9 6G **5**
Sowerby Cl. SE9 2D **4**
Spa at Beckenham, The 5A **8**
Spa Cl. SE25 5D **6**
Spa Hill SE19 5C **6**
Sparkes Cl. BR2: Brom 7D **35** (1J **17**)
Sparrow Dr. BR5: Farnb 5F **19**
Sparrow's Farm Leisure Cen. 4H **5**
Sparrows La. SE9 4H **5**
Speakers Ct. CR0: Croy 5C **14**
Speke Hill SE9 7E **4**
Speke Rd. CR7: Thor H 6C **6**
Speldhurst Cl. BR2: Brom 2G **17**
Spencer Cl. BR6: Orp 6H **19**
Spencer Ct. BR6: Farnb 2F **25**
Spencer Gdns. SE9 2E **4**
Spencer Pl. CR0: Croy 4C **14**
Spencer Rd. BR1: Brom 4G **9**
Spinney, The BR8: Swan 6K **13**
DA14: Sidc 2D **12**
Spinney Cl. BR3: Beck 1C **16**
Spinney Gdns. SE19 2E **6**
Spinney Oak BR1: Brom 6B **10**
Spinneys, The BR1: Brom 6C **10**
Spinney Way TN14: Cud 7G **25**
Spire Ct. *BR3: Beck* *6C* ***8***
(off Crescent Rd.)
Sport Croydon 1B **14**
Spout Hill CR0: Addtn 2B **22**
Springbourne Ct. BR3: Beck 5D **8**
(not continuous)
Springfield Av. BR8: Swan 6A **34**
Springfield Gdns. BR1: Brom 1C **18**
BR4: W W'ck 6C **16**
Springfield Ri. SE26 1G **7**
Springfield Rd. BR1: Brom 1C **18**
CR7: Thor H 5B **6**
SE26 2G **7**
Springfield Wlk. *BR6: Orp* *5G* ***19***
(off Place Farm Av.)
Spring Gdns. BR6: Chels 3A **26**
TN16: Big H 7E **28**
Spring Gro. SE19 4E **6**
Spring Hill SE26 1H **7**
Springholm Cl. TN16: Big H 7E **28**
Springhurst Cl. CR0: Croy 1A **22**
Spring La. SE25 3G **15**
SPRING PARK 7B **16**
Spring Pk. Av. CR0: Croy 6J **15**
Springpark Dr. BR3: Beck 7D **8**
Spring Pk. Rd. CR0: Croy 6J **15**
Spring Shaw Rd. BR5: St P 5K **11**
Spring Va. Cl. BR8: Swan 3A **34**
Springvale Retail Pk. BR5: St P 7B **12**
(not continuous)
Springvale Way BR5: St P 7B **12**
Sprucedale Cl. BR8: Swan 6K **13**
Sprucedale Gdns. CR0: Croy 7J **15**
Spruce Pk. BR2: Brom 7A **35** (1G **17**)
Spruce Rd. TN16: Big H 5F **29**
Spurgeon Av. SE19 5C **6**
Spurgeon Rd. SE19 5C **6**
Spurrell Av. DA5: Bexl 1J **13**
Spur Rd. BR6: Orp 6K **19**
Square, The BR8: Swan 7J **13**
TN16: Tats 2B **32**
Squires Fld. BR8: Swan 3B **34**
Squires Way DA2: Dart 1J **13**
Squires Wood Dr. BR7: Chst 4B **10**
Squirrels Cl. BR6: Orp 5H **19**
Squirrels Drey *BR2: Brom* *6F* ***9***
(off Park Hill Rd.)
Stables End BR6: Farnb 7F **19**
Stables M. SE27 2B **6**
Staddon Cl. BR3: Beck 1K **15**
Stafford Rd. DA14: Sidc 1H **11**
Stainer Ho. SE3 1B **4**
Staines Wlk. DA14: Sidc 3B **12**
Stainmore Cl. BR7: Chst 5G **11**
Stalisfield Pl. BR6: Downe 6D **24**
Stambourne Way BR4: W W'ck 6D **16**
SE19 4D **6**
Stambourne Woodland Wlk. SE19 4D **6**
Stamford Dr. BR2: Brom 7A **35** (1G **17**)
Standard Rd. BR6: Downe 6D **24**
Standish Ho. *SE3* *1A* ***4***
(off Elford Cl.)
Stanger Rd. SE25 1F **15**
Stanhill Cotts. DA2: Dart 4J **13**
Stanhope Av. BR2: Hayes 5G **17**
Stanhope Gro. BR3: Beck 2A **16**
Stanhope Rd. CR0: Croy 7D **14**
DA15: Sidc 1K **11**
Stanley Av. BR3: Beck 6D **8**
Stanley Gro. CR0: Croy 3A **14**
Stanley Rd. BR2: Brom 7E **35** (1J **17**)
BR6: Orp 5K **19**
CR0: Croy 3A **14**
DA14: Sidc 1K **11**
Stanley Way BR5: St M Cry 2A **20**
Stanmore Ter. BR3: Beck 6B **8**
Stanstead Cl. BR2: Brom 2G **17**
Stanton Cl. BR5: Orp 4B **20**
Stanton Rd. CR0: Croy 4B **14**
SE26 1A **8**
Stanton Sq. SE26 1A **8**
Stanton Way SE26 1A **8**
Staples, The BR8: Swan 3C **34**
Stapleton Rd. BR6: Orp 1J **25**
Starbeck Cl. SE9 4F **5**
Star Hill Rd. TN14: Dun G 5K **31**
Star La. BR5: St M Cry 1B **20**
Starling Cl. CR0: Croy 3K **15**
Starts Cl. BR6: Farnb 7D **18**
Starts Hill Av. BR6: Farnb 1E **24**
Starts Hill Rd. BR6: Farnb 7D **18**
State Farm Av. BR6: Farnb 1E **24**
Station App. *BR1: Brom* *6C* ***35***
(off High St.)
BR2: Hayes 5H **17**
BR3: Beck 5B **8**
BR4: W W'ck 4D **16**
BR5: St M Cry 1A **20**
BR6: Chels 2A **26**
BR6: Orp 6J **19**
BR7: Chst 3B **10**
(Elmstead La.)
BR7: Chst 5D **10**
(Vale Rd.)
BR8: Swan 1K **21**
SE3 1A **4**
SE9 6H **5**
(Bercta Rd.)
SE9 5E **4**
(Crossmead)
SE26 1H **7**
Station Cotts. BR6: Orp 6J **19**
Station Est. BR3: Beck 7J **7**
Station Hill BR2: Hayes 6H **17**
Station Rd. BR1: Brom 2C **35** (5H **9**)
BR2: Brom 6F **9**
BR4: W W'ck 5D **16**
BR5: St P 1B **20**
BR6: Orp 6J **19**
BR8: Swan 1K **21**
CR0: Croy 5B **14**
DA15: Sidc 1K **11**
SE20 3H **7**
SE25 1E **14**
TN14: Hals 6E **26**
Station Sq. BR5: Pet W 2F **19**
Stedman Cl. DA5: Bexl 1K **13**
Steep Cl. BR6: Chels 3J **25**
Steep Hill CR0: Croy 7D **14**
Steeple Hgts. Dr.
TN16: Big H 6F **29**
Stembridge Rd. SE20 6G **7**
Stephen Cl. BR6: Orp 7H **19**
Sterling Ho. SE3 1A **4**
Steve Biko La. SE6 1B **8**
Stevens Cl. BR3: Beck 3B **8**
DA5: Bexl 1J **13**
Stewart Cl. BR7: Chst 2E **10**
Steyning Gro. SE9 1C **10**
Stiles Cl. BR2: Brom 3C **18**
Stirling Cl. DA14: Sidc 1H **11**
Stirling Dr. BR6: Chels 2A **26**
Stockbury Rd. CR0: Croy 3H **15**
Stock Hill TN16: Big H 5F **29**
Stockwell Cl. BR1: Brom 4D **35** (6J **9**)
Stodart Rd. SE20 5H **7**
Stofield Gdns. SE9 7C **4**
Stokes Rd. CR0: Croy 3J **15**
Stoms Path *SE6* *2B* ***8***
(off Maroons Way)
Stonegate Cl. BR5: St P 7B **12**
STONEHILL GREEN 4H **13**
Stonehill Woods Pk. DA14: Sidc 3G **13**
Stonehouse La. TN14: Hals 5C **26**
Stonehouse Rd. TN14: Hals 6B **26**
Stoneings La. TN14: Knock 7D **30**
Stoneleigh Pk. Av. CR0: Croy 3J **15**
Stoneleigh Rd. BR1: Brom 7E **10**
Stone Pk. Av. BR3: Beck 1B **16**
Stone Rd. BR2: Brom 2G **17**
Stones Cross Rd. BR8: Crock 2H **21**
Stoney La. SE19 3E **6**
Storrington Rd. CR0: Croy 5E **14**
Stour Cl. BR2: Kes 1K **23**
Stowell Av. CR0: New Ad 6E **22**
Stowe Rd. BR6: Chels 1A **26**
Stowting Rd. BR6: Orp 1H **25**
Stratford Ho. Av. BR1: Brom 7B **10**
Stratford Rd. CR7: Thor H 1A **14**
Strathaven Rd. SE12 3A **4**
Strathmore Rd. CR0: Croy 4C **14**
Strathyre Av. SW16 7A **6**
Strawberry Flds. BR8: Swan 5K **13**
Streamside Cl. BR2: Brom 7C **35** (1H **17**)
Stretton Rd. CR0: Croy 4D **14**
Strickland Way BR6: Orp 1J **25**
Strongbow Cres. SE9 2E **4**
Strongbow Rd. SE9 2E **4**
Stroud Grn. Gdns. CR0: Croy 4H **15**
Stroud Grn. Way CR0: Croy 4G **15**
Stroud Rd. SE25 3F **15**
Stuart Av. BR2: Hayes 5H **17**
Stuart Cl. BR8: Swan 2A **34**
Stuart Ct. *CR0: Croy* *7A* ***14***
(off St John's Rd.)
Stuart Cres. CR0: Croy 7A **16**
Stuart Rd. CR7: Thor H 1B **14**
Stubbs Hill BR6: Prat B 2G **31**
Studio Arts & Media Cen., The 5K **7**
Studland Rd. SE26 2J **7**
Studley Ct. DA14: Sidc 2A **12**
Stumps Hill La. BR3: Beck 3B **8**
Sturges Fld. BR7: Chst 3G **11**
Styles Way BR3: Beck 1D **16**
Sudbury Cres. BR1: Brom 3H **9**
Sudbury Gdns. CR0: Croy 7D **14**
Suffield Rd. SE20 6H **7**
Suffolk Ho. *CR0: Croy* *6C* ***14***
(off George St.)
SE20 *5J* ***7***
(off Croydon Rd.)
Suffolk Rd. DA14: Sidc 3B **12**
SE25 1E **14**
Sultan St. BR3: Beck 6J **7**
Summerfield BR1: Brom 2E **35**
Summer Gro. BR4: W W'ck 6F **17**
Summer Hill BR7: Chst 6D **10**
Summerhill Cl. BR6: Orp 7H **19**
Summerhill Vs. *BR7: Chst* *5D* ***10***
(off Susan Wood)
Summerhouse Dr. DA2: Dart 1J **13**
DA5: Bexl, Dart 1J **13**
Summerlands Lodge BR6: Farnb 1D **24**
Summit Way SE19 4D **6**
Sumner Cl. BR6: Farnb 1F **25**
Sumner Gdns. CR0: Croy 5A **14**
Sumner Rd. CR0: Croy 5A **14**
Sumner Rd. Sth. CR0: Croy 5A **14**
Sundial Av. SE25 7E **6**
SUNDRIDGE 3J **9**
Sundridge Av. BR1: Brom 5A **10**
BR7: Chst 5A **10**
Sundridge Hill TN14: Knock, Sund 7G **31**
Sundridge La. TN14: Knock 6F **31**
Sundridge Pde. BR1: Brom 4J **9**
SUNDRIDGE PARK 4J **9**
Sundridge Park Station (Rail) 4J **9**
Sundridge Pl. CR0: Croy 5F **15**
Sundridge Rd. CR0: Croy 4E **14**
Sunningdale Rd. BR1: Brom 1B **18**
Sunningvale Av. TN16: Big H 4E **28**
Sunningvale Cl. TN16: Big H 4F **29**
Sunny Bank SE25 7F **7**
Sunnycroft Rd. SE25 7F **7**
Sunnydale BR6: Farnb 6D **18**
Sunnydale Rd. SE12 2A **4**
Sunnydene St. SE26 1K **7**
Sunnyfield Rd. BR7: Chst 7K **11**
Sunray Av. BR2: Brom 3B **18**
Sunset Gdns. SE25 6E **6**
Superior Dr. BR6: Chels 3J **25**
Surrey M. SE27 1D **6**
Surrey Rd. BR4: W W'ck 5C **16**

Surrey St. CR0: Croy 6B 14
Surridge Gdns. SE19 3C 6
Susan Wood BR7: Chst 5D 10
Sussex Rd. BR4: W W'ck 5C 16
BR5: Orp 3B 20
DA14: Sidc 2A 12
Sussex Ter. *SE20* *4H 7*
(off Graveney Gro.)
Sutcliffe Pk. Athletics Track 2B 4
Sutherland Av. BR5: St M Cry 3J 19
DA16: Well 1K 5
TN16: Big H 6F 29
Sutherland Rd. CR0: Croy 4A 14
Sutton Cl. BR3: Beck 5C 8
Sutton Ct. SE19 4E 6
Sutton Gdns. CR0: Croy 2E 14
Swain Rd. CR7: Thor H 2B 14
Swallands Rd. SE6 1B 8
(not continuous)
Swallowtail Cl. BR5: St P 1C 20
SWAN, THE 6D 16
Swan Cl. BR5: St P 7K 11
CR0: Croy 4D 14
SWANLEY 7K 13
Swanley By-Pass BR8: Swan 5G 13
DA14: Swan 5G 13
Swanley Cen. BR8: Swan 7K 13
SWANLEY INTERCHANGE 7C 34
Swanley La. BR8: Swan 5A 34
Swanley Station (Rail) 1J 21
SWANLEY VILLAGE 3C 34
Swanley Village Rd. BR8: Swan 3C 34
Sward Rd. BR5: St M Cry 3K 19
Sweeps La. BR5: St M Cry 2C 20
Swievelands Rd. TN16: Big H 1A 32
Swiftsden Way BR1: Brom 3F 9
Swinburne Cres. CR0: Croy 3H 15
Swires Shaw BR2: Kes 1A 24
Swithland Gdns. SE9 1D 10
Sycamore Cl. SE9 6D 4
Sycamore Dr. BR8: Swan 7K 13
Sycamore Gro. SE20 5F 7
Sycamore Ho. BR2: Brom 6F 9
Sycamore Lodge BR6: Orp 6J 19
SYDENHAM 1H 7
Sydenham Av. SE26 2G 7
Sydenham Cotts. SE12 6B 4
Sydenham Ct. *CR0: Croy* *5C 14*
(off Sydenham Rd.)
Sydenham Hill SE26 1E 6
Sydenham Hill Station (Rail) 1E 6
Sydenham Pk. SE26 1H 7
Sydenham Pk. Rd. SE26 1H 7
Sydenham Rd. CR0: Croy 5B 14
SE26 1H 7
Sydenham Station (Rail) 1H 7
Sydney Rd. DA14: Sidc 1H 11
Sylvan Est. SE19 5E 6
Sylvan Hill SE19 5D 6
Sylvan Rd. SE19 5E 6
Sylvan Wlk. BR1: Brom 7C 10
Sylvan Way BR4: W W'ck 1F 23
Sylverdale Rd. CR0: Croy 7A 14
Sylvester Av. BR7: Chst 3C 10

T

Tait Rd. CR0: Croy 4D 14
Tait Rd. Ind. Est. *CR0: Croy* *4D 14*
(off Tait Rd.)
Talbot Rd. CR7: Thor H 1C 14
Talisman Sq. SE26 1F 7
Tall Elms Cl. BR2: Brom 2G 17
Tamworth Pl. CR0: Croy 6B 14
Tamworth Rd. CR0: Croy 6A 14
Tandridge Dr. BR6: Orp 5G 19
Tandridge Pl. BR6: Orp 5G 19
Tanfield Rd. CR0: Croy 7B 14
Tangleberry Cl. BR1: Brom 1C 18
Tanglewood Cl. CR0: Croy 7H 15
Tanglewood Ct. BR5: St P 7B 12
Tannery Cl. BR3: Beck 2J 15
Tannsfeld Rd. SE26 2J 7
Tara Ct. BR3: Beck 6C 8
Tarling Cl. DA14: Sidc 1A 12
Tarnwood Pk. SE9 4E 4
Tarquin Ho. *SE26* *1F 7*
(off High Level Dr.)
Tarragon Gro. SE26 3J 7
TATSFIELD 3B 32
TATSFIELD GREEN 3D 32
Tatsfield La. TN16: Tats 3E 32
Tattersall Cl. SE9 2D 4
Tavistock Ct. *CR0: Croy* *5C 14*
(off Tavistock Rd.)
Tavistock Ga. CR0: Croy 5C 14
Tavistock Gro. CR0: Croy 4C 14
Tavistock Rd. BR2: Brom 7A 35 (1G 17)
CR0: Croy 5C 14
Taylor Cl. BR6: Orp 1J 25
Taylor Ct. *SE20* *6H 7*
(off Elmers End Rd.)
Taylors Cl. DA14: Sidc 7K 5
Taylor's La. SE26 1G 7
Teal Av. BR5: St P 1C 20
Teardrop Cen. BR8: Swan 7C 34
Teasel Cl. CR0: Croy 5J 15
Teesdale Gdns. SE25 6D 6
Teevan Cl. CR0: Croy 4F 15
Teevan Rd. CR0: Croy 5F 15
Telegraph Path BR7: Chst 2E 10
Telemann Sq. SE3 1A 4
Telford Cl. SE19 3E 6
Telford Rd. SE9 6J 5
Telscombe Cl. BR6: Orp 6H 19
Temple Av. CR0: Croy 6A 16
Temple Rd. TN16: Big H 6F 29
Templeton Cl. SE19 5C 6
Tennison Rd. SE25 1E 14
Tennyson Rd. SE20 4J 7
Tenterden Cl. SE9 1C 10
Tenterden Gdns. CR0: Croy 4F 15
Tenterden Rd. CR0: Croy 4F 15
Tent Peg La. BR5: Pet W 2F 19
Terrace Hill *CR0: Croy* *7A 14*
(off Hanover St.)
Tetty Way BR2: Brom 3B 35 (6H 9)
Teynham Ct. BR3: Beck 7C 8
Teynham Grn. BR2: Brom 2H 17
Thakeham Cl. SE26 1G 7
Thanescroft Gdns. CR0: Croy 7D 14
Thanet Dr. BR2: Kes 7A 18
Thanet Ho. *CR0: Croy* *7B 14*
(off Coombe Rd.)
Thanet Pl. CR0: Croy 7B 14
Thanington Ct. SE9 3K 5
Thaxted Rd. SE9 7H 5
Thayers Farm Rd. BR3: Beck 5K 7
Theobald Rd. CR0: Croy 6A 14
Thesiger Rd. SE20 4J 7
Thicket Gro. SE20 4F 7
Thicket Rd. SE20 4F 7
Thirlmere Ri. BR1: Brom 3G 9
Thirsk Rd. SE25 1C 14
Thistlemead BR7: Chst 6E 10
Thistlewood Cres. CR0: New Ad 7E 22
Thomas Dean Rd. SE26 1A 8
Thomas Dinwiddy Rd.
SE12 6A 4
Thomas Turner Path *CR0: Croy* *6B 14*
(off George St.)
Thorn Cl. BR2: Brom 3D 18
Thorndon Cl. BR5: St P 6J 11
Thorndon Rd. BR5: St P 6J 11
Thornes Cl. BR3: Beck 7D 8
Thornet Wood Rd. BR1: Brom 7D 10
Thornhill Rd. CR0: Croy 4B 14
Thornlaw Rd. SE27 1A 6
Thornsett Pl. SE20 6G 7
Thornsett Rd. SE20 6G 7
Thornsett Ter. *SE20* *6G 7*
(off Croydon Rd.)
Thornton Dene BR3: Beck 6B 8
THORNTON HEATH 1B 14
Thornton Heath Station (Rail) 1B 14
Thornton Rd. BR1: Brom 2H 9
Thorpe Cl. BR6: Orp 6H 19
CR0: New Ad 7D 22
Thorpe Cl. SE26 1J 7
Thorsden Way SE19 2D 6
Thriffwood SE26 1H 7
Thrift La. TN14: Cud 6C 30
Thurbarn Rd. SE6 2C 8
Thurlby Rd. SE27 1A 6
Thurlestone Rd. SE27 1A 6
Thursland Rd. DA14: Sidc 2D 12
Thursley Cres. CR0: New Ad 4D 22
Thursley Rd. SE9 7E 4
Thurston Ho. BR3: Beck 3C 8
Thyer Cl. BR6: Farnb 1F 25
Ticehurst Cl. BR5: St P 4K 11
Tidenham Gdns. CR0: Croy 7D 14
Tideswell Rd. CR0: Croy 7B 16
Tiepigs La. BR2: Hayes 6F 17
BR4: W W'ck 6F 17
Tierney Ct. CR0: Croy 6D 14
Tiger La. BR2: Brom 7D 35 (1J 17)
Tilbrook Rd. SE3 1B 4
Tilbury Cl. BR5: St P 6A 12
Tile Farm Rd. BR6: Orp 7G 19
Tile Kiln La. DA5: Bexl 1K 13
Tilford Av. CR0: New Ad 5D 22
Tillingbourne Grn. BR5: St M Cry 1J 19
Tilt Yd. App. SE9 3E 4
Timber Cl. BR7: Chst 6D 10
TIMBERDEN BOTTOM 6K 27
Timbertop Rd. TN16: Big H 7E 28
Tinsley Cl. SE25 7G 7
Tintagel Rd. BR5: Orp 6B 20
Tipton Dr. CR0: Croy 7D 14
Tirrell Rd. CR0: Croy 3B 14
TITSEY 7A 32
Titsey Hill RH8: T'sey 5A 32
Titsey Place & Gardens 6A 32
Titsey Rd. RH8: Limp, T'sey 7A 32
Tiverton Cl. CR0: Croy 4E 14
Tiverton Dr. SE9 5H 5
Tivoli Rd. SE27 2B 6
Tom Coombs Cl. SE9 1D 4
Tonge Cl. BR3: Beck 2B 16
Tony Law Ho. SE20 5G 7
Tootswood Rd. BR2: Brom 2F 17
Topcliffe Dr. BR6: Farnb 1G 25
Top Dartford Rd. BR8: Swan 2A 34
DA2: Dart 2A 34
Topley St. SE9 1B 4
Top Pk. BR3: Beck 2F 17
Torridge Rd. CR7: Thor H 2A 14
Torrington Ct. *SE26* *2F 7*
(off Crystal Pal. Pk. Rd.)
Torrington Sq. CR0: Croy 4C 14
Torr Rd. SE20 4J 7
Torver Way BR6: Orp 7G 19
Totton Rd. CR7: Thor H 7A 6
Tourist Info. Cen.
Croydon 7B 14
Swanley 7K 13
Tovil Cl. SE20 6G 7
Tower Cl. BR6: Orp 6J 19
SE20 4G 7
Tower Rd. BR6: Orp 6J 19
Tower Vw. CR0: Croy 4K 15
Towncourt Cres. BR5: Pet W 2F 19
Towncourt La. BR5: Pet W 3G 19
Townshend Cl. DA14: Sidc 3A 12
Townshend Rd. BR7: Chst 2E 10
Towpath Way CR0 3E 14
Toynbec Cl. BR7: Chst 1E 10
Tramway Cl. SE20 5H 7
Transmere Cl. BR5: Pet W 3F 19
Transmere Rd. BR5: Pet W 3F 19
Tredown Rd. SE26 2H 7
Tredwell Cl. BR2: Brom 1B 18
Tredwell Rd. SE27 1A 6
Treebourne Rd. TN16: Big H 6E 28
Treeview Cl. SE19 5D 6
Treewall Gdns. BR1: Brom 1J 9
Tregony Rd. BR6: Chels 1J 25
Treloar Gdns. SE19 3C 6
Tremaine Rd. SE20 6G 7
Trenear Cl. BR6: Chels 1K 25
Trenholme Cl. SE20 4G 7
Trenholme Rd. SE20 4G 7
Trenholme Ter. SE20 4G 7
Trentham Dr. BR5: St M Cry 1K 19
Tresco Cl. BR1: Brom 3F 9
Trevenna Ho. *SE23* *1J 7*
(off Dacres Rd.)
Trevor Cl. BR2: Hayes 4G 17
Trewsbury Rd. SE26 2J 7
Trinity Cl. BR2: Brom 5B 18
Trinity Ct. CR0: Croy 6B 14
SE25 3D 14
Trinity M. SE20 5G 7
Tristram Rd. BR1: Brom 1G 9
Tritton Rd. SE21 1C 6
Troy Rd. SE19 3C 6
Trumble Gdns. CR7: Thor H 1A 14
Trunks All. BR8: Swan 6G 13
Truslove Rd. SE27 2A 6
Tubbenden Cl. BR6: Orp 7H 19
Tubbenden Dr. BR6: Orp 1G 25
Tubbenden La. BR6: Orp 1G 25
Tubbenden La. Sth. BR6: Farnb 2G 25
Tudor Cl. BR7: Chst 5C 10

Tudor Ct. BR8: Crock 4H **21**
SE9 1D **4**
TN16: Big H 7G **29**
Tudor Gdns. BR4: W W'ck 7D **16**
Tudor Pde. SE9 1D **4**
Tudor Pl. SE19 4E **6**
Tudor Rd. BR3: Beck 7D **8**
SE19 4E **6**
SE25 2G **15**
Tudor Way BR5: Pet W 3G **19**
Tudway Rd. SE3 1A **4**
Tugela Rd. CR0: Croy 3C **14**
Tugmutton Cl. BR6: Farnb 1E **24**
Tulip Cl. CR0: Croy 5J **15**
Tulse Cl. BR3: Beck 7D **8**
Tummons Gdns. SE25 6D **6**
Tunstall Cl. BR6: Orp 1H **25**
Tunstall Rd. CR0: Croy 5D **14**
Turkey Oak Cl. SE19 5D **6**
Turnberry Way BR6: Orp 5G **19**
Turner Cl. TN16: Big H 1E **28**
Turners Mdw. Way BR3: Beck 5A **8**
Turnpike Dr. BR6: Prat B 5B **26**
Turnpike Link CR0: Croy 6D **14**
Turpington Cl. BR2: Brom 3B **18**
Turpington La. BR2: Brom 4B **18**
Tweedy Rd. BR1: Brom 2B **35** (5H **9**)
Tye La. BR6: Farnb 2F **25**
Tylers Grn. Rd. BR8: Crock 3H **21**
Tylney Av. SE19 2E **6**
(not continuous)
Tylney Rd. BR1: Brom 6A **10**
Tynwald Ho. SE26 1F **7**
Tyrell Ho. *BR3: Beck* *2C **8***
(off Beckenham Hill Rd.)
Tyron Way DA14: Sidc 1H **11**

U

Uffington Rd. SE27 1A **6**
Ullswater Cl. BR1: Brom 4F **9**
Undershaw Rd. BR1: Brom 1G **9**
Underwood CR0: New Ad 2D **22**
Underwood, The SE9 6E **4**
Union Rd. BR2: Brom 2A **18**
CR0: Croy 4B **14**
Unity Cl. CR0: New Ad 5C **22**
SE19 2B **6**
University of Greenwich
Avery Hill Campus 3H **5**
Upchurch Cl. SE20 4G **7**
Updale Rd. DA14: Sidc 1J **11**
Upfield CR0: Croy 7G **15**
Uphill *BR2: Brom* *1G **17***
(off Westmoreland Rd.)
Uplands BR3: Beck 6B **8**
Uplands Rd. BR6: Orp 5A **20**
Up. Beulah Hill SE19 5D **6**
Upper Dr. TN16: Big H 7E **28**
UPPER ELMERS END 2A **16**
Up. Elmers End Rd. BR3: Beck 1K **15**
Upper Gro. SE25 1D **14**
UPPER NORWOOD 5D **6**
Upper Pk. Rd. BR1: Brom 2E **35** (5J **9**)
UPPER RUXLEY 4F **13**
Up. Shirley Rd. CR0: Croy 6H **15**
UPPER SYDENHAM 1G **7**
Upperton Rd. DA14: Sidc 2J **11**
Upton Ct. *SE20* *4H **7***
(off Blean Gro.)
Upton Rd. CR7: Thor H 6C **6**
Upwood Rd. SE12 3A **4**
Urquhart Ct. BR3: Beck 4A **8**
Ursula Lodges DA14: Sidc 2A **12**
Uvedale Cl. CR0: New Ad 7E **22**
Uvedale Cres. CR0: New Ad 7E **22**

V

Valan Leas BR2: Brom 7F **9**
Vale, The CR0: Croy 6J **15**
Vale Cl. BR6: Farnb 1D **24**
Valentyne Cl. CR0: New Ad 7F **23**
Vale Rd. BR1: Brom 5D **10**
Vale St. SE27 1C **6**
Valeswood Rd. BR1: Brom 2G **9**
Valley Rd. BR2: Brom 6F **9**
BR5: St P 5A **12**
Valley Vw. TN16: Big H 7E **28**
Valley Wlk. CR0: Croy 6H **15**
Valliers Wood Rd. DA15: Sidc 5K **5**
Vanbrugh Cl. BR6: Orp 5H **19**
Vancouver Cl. BR6: Chels 1K **25**
Vandyke Cross SE9 2D **4**
Vanessa Way DA5: Bexl 1J **13**
Vanguard Cl. CR0: Croy 5A **14**
Vanoc Gdns. BR1: Brom 1H **9**
Venner Rd. SE26 3H **7**
(not continuous)
Verdayne Av. CR0: Croy 5J **15**
Vermont Rd. SE19 3C **6**
Vernon Cl. BR5: St P 7A **12**
Versailles Rd. SE20 4F **7**
Veryan Cl. BR5: St P 1B **20**
Vicarage Ct. BR3: Beck 7K **7**
Vicarage Dr. BR3: Beck 5B **8**
Vicarage Rd. CR0: Wadd 7A **14**
Vicars Oak Rd. SE19 3D **6**
Viceroy Ct. CR0: Croy 5C **14**
Victoria Ct. SE26 3H **7**
Victoria Cres. SE19 3D **6**
Victoria Gdns. TN16: Big H 4E **28**
Victoria Hill Rd. BR8: Swan 3A **34**
Victoria Rd. BR2: Brom 2A **18**
BR7: Chst 2D **10**
DA15: Sidc 1J **11**
Victor Rd. SE20 4J **7**
Victory Pl. SE19 4D **6**
View Cl. TN16: Big H 5E **28**
View Ct. SE12 7B **4**
Viewlands Av. TN16: Westrm 2K **33**
Vigilant Cl. SE26 1F **7**
Village Grn. Av. TN16: Big H 6G **29**
Village Grn. Way TN16: Big H 6G **29**
Village Way BR3: Beck 6B **8**
Villiers Rd. BR3: Beck 6J **7**
Vincennes Est. SE27 1C **6**
Vincent Cl. BR2: Brom 7E **35** (1J **17**)
DA15: Sidc 5K **5**
Vincent Rd. CR0: Croy 4D **14**
Vincent Sq. TN16: Big H 2E **28**
Vine Rd. BR6: Chels 3J **25**
Viney Bank CR0: Sels 5A **22**
Vinson Cl. BR6: Orp 5K **19**
Virginia Rd. CR7: Thor H 5A **6**
Vista, The DA14: Sidc 2J **11**
SE9 3C **4**
Vogue Ct. BR1: Brom 2E **35** (5J **9**)
Vue Cinema
Croydon 7B **14**
Vulcan Bus. Cen. CR0: New Ad 5F **23**
Vulcan Way CR0: New Ad 6F **23**

W

Wadard Ter. BR8: Swan 7D **34**
Waddington Way SE19 4B **6**
WADDON 6A **14**
Waddon Cl. CR0: Wadd 7A **14**
Waddon New Rd. CR0: Croy 7A **14**
Waddon Pk. Av. CR0: Wadd 7A **14**
Waddon Rd. CR0: Croy, Wadd 7A **14**
Wade Av. BR5: Orp 4C **20**
Wadhurst Cl. SE20 6G **7**
Wagtail Wlk. BR3: Beck 2D **16**
Wagtail Way BR5: St P 1C **20**
Wakefield Ct. SE26 3H **7**
Wakefield Gdns. SE19 4D **6**
Wakely Cl. TN16: Big H 7E **28**
Waldegrave Rd. BR1: Brom 1B **18**
SE19 4E **6**
Waldegrove CR0: Croy 7E **14**
Walden Av. BR7: Chst 1C **10**
Waldenhurst Rd.
BR5: St M Cry 4C **20**
Walden Pde. BR7: Chst 3C **10**
(not continuous)
Walden Rd. BR7: Chst 3C **10**
Waldens Cl. BR5: St M Cry 4C **20**
Waldens Rd. BR5: St M Cry 4D **20**
Waldo Ind. Est. BR1: Brom 7A **10**
Waldo Rd. BR1: Brom 7A **10**
Waldron Gdns. BR2: Brom 7E **8**
Waldrons, The CR0: Croy 7A **14**
Walkden Rd. BR7: Chst 2D **10**
Walled Gdn. Cl. BR3: Beck 1C **16**
Walmer Cl. BR6: Farnb 1G **25**
Walnuts, The BR6: Orp 5K **19**
Walnuts Leisure Cen. 5K **19**
Walnuts Rd. BR6: Orp 5A **20**
Walnut Tree Cl. BR7: Chst 5G **11**
Walnut Way BR8: Swan 6J **13**
Walpole Rd. BR2: Brom 2A **18**
CR0: Croy 6C **14**
Walsh Cres. CR0: New Ad 1A **28**
Walsingham Pk. BR7: Chst 6G **11**
Walsingham Rd. BR5: St P 5A **12**
CR0: New Ad 6D **22**
Walters Rd. SE25 1D **14**
Walters Yd. BR1: Brom 3B **35** (6H **9**)
Waltham Cl. BR5: Orp 5C **20**
Walton Grn. CR0: New Ad 5C **22**
Walton Rd. DA14: Sidc 1A **12**
Walwyn Av. BR1: Brom 7A **10**
Wandle Ho. BR1: Brom 2E **8**
Wandle Park Stop (CT) 6A **14**
Wandle Pk. Trad. Est., The
CR0: Croy 5A **14**
Wandle Rd. CR0: Croy 7B **14**
Wansbury Way BR8: Swan 7B **34**
Wanstead Cl. BR1: Brom 6K **9**
Wanstead Rd. BR1: Brom 6K **9**
Warbank Cl. CR0: New Ad 6F **23**
Warbank Cres. CR0: New Ad 6F **23**
Wardens Fld. Cl. BR6: Chels 3H **25**
Warehouse Theatre 6C **14**
Waring Cl. BR6: Chels 3J **25**
Waring Dr. BR6: Chels 3J **25**
Waring Rd. DA14: Sidc 3B **12**
Waring St. SE27 1B **6**
Warlingham Rd. CR7: Thor H 1A **14**
Warminster Gdns. SE25 6F **7**
Warminster Rd. SE25 6E **6**
Warminster Sq. SE25 6F **7**
Warner Ho. BR3: Beck 3C **8**
Warner Rd. BR1: Brom 4G **9**
Warnford Rd. BR6: Chels 2J **25**
Warren Av. BR1: Brom 4F **9**
BR6: Chels 2J **25**
Warren Ct. BR3: Beck 4B **8**
CR0: Croy 5D **14**
Warren Ct. Farm TN14: Hals 2J **31**
Warren Dr. BR6: Chels 2A **26**
Warren Gdns. BR6: Chels 2K **25**
Warren Rd. BR2: Hayes 6H **17**
BR6: Chels 2J **25**
CR0: Croy 5D **14**
DA14: Sidc 1B **12**
Warren Wood Cl. BR2: Hayes 6G **17**
Warrington Ct. *CR0: Wadd* *7A **14***
(off Warrington Rd.)
Warrington Rd. CR0: Wadd 7A **14**
Warwick Cl. BR6: Chels 7K **19**
Warwick Ct. BR2: Brom 6F **9**
Warwick Ho. BR8: Swan 1K **21**
Warwick Rd. CR7: Thor H 7A **6**
DA14: Sidc 2A **12**
SE20 7G **7**
Washneys Rd. BR6: Prat B 3E **30**
Watcombe Pl. SE25 2G **15**
Watcombe Rd. SE25 2G **15**
Waterbank Rd. SE6 1C **8**
Watercroft Rd. TN14: Hals 6E **26**
Waterer Ho. SE6 1D **8**
Waterfield Gdns. SE25 1C **14**
Wateringbury Cl. BR5: St P 7A **12**
Watermead Rd. SE6 1D **8**
Watermen's Sq. SE20 4H **7**
Watermint Cl. BR5: St P 1C **20**
Waterside BR3: Beck 5A **8**
Waterside Av. *BR3: Beck* *2D **16***
(off Adamson Way)
Waterton BR8: Swan 1J **21**
Water Twr. Hill CR0: Croy 7C **14**
Waterworks Yd. *CR0: Croy* *7B **14***
(off Surrey St.)
Watery La. DA14: Sidc 3A **12**
Watlings Cl. CR0: Croy 3K **15**
Watlington Gro. SE26 2K **7**
Watsons Yd. BR6: Orp 4A **20**
Watts La. BR7: Chst 5E **10**
Wavell Dr. DA15: Sidc 3K **5**
Wavel Pl. SE26 1E **6**
Waverley Cl. BR2: Brom 2A **18**
Waverley Ct. SE26 2H **7**
Waverley Rd. SE25 1G **15**
Wayfield Link SE9 3J **5**
Waylands BR8: Swan 6A **34**
Waylands Cl. TN14: Knock 4J **31**
Waylands Mead BR3: Beck 5C **8**
Wayne Cl. BR6: Orp 7J **19**
Waynflete Av. CR0: Wadd 7A **14**
Wayside CR0: New Ad 3C **22**

Wayside Gro. SE9 1C **10**
Weald, The BR7: Chst 3C **10**
Weald Cl. BR2: Brom 6B **18**
Weaver Cl. CR0: Croy 7E **14**
Weaver Wlk. SE27 1B **6**
Wedgewood Ct. *BR2: Brom* *7G* ***9***
(off Cumberland Rd.)
Wedgwoods TN16: Tats 3B **32**
Wedgwood Way SE19 4B **6**
Weigall Rd. SE12 1A **4**
Weighton M. SE20 6G **7**
Weighton Rd. SE20 6G **7**
Welbeck Av. BR1: Brom 1H **9**
Wellands Cl. BR1: Brom 6C **10**
Wellbrook Rd. BR6: Farnb 1D **24**
Weller Pl. BR6: Downe 7D **24**
Wellesley Ct. Rd. CR0: Croy 6C **14**
Wellesley Gro. CR0: Croy 6C **14**
Wellesley Pas. CR0: Croy 6B **14**
Wellesley Rd. CR0: Croy 5B **14**
Wellesley Road Stop (CT) **6C 14**
Well Hall Pde. SE9 1E **4**
Well Hall Rd. SE9 1D **4**
WELL HALL RDBT. **1D 4**
WELL HILL **3G 27**
Well Hill BR6: Orp 3G **27**
Well Hill La. BR6: Chels 3G **27**
Wellhouse Rd. BR3: Beck 1B **16**
Wellhurst Cl. BR6: Chels 4J **25**
Wellington Rd. BR2: Brom 1K **17**
BR5: St M Cry 3A **20**
CR0: Croy 4A **14**
Welling Way DA16: Well 1H **5**
SE9 1H **5**
Wells Ct. BR2: Brom 6E **8**
Wells Ho. *BR1: Brom* *2J* ***9***
(off Pike Cl.)
Wellsmoor Gdns. BR1: Brom 7D **10**
Wells Pk. Rd. SE26 1F **7**
Wells Rd. BR1: Brom 6C **10**
Wendover Ct. BR2: Brom 6E **35**
Wendover Rd. BR2: Brom 7E **35** (1J **17**)
SE9 1C **4**
Wendover Way BR6: St M Cry 3K **19**
Wensley Cl. SE9 3E **4**
Wentworth Cl. BR2: Hayes 6H **17**
BR6: Farnb 2H **25**
Werndee Rd. SE25 1F **15**
Wesley Cl. BR5: St P 7B **12**
Wessex Ct. BR3: Beck 5K **7**
West App. BR5: Pet W 2F **19**
Westbourne Rd. CR0: Croy 3E **14**
SE26 3J **7**
Westbrook Dr. BR5: Orp 5C **20**
Westbrooke Rd. DA15: Sidc 6J **5**
Westbrook Rd. CR7: Thor H 5C **6**
Westbury Rd. BR1: Brom 5A **10**
BR3: Beck 7K **7**
CR0: Croy 3C **14**
SE20 5J **7**
West Comn. Rd. BR2: Hayes 5H **17**
BR2: Kes 5H **17**
Westcott Cl. BR1: Brom 2C **18**
CR0: New Ad 5C **22**
West Croydon Station (Rail & CT) **5B 14**
Westdean Av. SE12 5A **4**
Wested La. BR8: Crock 7B **34**
(not continuous)
WESTERHAM **7J 33**
WESTERHAM HILL **2F 33**
Westerham Hill TN16: Westrm 3G **33**
Westerham Lodge *BR3: Beck* *4B* ***8***
(off Park Rd.)
Westerham Rd. BR2: Kes 4A **24**
Westerham Trade Cen. TN16: Westrm 7J **33**
Westerley Cres. SE26 2A **8**
Westfield Rd. BR3: Beck 6A **8**
CR0: Croy 6A **14**
Westgate Ct. *SE12* *5A* ***4***
(off Burnt Ash Hill)
Westgate Rd. BR3: Beck 5D **8**
SE25 1G **15**
West Hallowes SE9 5C **4**
Westharold BR8: Swan 7J **13**
West Hill BR6: Downe 1H **29**
Westholme BR6: Orp 4H **19**
Westhorne Av. SE9 4A **4**
SE12 4A **4**
Westhurst Dr. BR7: Chst 2E **10**
Westland Dr. BR2: Hayes 6G **17**
Westleigh Dr. BR1: Brom 5B **10**
Westminster Av. CR7: Thor H 6A **6**
Westmoat Cl. BR3: Beck 4D **8**
Westmore Grn. TN16: Tats 2B **32**
Westmoreland Av. DA16: Well 1K **5**
Westmoreland Pl. BR1: Brom 6C **35** (7H **9**)
Westmoreland Rd. BR2: Brom 7A **35** (2F **17**)
Westmore Rd. TN16: Tats 3B **32**
Westmorland Ter. SE20 4G **7**
Westmount Rd. SE9 1F **5**
WEST NORWOOD **1B 6**
W. Norwood Crematorium SE27 1B **6**
West Norwood Station (Rail) **1A 6**
West Oak BR3: Beck 5E **8**
Weston Gro. BR1: Brom 1A **35** (5G **9**)
Weston Rd. BR1: Brom 1A **35** (4G **9**)
Westow Hill SE19 3D **6**
Westow St. SE19 3D **6**
West Pk. SE9 6D **4**
West St. BR1: Brom 2B **35** (5H **9**)
CR0: Croy 7B **14**
West St. Pl. *CR0: Croy* *7B* ***14***
(off West St.)
West Ter. DA15: Sidc 5K **5**
West Vw. Rd. BR8: Crock 3J **21**
BR8: Swan 6B **34**
West Way BR4: W W'ck 3E **16**
CR0: Croy 6K **15**
Westway BR5: Pet W 2G **19**
W. Way Gdns. CR0: Croy 6J **15**
Westwell Cl. BR5: Orp 5C **20**
WEST WICKHAM **5D 16**
West Wickham Pools **5D 16**
West Wickham Station (Rail) **4D 16**
Westwood Av. SE19 5B **6**
Westwood Cl. BR1: Brom 6A **10**
Westwood Hill SE26 2F **7**
Westwood Pl. SE26 1F **7**
Weybridge Rd. CR7: Thor H 1A **14**
Weymouth Ho. BR2: Brom 3A **35**
Wharncliffe Gdns. SE25 6D **6**
Wharncliffe Rd. SE25 6D **6**
Wharton Rd. BR1: Brom 2D **35** (5J **9**)
Whateley Rd. SE20 4J **7**
Wheathill Ho. *SE20* *6G* ***7***
(off Croydon Rd.)
Wheathill Rd. SE20 7G **7**
Wheatsheaf Hill TN14: Hals 5E **26**
Wheeler Pl. BR2: Brom 6D **35** (1J **17**)
Whinyates Rd. SE9 1D **4**
Whippendell Cl. BR5: St P 5A **12**
Whippendell Way BR5: St P 5A **12**
Whitby Cl. TN16: Big H 1A **32**
Whitebeam Av. BR2: Brom 4D **18**
White Cft. BR8: Swan 6K **13**
Whitecroft Cl. BR3: Beck 1E **16**
Whitecroft Way BR3: Beck 2D **16**
Whitefield Cl. BR5: St P 7B **12**
Whitefoot La. BR1: Brom 1D **8**
Whitehall Rd. BR2: Brom 2A **18**
White Hart Rd. BR6: Orp 4K **19**
White Hart Slip BR1: Brom 3C **35** (6H **9**)
Whitehaven Cl. BR2: Brom 7B **35** (1H **17**)
White Horse Hill BR7: Chst 1D **10**
Whitehorse La. SE25 1C **14**
Whitehorse Rd. CR0: Croy 4B **14**
CR7: Thor H 4B **14**
White La. RH8: T'sey 5A **32**
TN16: Tats, T'sey 5A **32**
Whiteley Rd. SE19 2C **6**
White Lodge SE19 4A **6**
White Oak Ct. BR8: Swan 7K **13**
Whiteoak Ct. BR7: Chst 3D **10**
White Oak Dr. BR3: Beck 6D **8**
White Oak Leisure Cen. **6J 13**
White Oak Sq. *BR8: Swan* *7K* ***13***
(off London Rd.)
White's Mdw. BR1: Brom 1D **18**
Whitethorn Gdns. CR0: Croy 6G **15**
Whitewebbs Way BR5: St P 5J **11**
Whitewood Cotts. TN16: Tats 2B **32**
Whitgift Cen. CR0: Croy 6B **14**
Whitgift Sq. CR0: Croy 6B **14**
Whitgift St. CR0: Croy 7B **14**
Whitmore Rd. BR3: Beck 7A **8**
Whitney Wlk. DA14: Sidc 3D **12**
Whitstable Cl. BR3: Beck 5A **8**
Whitstone La. BR3: Beck 2C **16**
Whittell Gdns. SE26 1H **7**
Whitworth Rd. SE25 7D **6**
Wichling Cl. BR5: Orp 5C **20**
Wickers Oake SE19 1E **6**
Wicket, The CR0: Addtn 2B **22**
Wickham Av. CR0: Croy 6K **15**
Wickham Chase BR4: W W'ck 5E **16**
Wickham Ct. Rd. BR4: W W'ck 6D **16**
Wickham Cres. BR4: W W'ck 6D **16**
Wickham Rd. BR3: Beck 6C **8**
CR0: Croy 6J **15**
Wickham Way BR3: Beck 1D **16**
Wicks Cl. SE9 1A **10**
Widecombe Rd. SE9 7D **4**
WIDMORE **7K 9**
WIDMORE GREEN **6A 10**
Widmore Lodge Rd. BR1: Brom 6A **10**
Widmore Rd. BR1: Brom 3C **35** (6H **9**)
Wilberforce Ct. BR2: Kes 4A **24**
Wilderness Rd. BR7: Chst 4E **10**
Wilford Rd. CR0: Croy 3B **14**
Wilkinson Gdns. SE25 5D **6**
Wilks Gdns. CR0: Croy 5K **15**
Will Crooks Gdns. SE9 1B **4**
Willersley Av. BR6: Orp 7G **19**
DA15: Sidc 5K **5**
Willett Cl. BR5: Pet W 3H **19**
Willett Way BR5: Pet W 2G **19**
William Barefoot Dr. SE9 1D **10**
William Booth Rd. SE20 5F **7**
William Nash Ct. BR5: St P 7B **12**
William Petty Way BR5: Orp 5B **20**
William Wood Ho. *SE26* *1H* ***7***
(off Shrublands Cl.)
Willis Ct. BR4: W W'ck 6E **16**
Willis Rd. CR0: Croy 4B **14**
Willow Av. BR8: Swan 5A **34**
Willow Bus. Pk. SE26 1H **7**
Willow Cl. BR2: Brom 2C **18**
BR5: St M Cry 4A **20**
Willow Grange DA14: Sidc 1A **12**
Willow Gro. BR7: Chst 3D **10**
Willow Ho. BR2: Brom 6F **9**
Willow Mt. CR0: Croy 7D **14**
Willows, The BR3: Beck 5B **8**
Willow Tree Ct. DA14: Sidc 2K **11**
Willow Tree Wlk. BR1: Brom 2E **35** (5J **9**)
Willow Va. BR7: Chst 3E **10**
Willow Wlk. BR6: Farnb 7E **18**
Willow Way SE26 1H **7**
Willow Wood Cres. SE25 3D **14**
Wilmar Gdns. BR4: W W'ck 5C **16**
Wilmington Av. BR6: Orp 6B **20**
Wiltshire Rd. BR6: Orp 4K **19**
CR7: Thor H 7A **6**
Wimborne Av. BR5: St P 1J **19**
BR7: Chst 7J **11**
Wimborne Way BR3: Beck 7J **7**
Wimpole Cl. BR2: Brom 7E **35** (1K **17**)
Winchcomb Gdns. SE9 1C **4**
Winchester Cl. BR2: Brom 7G **9**
Winchester Pk. BR2: Brom 7G **9**
Winchester Rd. BR2: Brom 6A **35** (7G **9**)
BR6: Chels 1B **26**
Winchet Wlk. CR0: Croy 3H **15**
Winchfield Rd. SE26 2K **7**
Wincrofts Dr. SE9 1J **5**
Windall Cl. SE19 5F **7**
Windermere Cl. BR6: Farnb 7E **18**
Windermere Rd. BR4: W W'ck 6F **17**
CR0: Croy 5E **14**
Windfield Cl. SE26 1J **7**
Windham Av. CR0: New Ad 6E **22**
Windmill Bri. Ho. *CR0: Croy* *5D* ***14***
(off Freemasons Rd.)
Windmill Dr. BR2: Kes 1K **23**
Windmill Gro. CR0: Croy 3B **14**
Windmill Rd. CR0: Croy 4B **14**
Windsor Cl. BR7: Chst 2E **10**
SE27 1B **6**
Windsor Dr. BR6: Chels 3K **25**
Windsor Gro. SE27 1B **6**
Windsor Rd. CR7: Thor H 6A **6**
Windy Ridge BR1: Brom 5B **10**
Wingate Rd. DA14: Sidc 3B **12**
Winlaton Rd. BR1: Brom 1E **8**
Winnipeg Dr. BR6: Chels 3J **25**
Winn Rd. SE12 5A **4**
Winston Ct. BR1: Brom 2E **35**
Winterborne Av. BR6: Orp 7G **19**
Winterbourne Rd. CR7: Thor H 7A **6** & 1A **14**
Winterton Ct. SE20 6F **7**
Winton Ct. BR8: Swan 1K **21**
Winton Rd. BR6: Farnb 1E **24**
Winton Way SW16 2A **6**
Wireless Rd. TN16: Big H 4F **29**
Wirrall Ho. SE26 1F **7**
Wirral Wood Cl. BR7: Chst 3D **10**

Wisbeach Rd. CR0: Croy 2C **14**
Wisley Rd. BR5: St P 4K **11**
Wistaria Cl. BR6: Farnb 6E **18**
Wisteria Gdns. BR8: Swan 6J **13**
Witham Rd. SE20 . . . . 7H **7**
Withens Cl. BR5: St M Cry 1B **20**
Witherston Way SE9 . . . . 6F **5**
Witley Cres. CR0: New Ad 3D **22**
Wittersham Rd. BR1: Brom 2G **9**
Wiverton Rd. SE26 . . . . 3H **7**
Wixom Ho. SE3 . . . . 1B **4**
Woburn Ct. CR0: Croy 5B **14**
Woburn Rd. CR0: Croy 5B **14**
Woldham Pl. BR2: Brom 1K **17**
Woldham Rd. BR2: Brom 1K **17**
Wolds Dr. BR6: Farnb 1D **24**
Wolfe Cl. BR2: Hayes 3H **17**
Wolfington Rd. SE27 . . . . 1A **6**
Wolsey Cres. CR0: New Ad 5D **22**
Wolsey M. BR6: Chels 2J **25**
Woodbank Rd. BR1: Brom 1G **9**
Woodbastwick Rd. SE26 . . . . 2J **7**
Woodberry Gro. DA5: Bexl 1J **13**
Woodbine Gro. SE20 . . . . 4G **7**
Woodbine Rd. DA15: Sidc 5K **5**
Woodbury Cl. CR0: Croy 6E **14**
TN16: Big H 7H **29**
Woodbury Ho. SE26 . . . . 1F **7**
Woodchurch Cl. DA14: Sidc 7J **5**
Woodchurch Dr. BR1: Brom 4A **10**
Wood Cl. DA5: Bexl 1K **13**
Woodclyffe Dr. BR7: Chst 6D **10**
Woodcote Av. CR7: Thor H 1A **14**
Woodcote Dr. BR6: Orp 5G **19**
Woodcote Pl. SE27 . . . . 2A **6**
Woodcote Vs. *SE27* *2B 6*
(off Woodcote Pl.)
Woodcroft SE9 . . . . 7E **4**
Woodcroft Rd. CR7: Thor H 2A **14**
Wood Dr. BR7: Chst 3B **10**
Wood End BR8: Swan 1H **21**
Woodend SE19 . . . . 3B **6**
Wooderson Cl. SE25 . . . . 1D **14**
Woodfield Cl. SE19 . . . . 4B **6**
Woodfield Ho. *SE23* *1J 7*
(off Dacres Rd.)
Woodgers Gro. BR8: Swan 4A **34**
Woodhead Dr. BR6: Orp 7H **19**
Woodhurst Av.
BR5: Pet W 3F **19**
Woodington Cl. SE9 . . . . 3F **5**
Woodknoll Dr. BR7: Chst 5C **10**
Woodland Cl. SE19 . . . . 3D **6**
Woodland Hill SE19 . . . . 3D **6**
Woodland Rd. CR7: Thor H 1A **14**
SE19 . . . . 2D **6**
Woodlands BR2: Brom 1G **17**
Woodlands, The BR6: Chels 3A **26**
SE19 . . . . 4B **6**
Woodlands Av. DA15: Sidc 5K **5**
Woodlands Cl. BR1: Brom 6C **10**
BR8: Swan 5A **34**
Woodlands Ct. BR1: Brom 5G **9**
Woodlands Pk. DA5: Bexl 1J **13**
Woodlands Ri. BR8: Swan 4A **34**
Woodlands Rd. BR1: Brom 6B **10**
BR6: Chels 3K **25**
Woodlands Ter. BR8: Crock 3G **21**
Woodlands Vw. TN14: Hals 6G **27**
Woodland Wlk. BR1: Brom 1E **8**
(not continuous)
Woodland Way BR4: W W'ck 1C **22**
BR5: Pet W 1F **19**
CR0: Croy 5K **15**
Woodlea Dr. BR2: Brom 2F **17**
Woodley Rd. BR6: Chels 6B **20**
Wood Lodge Gdns. BR1: Brom 4B **10**
Wood Lodge La. BR4: W W'ck 7D **16**
Woodmere SE9 . . . . 5E **4**
Woodmere Av. CR0: Croy 4H **15**
Woodmere Cl. CR0: Croy 4J **15**
Woodmere Gdns. CR0: Croy 4J **15**
Woodmere Way BR3: Beck 2E **16**
Woodmount BR8: Crock 4J **21**
Woodpecker Mt. CR0: Sels 5A **22**
Wood Ride BR5: Pet W 1G **19**
Wood Rd. TN16: Big H 7E **28**
WOODSIDE **3F 15**
Woodside BR6: Chels 2K **25**
Woodside Av. BR7: Chst 2F **11**
SE25 . . . . 3G **15**
Woodside Ct. Rd. CR0: Croy 4F **15**
Woodside Cres. DA15: Sidc 7K **5**
Woodside Dr. DA2: Dart 1K **13**
Woodside Grn. SE25 . . . . 3F **15**
(not continuous)
Woodside Pde. DA15: Sidc 7K **5**
Woodside Pk. SE25 . . . . 3G **15**
Woodside Rd. BR1: Brom 2B **18**
DA15: Sidc 7K **5**
SE25 . . . . 3G **15**
Woodside Stop (CT) **3G 15**
Woodside Way CR0: Croy 3H **15**
Woodstock Gdns. BR3: Beck 5C **8**
Woodstock Rd. CR0: Croy 7C **14**
Wood St. BR8: Swan 4D **34**
Woodsyre SE26 . . . . 1E **6**
Woodvale Av. SE25 . . . . 7E **6**
Woodvale Ct. BR1: Brom 2D **35**
Woodvale Wlk. SE27 . . . . 2B **6**
Woodview Cl. BR6: Farnb 6F **19**
Woodview Rd. BR8: Swan 6H **13**
Woodville Ct. SE19 . . . . 5E **6**
Woodville Rd. CR7: Thor H 1B **14**
Wood Way BR6: Farnb 6D **18**
Woodyates Rd. SE12 . . . . 3A **4**
Worbeck Rd. SE20 . . . . 6G **7**
Worcester Cl. CR0: Croy 6B **16**
Wordsworth Rd. SE20 . . . . 4J **7**
Worlds End La. BR6: Chels 3J **25**
Worleys Dr. BR6: Orp 1G **25**
Worsley Bri. Rd. BR3: Beck 4B **8**
SE26 . . . . 1A **8**
Worsley Grange BR7: Chst 3F **11**
Worth Cl. BR6: Orp 1H **25**
Wotton Grn. BR5: St M Cry 1C **20**
Wren Cl. BR5: St P 7C **12**
Wren Ct. *CR0: Croy* *7C 14*
(off Coombe Rd.
Wren Rd. DA14: Sidc 1B **12**
Wrenthorpe Rd. BR1: Brom 1F **9**
Wrights Rd. SE25 . . . . 7D **6**
Wrotham Ho. *BR3: Beck* *4A 8*
(off Sellindge Cl.
Wych Elm Lodge BR1: Brom 4G **9**
Wychwood Av. CR7: Thor H 7B **6**
Wychwood Way SE19 . . . . 3C **6**
Wydehurst Rd. CR0: Croy 4F **15**
Wydeville Mnr. Rd. SE12 . . . . 1J **9**
Wye Cl. BR6: Orp 4J **19**
Wyncham Av. DA15: Sidc 5K **5**
Wyncroft Cl. BR1: Brom 7C **10**
Wyndham Cl. BR6: Farnb 5F **19**
Wynford Gro. BR5: St P 7A **12**
Wynford Way SE9 . . . . 7E **4**
Wynton Gdns. SE25 . . . . 2E **14**
Wythens Wlk. SE9 . . . . 3G **5**
Wythes Cl. BR1: Brom 6C **10**
Wythfield Rd. SE9 . . . . 3E **4**
Wyvern Cl. BR6: Chels 7A **20**

Y

Yalding Gro. BR5: St M Cry 1C **20**
Yeoman Cl. SE27 . . . . 1A **6**
Yeovil Cl. BR6: Orp 6H **19**
Yester Dr. BR7: Chst 4B **10**
Yester Pk. BR7: Chst 4C **10**
Yester Rd. BR7: Chst 4B **10**
Yewdale Cl. BR1: Brom 3F **9**
Yew Tree Cotts. TN14: Hals 1K **31**
Yewtree Rd. BR3: Beck 7A **8**
Yew Tree Way CR0: Sels 6A **22**
(not continuous
Yolande Gdns. SE9 . . . . 2D **4**
York Av. DA15: Sidc 6K **5**
Yorkland Av. DA16: Well 1K **5**
York Ri. BR6: Orp 6H **19**
York Rd. TN16: Big H 1A **32**
YORKSHIRE GREY **2C 4**

Z

Zelah Rd. BR5: Orp 4B **20**
Zermatt Rd. CR7: Thor H 1B **14**
Zion Pl. CR7: Thor H 1C **14**
Zion Rd. CR7: Thor H 1C **14**

The representation on the maps of a road, track or footpath is no evidence of the existence of a right of way.

The Grid on this map is the National Grid taken from Ordnance Survey mapping with the permission of the Controller of Her Majesty's Stationery Office.